Praise For Previous Editions Of The
CONSUMER GUIDE TO HOME ENERGY SAVINGS

"The *Consumer Guide to Home Energy Savings* suffers from a modest title...the guide reveals how to buy and operate just about everything in your house that's connected to an electric or gas meter." — *Today's Homeowner*

"One of the best resources for homeowners that we've ever seen."
— Anne Ducey, Conservation Marketing Coordinator, Seattle City Light

"Face it, most of us don't have the inclination—or the time—to become experts...about energy efficiency and its impact on the environment. But whether we're sealing a drafty doorway, remodeling a bathroom or shopping among rows of gleaming new refrigerators, we know our actions have an impact—on the planet, as well as on our pocketbook. This book offers practical advice that will help you make smart decisions about how you build or buy.

Not a textbook in volume or style, this paperback makes for handy toting—perhaps for perusing during your energy-efficient commute on BART or Muni."
— Beth Bourland, *The San Francisco Chronicle*

"It tells you which appliances you can replace for the biggest energy savings...in words anyone can comprehend in real sentences and nice, neat diagrams." — *Coastal Maine News*

" A comprehensive reference guide (in plain English, no less) for homeowners who've chosen to wade through the sometimes murky waters of buying green, and money-saving, home improvement products." — *The Flint Journal*

"Not only does the Guide rate all the brands of major home appliance~ and fixtures for energy efficiency, it also shows how to insulate. ' scape and maintain your home in the manner that will make v~ and your planet greener."

"This compact little book is full of tips on saving energv ' and the planet. And speaking of energy, an ever' before you decide which major appliance to h of yours." .yns

"If you own one book on saving energy at ho.

.nunications

"An indispensable handbook for consumers who wa,,t to reduce their home energy use." — *The Consumer's Guide to Effective Environmental Choices*

"The most comprehensive guide to saving money and the environment available today." —Diane MacEachern, Tips for Planet Earth (syndicated column)

"Full of brand name evaluations to help a homeowner make more knowledgeable purchases..." — *The New York Times*

"A comprehensive, easy-to-use resource..." —*Science News*

CONSUMER GUIDE
TO
HOME ENERGY SAVINGS

The **American Council for an Energy-Efficient Economy (ACEEE)** is an independent, nonprofit organization dedicated to advancing energy efficiency as a means of promoting both economic prosperity and environmental protection. Support for our work comes from a wide range of foundations, government organizations, research institutes, utilities, and corporations.

ACEEE publishes guides for consumers and procurement officials buying equipment and vehicles: *Consumer Guide to Home Energy Savings; The Most Energy-Efficient Appliances* (updated periodically); *Guide to Energy-Efficient Commercial Equipment, 2nd edition*; and *ACEEE's Green Book®: The Environmental Guide to Cars and Trucks* (updated annually).

To request the ACEEE Publications Catalog, write:

ACEEE
1001 Connecticut Avenue, N.W., Suite 801
Washington, D.C. 20036
Phone: (202) 429-0063
Fax: 202-429-0193
E-mail: aceee_publications@aceee.org

Home Energy is a nonprofit magazine about residential energy conservation. Articles cover topics ranging from research into new energy-saving technologies to tips on how to save energy in the home. Written for the professional and the homeowner, it is "the best magazine in America on home energy," according to John Javna, author of *50 Simple Things You Can Do to Save the Earth*. To subscribe, write:

Home Energy
2124 Kittredge Street, Suite 95
Berkeley, California 94704

CONSUMER GUIDE TO HOME ENERGY SAVINGS

by
Alex Wilson, Jennifer Thorne, and John Morrill

Eighth Edition

American Council for an Energy-Efficient Economy
Washington, D.C.

IN COOPERATION WITH:
Home Energy magazine
Berkeley, California

Consumer Guide to Home Energy Savings, 8th Edition

Published by the American Council for an Energy-Efficient Economy
1001 Connecticut Avenue, N.W., Suite 801, Washington, D.C. 20036

Printed in the United States of America

Cover and book design by Chuck Myers
Illustrations by David Conover
Printed in the United States of America

Portions of this book have been reprinted with the permission of Massachusetts Audubon Society from the following guides: *Saving Energy and Money with Home Appliances; Oil and Gas Heating Systems; How to Weatherize Your Home or Apartment; All About Insulation;* and *Contractor's Guide to Sealing Air Leaks.*

Listings of the most efficient appliances are necessarily incomplete. Smaller manufacturers often do not have efficiency data independently monitored. Also, new, more efficient models are constantly joining the market. Please use this book as a guide, not a bible.

Written comments on this publication are welcome; send your comments to:

Consumer Guide to Home Energy Savings Editor
American Council for an Energy-Efficient Economy
1001 Connecticut Avenue, N.W., Suite 801
Washington, D.C. 20036-5525
aceee.org/consumerguide

ISBN 0-918249-46-5

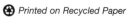 *Printed on Recycled Paper*

TABLE OF CONTENTS

Home Energy Checklist for Action............inside front and back covers

Lists of Tables viii

Acknowledgments xi

PART I — Consumer Guide to Home Energy Savings

Chapter 1   Saving Energy and Saving the Environment....................1

Chapter 2   Buttoning Up Your House...11

Chapter 3   New Windows...29

Chapter 4   Heating Systems...43

Chapter 5   Cooling Systems...77

Chapter 6   Water Heating...97

Chapter 7   Food Storage..117

Chapter 8   Cooking...123

Chapter 9   Dishwashing..131

Chapter 10   Laundry...137

Chapter 11   Lighting...145

Chapter 12   Other Energy Uses in the Home................................165

Part II — The Most Energy-Efficient Appliances

Refrigerators and Freezers..179

Dishwashers 184

Clothes Washers 186

Gas Water Heaters...190

Gas Combination Water Heaters/Space Heaters......................191

Oil Water Heaters..191

Room Air Conditioners 192

Central Air Conditioners 195

Conventional (Air-Source) Heat Pumps 200

Gas Furnaces 205

Gas Boilers—Hot Water 207

Gas Boilers—Steam 209

Oil Furnaces 211

Oil Boilers—Hot Water 212

Oil Boilers—Steam 215

Appendix 1 CO_2 Emissions and Energy Savings 217

Appendix 2   Understanding EnergyGuide Labels 219

Appendix 3   List of Manufacturers 227

Appendix 4   For More Information 233

Appendix 5   Choosing Heating and
              Air Conditioning Contractors 237

Index 239

LISTS OF TABLES

Table 1.1
Energy Conservation and CO_2 Savings in the Home 3

Table 3.1
Representative Window Sizes for NFRC Labeling 38

Table 4.1
Manufacturers of Ground-Source Heat Pumps 61

Table 5.1
Ceiling Fan Sizing 89

Table 6.1
Peak Hourly Hot Water Demand 104

Table 6.2
Manufacturers of Instantaneous ("Tankless") Gas Water Heaters 107

Table 6.3
Manufacturers of Heat Pump Water Heaters 108

Table 6.4
Manufacturers of Combination Water Heaters/Space Heaters 108

Table 6.5
North American Solar Water Heating Systems 109

Table 6.6
Life-Cycle Costs for 13-Year Operation of Different Types
of Water Heaters 110

Table 11.1
Compact Fluorescent Lamp Manufacturers 148

Table 11.2
Savings Achieved by Switching from Incandescent to
Compact Fluorescent 151

Table 11.3
Electronic Ballasts Manufacturers (for tube fluorescent lamps) 153

Table 11.4
High-Performance Tube Fluorescent Lamps 153

Table 11.5
Catalog Retailers Offering PV-Powered Lighting 156

Table 11.6
Lighting Controls Manufacturers 158

Table 11.7
Mail-Order Lighting Equipment Retailers 162

Table 11.8
Wholesaler of Energy-Conserving Lighting Products 162

Table 12.1
Typical Energy Consumption and Percent Saturation
of Miscellaneous Electricity Uses in the Home 166

Table 12.2
Residential Energy Consumption of Miscellaneous Appliances
in the United States 167

Table A.1
CO_2 Emissions from Different Energy Sources 217

ACKNOWLEDGMENTS

This book owes much to the energy conservation community: those hardworking folks who have worked diligently (and quietly) to increase the energy efficiency of the U.S. housing stock by one-third since 1973, and whose trials and errors have produced the knowledge compiled here.

The information in this guide has evolved with the steady improvements in residential appliances and changes in equipment efficiency standards. Each new edition benefits from the suggestions of experts in this field. We thank all the individuals who have reviewed this or previous editions for clarity and technical accuracy: Carl Blumstein, Fred Davis, Neal Elliott, Howard Geller, Roger Harris, John Hayes, Drew Kleibrink, Michael L'Ecuyer, Marc Ledbetter, Karina Lutz, Chris Mathis, Alan Meier, Steve Nadel, Nancy Schalch, Mike Thompson, and Hofu Wu.

We also thank our colleagues who have contributed to the production of this guide: David Conover for his illustrations; Harvey Sachs for his detailed review and input on updating material; Renee Nida for her copyediting and proofreading; Marycel Tuazon for her assistance with several of the tables; and Glee Murray for her overview of the entire process. As usual, the authors remain responsible for any errors or omissions that remain.

PART I

Consumer Guide to Home Energy Savings

CHAPTER 1
Saving Energy and Saving the Environment

A re you about to buy a new appliance? Remodel your house? Upgrade your heating or cooling system? If you're like most of us, you don't do these things very often. When you do, you want to make good choices, both for your pocketbook and for the environment. But you probably don't have time to become an expert. That's where this book can help.

The *Consumer Guide to Home Energy Savings* will help you make wise investment decisions and help you decide which products to buy and how to use them for maximum energy savings. We've sorted through the thousands of major home appliances and heating and cooling systems on the market and picked out those that are the most efficient. We've listed the best ways to tighten up your house so that your heating and cooling systems won't have to work as hard—or use as much energy. We've pulled together tips on operating new and existing appliances to reduce energy use and improve performance. But before getting into the details, let's take a look at why it makes sense to buy the most efficient appliances and conserve energy in the home.

ENERGY USE AND THE ENVIRONMENT

Every time you buy a home appliance, tune up your heating system, or replace a burned-out light bulb, you're making a decision that affects the environment. You are probably already aware that most of our biggest environmental problems are directly associated with energy production and use: urban smog, oil spills, acid rain, and global warming, to mention a few. But you may not realize just how big a difference each of us can make by taking energy use into account in our household purchasing and maintenance decisions.

For example, did you know that every kilowatt-hour (kWh) of electricity you avoid using saves over two pounds of carbon dioxide (CO_2) that would otherwise be pumped into the atmosphere?[1] CO_2 is the number one contributor to global warming, a process that scientists say

---

[1] This assumes that your utility company produces electricity by burning coal. One-half of all U.S. electricity is generated by coal. If another fuel or hydropower is used, less CO_2 will be produced.

could raise the earth's temperatures by 5–9°F over the next hundred years. If you replace a typical 1980, 20-cubic-foot refrigerator with an energy-efficient 2003 model, you'll save more than 800 kWh and almost a ton of CO_2 emissions per year! Installing an 18-watt compact fluorescent light in place of a 75-watt incandescent light bulb will save about 570 kWh and over 1,300 pounds of CO_2 emissions over the life of the compact fluorescent.

Carbon dioxide is only one of the environmentally harmful gases resulting from energy use. Others, such as sulfur dioxide, nitrous oxide, carbon monoxide, and ozone, have much more direct effects—effects that can be seen and smelled in every major urban area of the country. That new refrigerator mentioned above will save each year over 20 pounds of sulfur dioxide emissions, the leading cause of acid rain.

Other energy-saving products and improvements around the home can help the environment. Table 1.1 shows the reductions in CO_2 emissions achieved from a few relatively easy energy improvements in the home. With some of these you'll notice different CO_2 savings depending on the type of fuel used. That's because some fuels give off less CO_2 than others. If you're interested in this kind of analysis, turn to Appendix 1 for details on the CO_2 emissions from different energy sources.

Worldwide, we pump some 26 billion tons of CO_2 into the atmosphere each year—more than four tons for every man, woman, and child on earth. The United States is responsible for one-quarter of that, or close to 6 billion tons per year. On a per-capita basis, that comes to 21 tons for each American, though some of us produce a lot more than others.

Reducing CO_2 emissions by a few tons per year may not seem like a lot, given the billions of tons released worldwide each year. But the collective actions of many will have a dramatic effect, particularly in a high energy-use country like the United States. For example, the appliance efficiency standards that took effect in the early 1990s saved more than 88 billion kWh in 2000—about 28 million tons of CO_2. Updates to these standards will save more than 250 billon kWh in 2010. If the roughly 40 million households in climates with large heating needs boosted their furnace or boiler efficiencies from 70% to 90%, some 45 million tons of CO_2 emissions would be eliminated each year. Substituting compact fluorescent lamps for the ten most frequently used incandescent lamps in every house in the country would reduce CO_2 emissions by about the same amount.

The U.S. Environmental Protection Agency (EPA) and U.S. Department of Energy (DOE) recognize the local and global environmental significance of residential appliances and equipment. Working in voluntary cooperation with manufacturers and retailers, these agencies

TABLE 1.1

ENERGY CONSERVATION AND CO_2 SAVINGS IN THE HOME

Energy Conservation Measure	CO_2 Savings (tons/yr)		
	Gas	Oil	Electric[1]
Installing 10 13-watt compact fluorescent light bulbs in place of 10 60-watt incandescent bulbs[2]	—	—	0.0
Replacing typical 1980 refrigerator with energy-efficient 2003 model[3]	—	—	0.0
Replacing a 65% efficient furnace or boiler with one that is 90% efficient[4]	2.0	3.0	—
Substituting gas or oil heat for electric resistance heat[1,4]	23.0	19.0	—
Replacing single-glazed windows with argon-filled double-glazed windows[4]	2.4	3.9	9.8
Planting shade trees around house and painting house a lighter color[5]	—	—	0.9–2.4
Installing a solar water-heating system[6]	0.8	1.4	4.9
Boosting energy efficiency of house being built from standard insulation levels to super-insulated standards[7]	5.5	8.8	23.0

1. Assumes electricity generated using coal.
2. Assumes lights on 2,000 hours per year (5½ hours per day).
3. Average 1980 model uses 1,300 kWh per year; energy-efficient 2003 model uses 450 kWh per year.
4. Assumes 1,850 square-foot house of average (good) energy efficiency (heating load of 6.95 Btu/ft²/°F-day) in a northern climate (6,300 heating degree-days).
5. Data from Lawrence Berkeley Laboratory, Berkeley, Calif. Based on computer simulations for various locations around the country.
6. Assumes two-panel system providing 14.25 million Btu/year (75% of demand).
7. Assumes 1,850 square-foot house in northern climate (6,300 degree-days). Boosting energy efficiency from 6.95 Btu/ft²/°F-day to 1.37 Btu/ft²/°F-day (going from R-19 walls, R-30 ceilings, double-glazed windows, and relatively loose construction to R-31 walls, R-38 ceilings, low-e windows, and tight construction).

have created a distinctive ENERGY STAR® label to help consumers identify energy-efficient appliances, computers, lighting, and home entertainment equipment. Some homebuilders are now constructing entire ENERGY STAR homes, which include a variety of energy-efficient features and equipment. ENERGY STAR homes are at least 30% more energy efficient than the current International Energy Conservation Code (formerly known as the Model Energy Code).

The ENERGY STAR logo identifies energy-efficient appliances and equipment. The ENERGY STAR distinction is now available for qualifying furnaces, central and room air conditioners, heat pumps, refrigerators, dishwashers, clothes washers, light fixtures, televisions and VCRs, audio equipment, computers and computer monitors, and a variety of other office equipment.

To get a sense of just how effective energy conservation can be, take a look at the 1970s and 1980s. From 1973 to 1986, the U.S. gross national product grew 36% with no increase in energy use at all. Had efficiencies remained at 1973 levels, we would be spending an extra $150 billion in energy bills each year and pumping $1\frac{1}{2}$ times more CO_2 into the atmosphere! We are already saving the equivalent of 13 million barrels of oil each day—half of the OPEC output—and, compared with 1973 projections, we're getting by with 250 fewer large power plants than would have otherwise been required.

SAVING THE EARTH— AND GETTING PAID TO DO IT

The wonderful thing about saving energy is that, in addition to helping the environment, you save money. It's like contributing to a good cause and ending up with more money in your pocket. Many of the energy-efficient appliances and heating or cooling systems covered in this book cost no more than their inefficient counterparts. With most others, the extra cost is easily repaid in energy savings over just a few years.

When you buy an appliance, you pay more than just the sales price—you commit yourself to paying the cost of running the appliance for as long as you own it. These energy costs can add up quickly. For

DEPENDENCE ON FOREIGN OIL

Although petroleum is generally not a source of energy for homes, most homeowners own and operate motor vehicles on a daily basis. Reliance on petroleum for our transportation needs is an important energy and environmental concern. The risks associated with heavy reliance on foreign oil are clear as terrorist activity and costly wars in the Middle East underscore our vulnerability to that unstable region.

Lest we forget: in the late 1970s, the United States imported over 40% of its oil, with a peak of 46.4% in 1977. Then dramatic price increases and supply shortages fueled highly effective energy conservation efforts. Net petroleum imports dropped to 28% by 1982. But by the mid-1980s, as fuel prices softened (due in part to successful conservation efforts), interest in conservation dropped and oil imports crept back up—to over 40% by 1990. From 1985 to 2000, oil imports doubled and by the mid-1990s dependence on foreign oil had grown to over 50% of oil supplies. This reliance on foreign oil cost about $110 billion in 2000, accounting for one-quarter of the total U.S. trade deficit.

The answer isn't to open up wilderness areas to oil exploration, but to use less energy more efficiently. A 1½ miles-per-gallon (mpg) increase in fuel economy by automobiles in the United States would save more oil than is estimated to lie under the Arctic National Wildlife Refuge. Indeed, energy efficiency improvements and aggressive energy conservation measures could totally eliminate U.S. dependency on foreign oil. We can't look just to the governing bodies to bring about these changes—it's up to each of us. And it should start in our homes and our cars.

---

example, running a refrigerator 15–20 years costs as much as the initial purchase price of the unit. That 100-watt light bulb you just put in will cost about $6 in electricity over its (short) life.

The sum of the purchase price and the energy cost of running an appliance or light bulb over its lifetime is called its life-cycle cost. The life-cycle costs of energy-efficient appliances are lower than those of average models even though the average-efficiency models may cost less to buy.

To increase the economic benefits of buying more energy-efficient appliances and boosting your overall home efficiency, your state or utility company may offer a rebate program for the purchase of energy-efficient appliances. Many states and utility companies have realized that it costs less money to conserve energy than to build new power plants and that they can save money by paying you to save energy. Rebates are most common for high-efficiency heat pumps, central air conditioners, refrigerators, and clothes washers. Rebate programs are much more common among electric companies than gas companies, although some gas utilities offer rebates for high-efficiency furnaces and boilers. If you plan to buy a major appliance soon, ask your utility if it offers rebates for efficient models.

Always consider how much it will cost to operate a new appliance or light bulb—not just how much it costs to buy.

HOW TO USE THIS BOOK

The *Consumer Guide to Home Energy Savings* is the most complete and up-to-date guide available on energy savings in the home. Following a review of measures to tighten up the building shell itself, the book focuses on the things you put in it—including major appliances, heating equipment, air conditioning, and lighting—and how the energy use of those products can be reduced.

If you're about to buy a new appliance or heating system, you'll be most interested in the tips on what to look for when buying new equipment and the listings in Part II of the most energy-efficient models available. Only the very highest rated models are listed within each appliance category. The models listed here represent only a small percentage of all the different models currently available. Many more appliances are better than average in terms of efficiency, but only the best are included here.

Our lists are based on information from the most recent product directories published by appliance industry associations, the ENERGY STAR program, and product manufacturers. The efficiency ratings are based on standardized laboratory tests that manufacturers are required to conduct on their products. The same test ratings are listed on the yellow EnergyGuide labels that are required for most home appliances. See Appendix 2 for information on how to read and interpret EnergyGuide

Based on standard U.S. Government tests

ENERGYGUIDE

Refrigerator-Freezer
With Automatic Defrost
With Side-Mounted Freezer
With Through-the-Door-Ice Service

XYZ Corporation
Model ABC-W
Capacity: 23 Cubic Feet

Compare the Energy Use of this Refrigerator
with Others Before You Buy.

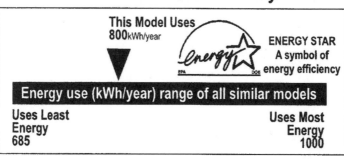

This Model Uses
800kWh/year

ENERGY STAR
A symbol of
energy efficiency

Energy use (kWh/year) range of all similar models

Uses Least
Energy
685

Uses Most
Energy
1000

kWh/year (kilowatt-hours per year) is a measure of energy (electricity) use.
Your utility company uses it to compute your bill. Only models with 22.5 and 24.4
cubic feet and the above features are used in this scale.

Refrigerators using more energy cost more to operate.
This model's estimated yearly operating cost is:

$65

Based on a 2000 U.S. Government national average cost of 8.03¢ per kWh for electricity. Your
actual operating cost will vary depending on your local utility rates and your use of the product.

Important: Removal of this label before consumer purchase violates the Federal Trade Commission's Appliance Labeling Rule (16 C.F.R. Part 305).

EnergyGuide labels provide a fast and easy way to
compare the energy efficiency of most home appliances.

labels, and read through the detailed information on energy performance in each chapter.

The lists of refrigerators, freezers, water heaters, clothes washers, and dishwashers include the estimated annual energy use. The lists of furnaces, boilers, air conditioners, and heat pumps include their efficiency ratings instead of estimated energy use. The energy use for these appliances varies greatly from house to house depending on climate, family size, and other factors, but the efficiency ratings provide a good way to compare the energy use of one model to another. The higher the efficiency, the lower the energy use and operating cost.

Keep in mind that energy performance is not the only consideration you should use when selecting home appliances. Consumers must consider how effectively the appliances perform their primary functions—cleaning dishes, keeping food cold, etc.—as well as how much energy they use in doing it. For example, you wouldn't consider buying a dishwasher that didn't get your dishes clean, even if it used just half as much energy. This book does not pretend to be a comprehensive review of product reliability or performance, or a guide to convenience features found in these products; there are other sources for that information. It is worth noting, however, that energy-efficient appliances are generally high-quality products due to the better materials and components used in their construction.

The model numbers in this book are used by manufacturers in their product literature. In some cases, appliance dealers use abbreviated model numbers (for example, dropping the first number or letter). An asterisk (*) appearing in a model number indicates a digit or letter that varies with features of the appliance not affecting its energy efficiency and capacity (for example, color).

When shopping for major home appliances, you may want to call several stores or dealers to check the price and availability of different models. Ask the salesperson for information about the efficiency of each model, but be aware that he or she may not know very much about energy performance. Take this guide along when you shop. Use it along with the yellow EnergyGuide labels to compare similar models.

Several new appliance makers have entered the U.S. market in recent years. These and some other companies manufacturing high-efficiency equipment are not exactly "household names," and it may not be easy to find their products in your local appliance store. Appendix 3 lists phone numbers and, where available, web sites for all the companies whose products are listed in this guide. Customer service representatives should be able to direct you to a local distributor.

If you cannot find some of the models listed in this book, you can still use the information provided here to your advantage. Compare the efficiencies of the models you can find to those that are listed here. Don't be satisfied if the salesperson tells you that one model is just as efficient as another unless he or she can demonstrate this to you. Indeed, some brand-new models may be as efficient as those in this book, but were introduced after this book went to press. Use the models listed here for comparison.

And thank you for taking the time to consider energy efficiency. Remember, every time you do something to save energy, you're helping the environment. All of us—and especially our children and their children—owe you a big thanks.

CHAPTER 2
Buttoning Up Your House

If you live in a cold climate, you probably spend something like two-thirds of your energy dollars on heat. Your old furnace or boiler chugs away burning the gas or oil like there's no tomorrow. So should you rush right out and buy a new super-efficient one? Not necessarily.

Replacing your existing heating system with one that's more efficient may well be a wise step, but it shouldn't necessarily be your first step. You should first try to lower your heating requirements. Tighten up. Weatherize. Insulate. By reducing your heating needs, you may increase comfort and you may be able to get by with a significantly smaller—and less expensive—furnace or boiler.

The same arguments hold true with air conditioning. If you live in a warm climate with high cooling requirements, it makes a lot of sense to tighten up the house to reduce your cooling load before investing in new air conditioning equipment.

A tight, well-insulated house saves energy and allows you to get by with smaller-capacity heating and air conditioning systems, and it is also more comfortable, with smaller temperature swings. No more cold drafts at your feet while temperatures at head level are a sweaty 80°F. With less of this temperature stratification during the winter months, you'll even find yourself comfortable at a lower thermostat setting than you're used to.

In the next few pages, we'll take a look at some of the measures you can take to improve the energy efficiency of your house and when it makes sense to consider such projects.

CONSIDER AN ENERGY AUDIT

Find out from a pro where heat is being lost through your home's shell and what you should do about it. Energy auditors use sophisticated equipment, like a blower door and infrared camera, to help pinpoint air leaks and areas with inadequate insulation. Trained energy auditors know what to look for in both newer and older houses, and the investment in their time is usually well worth the cost. Depending on the service, you may be able to have your heating or cooling system cleaned, tuned up, and tested at the same time (see Chapters 4 and 5). Some utility companies provide basic energy audits free of charge.

Some energy auditors and building scientists provide several services to improve the overall performance and comfort provided by houses. Sometimes called *house doctors* or *home performance contractors*, they address each building as a system. They understand how to improve a home's overall safety, comfort, energy efficiency, and indoor air quality. After all, many construction flaws can result in high energy bills, and some conditions that cause high energy bills can compromise building safety or resident health and comfort. For example, home performance contractors can diagnose and fix uneven

Have an energy audit done on your house to find out where the heat really goes—and what you should do about it.

heat distribution while lowering energy costs, or reduce cold drafts and moisture condensation problems while reducing energy bills. For more information on the services available from home performance contractors, visit http://www.homeenergy.org/perfbro.intro.html. Or contact your state energy office or cooperative extension service for information on qualified auditors and contractors in your area.

If you are a renter, encourage your landlord to have an energy audit conducted and follow through on the recommended energy improvements. You might offer to help your landlord by arranging for the audit and even doing some of the work in exchange for rent. After all, if you pay for heating, air conditioning, and electricity, energy improvements are very much in your interest. Even if your landlord won't pay for energy conservation projects, many of the suggestions in this chapter are inexpensive enough that they'll pay for themselves in just a year or two, justifying your out-of-pocket expenditures.

FIND AND SEAL AIR LEAKS

Hidden air leaks cause some of the largest heat losses in older homes. Common air leakage sites are listed below:

■ Plumbing penetrations through insulated floors and ceilings

■ Chimney penetrations through insulated ceilings and exterior walls

■ Along the sill plate and band joist at the top of foundation walls

■ Fireplace dampers

■ Attic access hatches

■ The tops of interior partition walls where they intersect with the attic space

■ Recessed lights and fans in insulated ceilings

■ Wiring penetrations through insulated floors, ceilings, and walls

■ Missing plaster

■ Electrical outlets and switches, especially on exterior walls

■ Window, door, and baseboard moldings

■ Dropped ceilings above bathtubs and cabinets

■ Kneewalls in finished attics, especially at access doors and built-in cabinets and bureaus.

What you should use in sealing these hidden air leaks depends on the size of the gaps and where they are located. Caulk is best for cracks and gaps less than about ¼" wide. In choosing caulks, read the label carefully to make sure that the caulk is suitable for the material to be sealed. Look for caulks that remain flexible over a 20-year lifetime. If the caulked joint will be visible, choose a paintable caulk or one that is the right color. In general, you should avoid the cheapest caulks, because they probably won't hold up well.

Expanding foam sealant is an excellent material to use for sealing larger cracks and holes that are protected from sunlight and moisture. One-part polyurethane foam is commonly available in hardware and building supply stores. Today's products are safe for atmospheric ozone.

Backer rod or crack filler is a flexible foam material, usually round in cross-section (¼" to 1" in diameter), and sold in long coils. Use it for sealing large cracks and to provide a backing in very deep cracks that are to be sealed with caulk.

Use rigid foam insulation for sealing very large openings such as plumbing chases and attic hatch covers. Fiberglass insulation can also be used for sealing large holes, but it will work better if wrapped in plastic or stuffed in plastic bags, because air can leak through exposed fiberglass. Don't use plastic in places where high temperatures may be

Watch for hidden air leaks around pipes— and seal them up.

Seal joint with silicone caulk

Sheet metal, as required by fire codes

A tremendous amount of heat can escape around the chimney if it isn't properly sealed.

reached, and always wear gloves and a dust mask when working with fiberglass.

Sheets of polyethylene can be taped over large holes to block air flow in some situations, but this is usually a fairly temporary measure, since the polyethylene may disintegrate over time if not protected.

**Get rid of drafts along the floor
by caulking along the sill and band joist
from the basement.**

Band joist

Sill plate

Drop-ceilings above closets, showers, and cabinets can be among the worst offenders when it comes to air leakage.

Specialized materials such as metal flashing and high-temperature silicone sealants may be required for sealing around chimneys and flue pipes. Check with your building inspector or fire marshal if unsure about fire-safe details in these locations.

Depending on the way your house was framed, a lot of warm air can escape into the attic through the partition walls. Seal from the attic.

Expanding foam sealant works best for sealing somewhat larger gaps—over ¼" wide.

Backer rod or crack filler can also be used for sealing deep cracks or as a backing for caulk.

UPGRADE INEFFICIENT WINDOWS AND DOORS

About one-third of the home's total heat loss usually occurs through windows and doors. In fact, the total energy lost through windows and doors in this country is about as much as the amount of energy we get from the Alaska Pipeline! Windows deserve the most attention because they outnumber doors. To reduce heat loss, you can either fix up your existing windows or replace them with new energy-efficient units. Which choice you should take depends on a number of factors.

If the existing windows have rotted or damaged wood, cracked glass, missing putty, poorly fitting sashes, or locks that don't work, you may be better off replacing them. The next chapter discusses the exciting advances in new window technology.

If the windows are generally in good shape, it will probably be more cost-effective to boost their efficiency by weatherstripping, caulking, and fitting them with storm panels rather than undergo the expense of

Outside

Inside

A tremendous amount of cold air can leak in through old windows.

window replacement. New windows, even when they replace very inefficient windows, rarely pay back their cost quickly enough to be a good investment just from energy saved. However, if you plan to replace windows for comfort, appearance, cleaning convenience, modernization, or any other reason, it almost always pays to invest in more efficient windows rather than minimum-performance ones.

There are a number of ways to improve the energy efficiency of existing windows. The quickest and least expensive option is to seal all window edges and cracks with rope caulk. This costs less than $1 per window and only takes a few minutes. Rope caulk may be taken off, stored in foil, and reused for two or three seasons, but once it hardens you should discard it. With double-hung windows, if you don't need to open the upper sash, you can permanently caulk them closed.

Compression type

V-type

Weatherstripping is the most permanent way to cut air leakage through windows and doors.

A more permanent solution is to weatherstrip the windows. This is more time-consuming and expensive than installing rope caulk ($8–$10 per window), but it only needs to be done once, it permits you to open the window, and the weatherstripping is out of sight. The type of weatherstripping to use depends on the type of window—both compression-type and V-strip weatherstripping are widely available in building supply stores. You usually get what you pay for with weatherstripping products, so spend the few extra dollars necessary to get a top-quality product that is likely to hold up over years of use.

The next step in improving window energy efficiency is to install some type of storm window. If you have single-glazed windows, storm panels will double their energy efficiency. If you heat with oil, the improved energy efficiency in a cold climate will save about a gallon of oil per square-foot of window per year. (That's an awful lot of oil that is otherwise leaking out of your house and adding to our air pollution woes.) With gas heat, the savings can top 1 therm per square foot per year.

The simplest type of storm window is a plastic film taped to the inside of the window frame. Inner storm window kits are readily available from hardware stores. They cost just $3–$8 per window and typically last for one to three years. Some are made of special shrink-tight plastic that you heat with a blow dryer after installation to get rid of wrinkles. These inexpensive plastic films are especially suitable for apartments and condominiums where exterior improvements are not allowed or not practical.

Removable or operable storm windows with glass or rigid acrylic panes generally make more sense if you plan to stay in the house for more than a few years. Both exterior and interior storm windows are available, though exterior units are far more common. Most people choose aluminum-framed combination storm/screen windows, which are very convenient to operate. Be careful, though. There are big differences among products on the market, especially relative to air tightness. The tightest units have air leakage rates as low as 0.01 cfm/ft, while the worst are over 1 cfm/ft. Don't settle for anything higher than 0.3 cfm/ft. Also look for units with low-e coatings on the glass to improve the energy performance.

Storm windows typically cost between $50 and $120, depending on size, quality, and labor for installation—far less than replacement windows. Before buying new storm windows, though, check to make sure you don't already have a stack in a dusty corner of your basement or attic. If these are older wood-framed storm windows, they probably just need a coat of paint. Although they aren't quite as convenient as combination storm/screen windows (they have to be taken down and put up

Weep holes

Outside

Duct tape seals edges

Inside

Permanent   Prime Window   Temporary Plastic

Storm windows can be installed on the inside or outside.

each year and separate screens are required), wooden storm windows are often more energy efficient. If aluminum combination storms are already in place, examine them to make sure they are tightly sealed where mounted to the window casings; if not, caulk all cracks (but do not seal the small weep holes on the bottom edges). Finally, you can boost the energy efficiency of windows by installing insulating curtains or drapes on the interior. These can be closed at night to significantly cut down on heat loss. They can also be closed on hot summer days to keep out unwanted heat gain. Look for

Install door sweeps to reduce airflow underneath doors.

shades or drapes that fit into tracks to keep air from passing around the edges.

Don't forget about your doors. As with windows, make sure your doors are in good shape. Weatherstrip around the whole perimeter to ensure a tight seal when closed. Install quality door sweeps on the bottom of the doors if they aren't already in place. On an old, uninsulated metal or fiberglass door, a storm door probably isn't cost-effective. In fact, a glass storm door may damage the plastic trim on some metal or fiberglass doors by trapping heat.

INSULATE

Insulation is your primary defense against heat loss through the house envelope. However, putting insulation into a house after it is built can be pretty difficult. Because of the large area involved, walls are most important. You may be able to tell if the walls are insulated by removing an outlet cover and peering into the wall cavity. Another way to check for insulation is to find a closet (or cabinet) along an exterior wall. Drill two ¼" holes into the wall about 4" apart, with one hole above the other. Shine a flashlight into one hole while looking into the other, and any insulation should be apparent. If there isn't any insulation, the best option is to bring in an insulation contractor to blow cellulose or fiberglass into the walls.

Adding insulation to an unheated attic is usually a lot easier. If there is no floor in the attic, simply add more insulation, either loose fill or unfaced fiberglass batts. If the existing insulation comes up to the top of the joists, add an additional layer of unfaced batts across the joists. This helps to cover gaps between the first layer of batts. If an attic floor is in place, you may need to remove that floor before adding insulation (be very careful not to step through the ceiling below!). In most of the country, a full foot of fiberglass or cellulose insulation is cost-effective in the attic floor.

If the attic is finished with a sloped cathedral ceiling, adding extra insulation is much more difficult. If there is no insulation there at present, it may be worth pulling off the drywall, insulating, and installing a new ceiling. Or, if you will be re-roofing in the near future, consider adding a layer of rigid foam insulation and decking on top of the existing roof and then shingling over that. In either case, it's a major project, and you will probably have to bring in a contractor to do the work. If there is already

Cellulose or fiberglass insulation can be blown into uninsulated walls by an insulation contractor.

Adding more attic insulation is often easy and can be done by homeowners.

Ventilation Out

POSSIBILITY #1
Fiberglas Batts

Ensure Adequate Ventilation

POSSIBILITY #2
Rigid Insulation

Drywall on Vapor Barrier

Permanent

Floor

Floor Insulation

Ventilation In

Insulating a sloped ceiling in a finished attic can be done from the inside, or by installing foam and new roofing on the outside.

some insulation in the roof, it may be hard to justify the cost of this work, in which case you can focus your energy efforts elsewhere.

Heat loss through foundation walls is often neglected even in new houses. But in fact, in an otherwise well-insulated and tight house, as much as 20% of the total heat loss can occur through uninsulated foundation walls. Insulating the foundation or floor can easily save several hundred gallons of oil or several hundred therms of gas per year in northern climates.

**To reduce heat loss to an unheated
crawl space or basement, insulate between your floor joists.
If pipes in the crawl space could freeze, insulate around
the perimeter, as shown in the top illustration.**

Insulation

Vapor Barrier

Drywall

Basement Wall

The best way to insulate a basement wall is to build a 2 x 4 frame on the inside and insulate with fiberglass.

If the basement or crawl space is unheated and you don't have plans to fix it up, you will do best to insulate between the floor joists instead of around the perimeter walls. Use unfaced fiberglass batt insulation supported from below with wire or metal rods if necessary. Fluff the insulation to ensure that it fills the joist cavities. Cover the underside of the joists with a moisture-permeable air barrier, such as Tyvek® or Typar®. In crawl spaces, cover the ground surface with 6-mil-thick polyethylene to keep moisture from getting into the crawl space from the ground.

If the basement is heated and used, you need to insulate the basement walls instead. The simplest method is to build 2 × 4 frames against the concrete foundation walls, insulate with fiberglass, and cover with drywall. Before doing this, you may need to correct drainage problems on the exterior if water leaks into the basement. Hire a reputable contractor who understands foundation drainage, or, if you do the work yourself, consult a good do-it-yourself manual.

ECONOMICS

The economics of all these energy improvements will depend on where you live, how large your heating or cooling requirements are, and how much you pay for energy. Most measures described in this chapter will pay for themselves in five years or less if you heat with gas or oil, or use air conditioning. If you have electric resistance heat, the payback will generally be much faster. Do-it-yourself energy improvements pay for themselves the fastest because the labor cost is eliminated—but make sure you know what you're doing! And, remember that the cost savings are not the total picture: Proper work will increase your comfort and yield significant environmental benefits for everyone.

PLANNING ENERGY IMPROVEMENTS

Some of the more involved energy improvements mentioned here, such as window replacement and insulating, make the most sense when you are planning other remodeling work. If you are going to extend a wall out to enlarge your kitchen or put in a larger dormer for a master bedroom expansion, by all means boost energy efficiency at the same time. Rebuild walls with high insulation levels. Put in high-performance insulating windows.

As long as you're ripping out walls, take advantage of the mess and go a little further, boosting the efficiency of some of the adjoining walls and windows as well. With a small addition, some of this work might even pay for itself right away if it means, for example, that you can get by without adding a separate heating system or expanding your current heat distribution system.

NEW CONSTRUCTION

If you are building a new house or a major addition, do it right the first time, saving money and the environment for decades to come. Today's state-of-the-art energy-efficient houses typically require less than a quarter as much energy for heating and cooling as most existing houses. There are thousands of homes in the northern United States and Canada with yearly energy bills that total just $200 to $300.

These homes cost more to build than a standard house, but not that much more. You might spend an extra $5,000–$10,000 to build a superefficient house with R-30 walls, R-38 ceilings, R-19 foundations, R-3 windows, and very low air leakage. But that extra cost will usually be recovered in just five to ten years through energy savings. Plus, you'll be more comfortable and you'll have the satisfaction of knowing that your house is dumping less pollution and carbon dioxide into the atmosphere.

Once you get an idea of what you want, contact builders or architects in your area and find out how experienced they are with energy-efficient construction. Special skills are required to build high-efficiency houses and to install features such as heat-recovery ventilation systems. You may need to spend a little extra time looking for the right builder, but the time and effort will be well worth it.

CHAPTER 3
New Windows

Whether replacing windows in an older house or choosing windows for a new house, your decisions on what type of windows to buy will be among the most important decisions you will make in terms of energy use. In older houses, it is not uncommon for windows to account for a third of the total heat loss from a house. In new houses, windows typically account for 15% to 40% of total heat loss. Also, those windows can account for as much as 75% of heat gain during the summer months, adding to air conditioning costs. On the positive side, windows can be used for passive solar heating in the winter months and help reduce heating costs, and of course windows provide natural daylighting and views to the outside world.

Because of the impact windows have on both heat loss and heat gain, proper selection of products can be confusing. To add to the complexity, window glazing technology has changed tremendously in recent years. The best window glazings today insulate almost four times as well as the best commonly available windows from just fifteen years ago. Because of the rapid pace of change, even skilled designers are often not fully aware of the potential these new glazings offer for energy-efficient building design. Fortunately, just as windows were becoming more complicated, two organizations began offering better data and guidance for consumers. The National Fenestration Rating Council (NFRC) provides the objective data for wise choices, and ENERGY STAR offers guidance tailored to your climate zone. Both are covered in this chapter.

UNDERSTANDING HOW WINDOWS WORK

To understand how windows affect heating and cooling costs, we need to know a little about how energy flows through them. The next illustration shows the primary mechanisms of heat transfer through windows.

■ *Sunlight* (solar radiation) is an important source of heat, and is transmitted directly through most windows. Solar radiation consists of visible light and a part of the solar spectrum that is heat but not visible light (infrared heat radiation). Glazings are available that *selectively*

How heat moves through windows.

Outside

Inside

transmit light of different wavelengths—for example, some appear totally clear (high visible light transmittance) while blocking infrared heat radiation. A window's solar heat gain coefficient (SHGC) is the measure of the amount of solar energy that passes through the window; typical values range from 0.4 to 0.9, and the higher the SHGC, the greater the percentage of solar energy that is transmitted to the inside.

■ *Radiant heat* is given off by warmer objects to colder objects. Things warmed by sunlight become stronger sources of radiant heat, and radiant heat is blocked by most window glazings. Greenhouses and passive solar heating illustrate the dynamic between sunlight and radiant heat: sunlight passes through glazings, warming objects indoors, but the heat from those objects does not quickly escape back through the glazings, and the space warms up. Special coatings on high-performance windows change the way heat radiation is absorbed and reradiated (see discussion on low-e glazings below).

■ *Conduction* is the mechanism of heat transfer through physical contact. Heat conducts from the warmer to the cooler side of a window as each molecule excites its neighbor, passing the energy along. Conduction occurs not only through solid materials (window glass and frames), but also through the air space between the layers of glass.

The amount of heat transmission through a material due to a temperature difference is given by its "U-value." The smaller the U-value, the less heat is transmitted. One of the major recent advances in window performance has been to use special gases between the layers of glass. These gases conduct heat less readily than air, resulting in lower U-values than simple double-glazed windows. **The NFRC uses the term "U-factor" in place of "U-value." The meaning is the same, and you should consider the terms interchangeable.**

■ *Convection* is the movement of heat in a fluid, such as air. The heat is transferred as the molecules of air are physically moved from one place to another. A warm glass surface heats the air next to it, causing the air to rise. A cold glass surface is warmed by the air next to it, and that air mass will fall as it gives up its heat. These convection currents occur on the inside of a window, on the outside, and even between layers of glass if they are separated too far from each other.

■ *Infiltration* is the process that carries heat through cracks and gaps around window frames. Infiltration through leaky windows can carry cold air into a house and warm air out. Infiltration is driven by wind and other differences in air pressure, such as warm air rising inside a house.

FEATURES TO LOOK FOR
IN ENERGY-SAVING WINDOWS

As mentioned above, window technology has improved dramatically in recent years, with the net result of lowering your energy bills. Some of the most important energy features of windows are explained below.

■ *Multiple layers of glazing.* Until the 1980s the primary way manufacturers improved the energy performance of windows was to add additional layers of glazing. Double glazing insulates almost twice as well as single glazing. Adding a third or fourth layer of glazing results in further improvement. In the 1970s, with rising concern over energy, triple-glazed and even quadruple-glazed windows entered the market. Some of these windows use glass only; others use thin plastic films as the inner glazing layer(s).

■ *Thickness of air space.* With double-glazed windows the air space between the panes of glass has a big effect on energy performance. A very thin air space does not insulate as well as a thicker air space because of heat conducted through that small space. During the 1970s a lot of window manufacturers increased the thickness of the air space in double-glazed windows from ¼" to ½" or more. If the air space is too wide, however, convection loops between the layers of glazing occur. Beyond about 1", you do not get any further gain in energy performance with thicker air spaces.

■ *Low-conductivity gas fill.* By substituting a denser, lower conductivity gas such as argon for the air in a sealed insulated glass window, heat loss can be reduced significantly. The largest window manufacturer in the country today, Andersen Windows, uses argon gas-fill in all of its insulated glass windows, and most major manufacturers offer argon gas-fill as an option. Other gases that are being used in windows include carbon dioxide, krypton, and argon-krypton mixtures.

■ *Tinted glass coatings.* Tinted glass and tinted window films have long been used in commercial buildings to reduce heat gain through windows. Improved, lightly tinted windows are becoming more common for the residential market in southern (cooling-dominated) climates. These new glazings reduce the solar heat gain without reducing visibility as much as older tinted glass and films.

LOW-E COATINGS

More than any other single improvement, the invention and commercial development of low-emissivity (low-e) coatings in the 1980s revolutionized window technology. Thin, transparent coatings of silver or tin oxide permit visible light to pass through, but they effectively reflect infrared heat radiation back into the room. This reduces heat loss through the windows in the winter.

A variety of low-e windows are now available for different climate zones and different applications in any particular location. Low-e windows with high solar heat gain coefficients are appropriate for northern climates where passive solar heating is advantageous, while "southern low-e" windows with low heat gain coefficients are appropriate in milder climates where summer cooling is more significant than winter heating. ENERGY STAR offers guidance for cold, moderate, and warm climates. For more information, see the "ENERGY STAR Windows" section later in this chapter.

The different properties of these low-e glazings sometimes make it advisable to choose different types of glazing for different sides of your house. We realize it may be difficult to find a builder or contractor interested in customizing window glazings for the four sides of your house. However, we encourage you to begin thinking about new windows from an informed energy perspective. For example, if you want to benefit from passive solar heating, for the south side choose windows containing a top-performing low-e glass with a high solar heat gain coefficient. On the north, install the lowest U-value windows you can afford. Or to keep things simpler, you can order the same glazings for the east-, west-, and north-facing windows.

Some window manufacturers now produce both "northern" and "southern" climate low-e products. But other window manufacturers may still offer just one type of low-e glazing as their standard, and charge extra for substitutions—if they provide options at all. So a decision to choose different glazings for windows of different orientations may require some extra shopping around. If you do order different glazings for your different windows, be sure to keep track of which windows have which type of glazing, because they will probably all look identical!

EDGE SPACERS

As window glazings have improved in performance, what happens at the edges of the windows becomes increasingly significant. The edge spacer is what holds the panes of glass apart and provides the airtight seal in an insulated glass window.

Different types of edge spacers.

Traditionally, these have been hollow aluminum channels, usually filled with desiccant beads (which absorb small amounts of moisture that might get into the glazing unit).

Aluminum has extremely high conductivity. That didn't matter when the glazing did not insulate very well, but as better performing glazings were developed, proportionately more heat was lost through the edges.

Since about 1990, a number of improved edge spacers have come onto the market. Some are made of thin-walled steel and have a thermal break. Others are made of silicone foam or butyl rubber. Generally, better edge seals are a low-cost option when ordering windows, and worth considering. The net effect of improved edge spacers can be a 2–10% improvement in window energy performance, depending on the other performance characteristics of the window. With new edge spacers, however, pay particular attention to warranties against seal failure, which results in fogging and loss of any low-conductivity gas-fill. Choose windows with long warranties.

WINDOW FRAME AND SASH CONSTRUCTION

Window frame and sash construction has a big impact on energy performance. Wood is still the most common material in use, and it insulates reasonably well. Aluminum has been used extensively, particularly in the western part of the U.S., but unless a thermal break is incorporated into the design, aluminum frames conduct heat very rapidly and are therefore inefficient. Vinyl (PVC) windows are gaining in popularity, especially in the replacement market, and some vinyl frames insulated with fiberglass insulate better than wood. "Pultruded" fiberglass frames are entering the residential market from the commercial sector. They insulate well, and generally cost less than wood but more than vinyl.

Another important property is the airtightness of windows. Windows vary dramatically in how effectively they block infiltration. Airtightness is usually measured in cubic feet of air per linear foot of crack (cfm/ft) at specified testing conditions. Look for the (optional) air tightness ratings on NFRC labels (www.nfrc.org/label.html). The tightest windows have air leakage rates as low as 0.01 cfm/ft, and the industry standard is 0.37 cfm/ft. Most of the better windows have leakage rates in the range of 0.01 to 0.06 cfm/ft. However, individual windows purchased off a shelf may have leakage rates as high as 1 cfm/ft!

In general, casement and awning windows are tighter than double-hung and other sliding windows. This is because when a casement or awning window is closed it is pulled in against a compression-type gasket. Sliding windows have to use seals that permit the sash to slide, so

Different window geometries.
1. Frame
2. Glazing edge
3. Center of glass
4. Divider edge
5. Divider

they are rarely as airtight. You will find, though, that double-hung windows from a few manufacturers are tighter than casement windows from others, so it makes a lot of sense to examine air leakage specifications carefully when selecting windows.

Consumers should recognize that the manufacturer's quality control at the factory and care during shipping can have a big impact on the window's air tightness at a site. Furthermore, it is senseless to invest thousands of dollars in new windows only to have amateurs install them in your home. The high-rated performance of a window is meaningless if it is installed improperly with gaps and air leaks around the window. Be sure to have experienced contractors install your high-tech windows.

WINDOW DIMENSIONS

With high-performance windows, the dimensions of the windows have a big impact on total energy performance. This is because the glazing (glass, low-e coatings, gas fill, etc.) generally insulates better than the edge of the window (edge spacer, sash, and frame). This aspect of window performance has led to a great deal of confusion. If you consider only the energy performance of the glazing itself (center-of-glass performance), you get a very high insulating value. But if you factor in the energy performance of the window edges to arrive at a unit or average performance value, the insulating value is significantly lower. The smaller the window in question, the more significant the effect of the window edges, because a small window has proportionately more edge area than glazing area. Windows with true divided lights have a great deal more edge area.

UNDERSTANDING NFRC WINDOW RATINGS

Beginning in 1993, some windows began carrying NFRC energy performance labels. The National Fenestration Rating Council is a nonprofit collaboration of window manufacturers, government agencies, and building trade associations, founded to establish a fair, accurate, and credible energy rating system for fenestration products (windows, doors, and skylights).

Before NFRC developed standardized rating procedures for heat loss through windows, there was little consistency in how manufacturers listed energy performance. For example, some manufacturers listed only the center-of-glass performance, while others averaged performance for the entire unit. Also, different methods were used by manufacturers to calculate energy performance, so you couldn't be sure that the performance numbers from one manufacturer could be fairly compared with those of another.

NFRC U-VALUE RATINGS

Windows that have been rated by NFRC-approved testing laboratories and certified by independent certification and inspection agencies carry labels with U-value (U-factor) ratings. U-value is the measure of the amount of heat (in Btus) that moves through a square foot of window in an hour for every degree Fahrenheit difference in temperature across the window (Btu/ft²Fhr). U-value is the inverse of R-value, which is familiar to many people as an indicator of levels of insulation. With wall and attic insulation, the higher the R-value the better the insulation. Since U-value is the *inverse* of R-value, **the lower the U-value rating, the better the overall insulating value of the window.**

The U-factor ratings listed on NFRC labels (and in the *NFRC Certified Products Directory*) are whole-window U-values. That is, they take into account heat loss through the glass, window edge, and window frame.

COMPARATIVE U-VALUE

Because the unit U-values differ depending on the size of the window and it is unrealistic to list a different rating for every window size offered, NFRC came up with two standard sizes for every window type (see

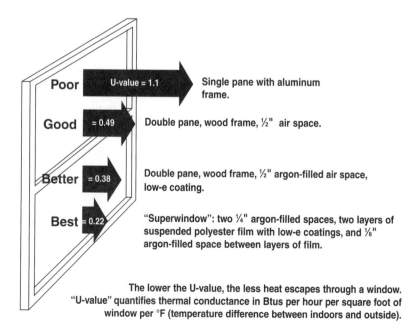

Poor U-value = 1.1 — Single pane with aluminum frame.

Good = 0.49 — Double pane, wood frame, ½" air space.

Better = 0.38 — Double pane, wood frame, ½" argon-filled air space, low-e coating.

Best = 0.22 — "Superwindow": two ¼" argon-filled spaces, two layers of suspended polyester film with low-e coatings, and ⅛" argon-filled space between layers of film.

The lower the U-value, the less heat escapes through a window. "U-value" quantifies thermal conductance in Btus per hour per square foot of window per °F (temperature difference between indoors and outside).

Table 3.1). For example, the representative residential casement window is 24" x 48", and the representative nonresidential casement window is 30" x 60". Showing two different sizes illustrates how sensitive the overall window U-value is to window size. If the U-values are very different for the residential and nonresidential samples of a single product, that product's thermal performance is sensitive to the actual product size. When comparing different products, be sure to compare ratings for the same size.

TABLE 3.1

REPRESENTATIVE WINDOW SIZES FOR NFRC LABELING

| | Size in inches (width × height) | |
	Residential	Nonresidential
Vertical Slider	36 × 60	48 × 72
Horizontal Slider	60 × 36	72 × 48
Casement	24 × 48	30 × 60
Projecting (Awning)	48 × 24	40 × 40
Fixed (includes unusual shapes)	48 × 48	48 × 72
Swinging Door with Frame	38 × 82	40 × 96
Sliding Patio Doors with Frames	72 × 82	72 × 96
Skylights and Sloped Glazings	24 × 48	48 × 48
Greenhouse/Garden	60 × 36	72 × 48

When a window manufacturer has its products certified, a great many different types and configurations of windows may be included. As defined by NFRC, a *product line* is a group of windows that have similar frame and operating characteristics (e.g., "Andersen Perma-Shield Casement windows"). Within each product line there may be various products. Differences among products include the number of layers of glazing, the use of or type of low-e coating, the type of gas-fill, edge spacer, etc.

UNDERSTANDING AN NFRC LABEL

NFRC labels describe the whole window U-factor (U-value), solar heat gain coefficient (SHGC), visible light transmittance, and air leakage for two representative sizes of windows.

NFRC SOLAR HEAT GAIN RATINGS

After heat loss, the most important energy property of glazings is how much solar heat gain they transmit. Solar heat gain can be beneficial—providing free passive solar heat during the winter

1. Official NFRC logo.
2. Window manufacturer.
3. Description of the individual product on which the label appears.
4. The certified U-factor (U-value) for the entire window; the *lower* the U-factor, the more efficient the window.
5. The certified solar heat gain coefficient (SHGC) for the entire window. A dimensionless number from 0 to 1.0 — the higher the SHGC, the greater the solar energy that passes through the window system (glazing and frame).
6. The certified visible light transmittance (VT) value for the entire window. A dimensionless number from 0 to 1.0 — the higher the VT, the greater the visible sunlight that passes through the window system (glazing and frame).
7. The certified air leakage rate. The air leakage rate is based on test conditions, and is given as the cubic feet (of air) per minute per foot of window edge (cfm/ft).

months—or it can be a problem, resulting in overheating during the summer. The solar heat gain coefficient introduced earlier describes how much solar energy is transmitted through a window. An SHGC of 0.8 means that 80% of the solar energy hitting the window gets through. (The window industry has used a similar term, "shading coefficient," but solar heat gain coefficient is becoming more common.)

NFRC has developed standard procedures for determining solar heat gain coefficients, and these ratings are listed on NFRC labels. These values make it easier to determine the suitability of windows for passive solar applications and the impact of windows on overheating and air conditioning loads.

But, as noted above, major window manufacturers have already started making low-e windows with different solar heat gain coefficients. Windows with high coefficients (above 0.70) are designed for colder climates, while windows with low coefficients are designed for hotter climates.

VISIBLE LIGHT TRANSMITTANCE

While SHGC describes the relative amount of solar energy that can pass through a window, the visible light transmittance is simply the relative amount of sunlight that can pass through. For example, tinted windows will have lower visible transmittance than clear windows, although the solar energy performance of tinted and clear windows might be similar. Also, a window with a large ratio of frame to glass will have a lower visible transmittance value than a window with a smaller ratio of frame to glass, since the frame will block visible sunlight.

NFRC INFILTRATION RATINGS

The third important energy property of windows is air leakage or air infiltration. Air leakage is already listed by many window manufacturers, in terms of cubic feet of air per minute per foot of crack. An optional air leakage value is now included on NFRC labels and in the *NFRC Certified Products Directory*. The NFRC has adopted the same basic procedures for measuring air leakage that have been used by the industry in the past.

ENERGY STAR WINDOWS

Windows, doors, and skylights qualifying for the ENERGY STAR label must meet requirements tailored for the country's three broad climate regions: northern, central, and southern. Window and door products that qualify in the heating-dominated northern states must have a U-factor of 0.35 or below and skylights must have a U-factor of 0.45 or below. In the central climate, where both heat loss and solar heat gain are important, qualifying products must have a U-factor of 0.40 or below and a SHGC of 0.55 or below. And in cooling-dominated southern states, qualifying products must have a U-factor of 0.75 or below and a SHGC of 0.40 or below. The Department of Energy is considering revisions to the ENERGY STAR windows criteria to increase energy savings. New specifications are anticipated to take effect by the end of 2003. For more information, visit the ENERGY STAR website (www.energystar.gov).

In addition, each ENERGY STAR window must carry the NFRC label, allowing comparisons of ENERGY STAR-qualified products on specific performance characteristics such as infiltration. To get efficiency gains beyond the ENERGY STAR levels, use the NFRC label or visit the NFRC website (www.nfrc.org/select.html) to find products with even tighter specifications.

RECOMMENDATIONS

1. If you're shopping for new windows, look for the NFRC label as your guide to their energy performance. Compare ratings on ENERGY STAR-labeled windows for your climate region.

2. Remember that a window's ability to insulate is given by its U-value, and the amount of solar energy it transmits is given by its solar heat gain coefficient—the lower the U-value and SHGC, the more efficient the window.

3. Look for windows with these energy-saving features: double panes; low-e coatings; low-conductivity gas-fill between panes; and wood, vinyl, or fiberglass frames.

4. Select windows with low air leakage ratings—between 0.01 and 0.06 cfm/ft.

5. Consider different glazings for windows on different sides of your house to benefit from passive solar and maximize energy benefits. Install the lowest U-value windows you can afford on north-facing windows. Select windows with appropriate low-e coatings for your local climate on the east, west, and south sides of your house.

6. To maximize energy performance, choose windows with larger unbroken glazing areas instead of multi-pane or true-divided-light windows. Applied grills that simulate true-divided-light windows are fine; they do not reduce energy efficiency.

7. Choose windows with good warranties against the loss of the air seal. If the glazing seal is lost, not only will fogging occur, but also any low-conductivity gas between the layers of glass will immediately be lost.

8. To ensure that your new windows perform as well as they should, hire skilled contractors to install them.

CHAPTER 4
Heating Systems

Heating is the largest energy expense in most homes, accounting for around two-thirds of annual energy bills in colder parts of the country. Reducing your energy use for heating, therefore, provides your single most effective way to reduce your home's contribution to global environmental problems. Heating systems in the United States spew over a billion tons of CO_2 into the atmosphere each year and about 12% of the nation's sulfur dioxide and nitrogen oxides.

A combination of conservation efforts and a new high-efficiency heating system can often cut your pollution output and fuel bills in half. Just upgrading your furnace or boiler from 56% to 90% efficiency in an average cold-climate house will save 1.5 tons of CO_2 emissions each year if you heat with gas, or 2.5 tons of CO_2 emissions every year if you heat with oil.

Very basically, a heating system replaces heat that is lost through the shell of your house. How much energy your heating system requires to replace that lost heat depends on four factors: where the house is located (in colder places, the house will lose more heat); how big the house is; the energy efficiency of the house; and how energy-efficient the heating system is.

You can't do much about the first factor. As for size, the bigger the house, the more energy it will take to heat it, but you aren't likely to change the size of your house, except perhaps to make it bigger.

You can do something about energy efficiency levels. Improving your home's energy efficiency is an excellent idea and offers the greatest opportunity for savings in heating costs. Some of the most effective measures, such as rope-caulking windows, cost next to nothing, while others, such as insulating, can be both expensive and time-consuming. These measures are addressed in Chapter 2.

That leaves your heating system itself, the focus of this chapter. Whether or not you've buttoned up your house, you can probably save a great deal by upgrading your heating system, either by installing a new high-efficiency system or by boosting the efficiency of your present system. Both of these options are addressed in this chapter.

HEATING SYSTEM BASICS

In considering the various options for improving or replacing your heating system, it helps to know some of the lingo. A lot of confusing terms and concepts are going to get thrown around by salespeople or heating system technicians, and you don't want to get left behind. Central heating systems have three basic parts: the heating plant itself where fuel is converted into useful heat, a distribution system to deliver heat to where it is needed, and controls to regulate when the fans and pumps controlling it all turn on and off.

TYPES OF HEATING SYSTEMS

Gas and Oil Heating Systems

Gas- and oil-fired heating systems generate heat in a boiler or furnace. Many people are confused about the difference between furnaces and boilers. A furnace heats air that is blown through air ducts and delivered to

Furnaces heat air, while boilers heat water.

Exit to supply plenum

Primary heat exchanger

Condensing heat exchanger

Furnace fan

Exhaust gas outlet

Gas burners

Flue gas fan

Condensate drain filter

The best furnaces today have efficiencies over 95%.

rooms through registers or grills. This type of heating system is called a ducted warm-air or forced warm-air distribution system. A boiler heats water or steam that circulates through pipes to radiators or baseboards. Hot-water heating systems, sometimes called hydronic systems, are more common today than steam systems. Some hot-water systems circulate water through plastic tubing in the floor, a system called radiant floor heating. Furnaces and boilers are both widely available in gas- and oil-fired models.

Inside a furnace or boiler, fuel is sprayed into a combustion chamber where it is mixed with air and burned. The combustion products are vented out of the building through a flue pipe. The flames heat a metal box called a heat exchanger. In a furnace, air is heated in the heat exchanger, while in a boiler, water is heated in the heat exchanger. For hot-water

Boilers work like furnaces, except that water instead of air is heated.

systems, the water is heated to about 180°F; in steam systems, the water is boiled, creating steam.

Heating system controls regulate when the various components of the heating system turn on and off. The most important control from your standpoint is the thermostat, which turns the system—or at least the distribution system—on and off to keep you comfortable. But there are other controls in a heating system, including aquastats, valves, vents, fan thermostats, and dampers. These control devices are described later in this chapter.

In some areas, gas-fired *direct heating equipment* is popular. This includes wall-mounted, free-standing, and floor furnaces, all characterized by their lack of ductwork and relatively small heat output (usually less than 40,000 Btuh). Because they lack ducts, they are most useful for warming a single room. If heating several rooms is required, either the doors between rooms must be left open, or another heating method should be sought. Better models use "sealed combustion air" systems, with a concentric pipe installed through the wall to both provide combustion air and carry off the combustion products. These units can provide acceptable performance, particularly for cabins and other buildings where large temperature differences between bedrooms and main rooms are acceptable. The models can be fired with natural gas or propane, and some burn kerosene.

Efficiency. The efficiency of a gas or oil heating system is a measure of how effectively it converts fuel into useful heat. There are

60–95% useful
heat out

5–30% lost
up flue

0–10% lost
thru jacket

100% ENERGY IN
(FUEL)

Combustion efficiency is a measure of
efficiency while the system is operating.

Annual fuel utilization efficiency (or
AFUE) accounts for on-and-off cycling
throughout the heating season.

5–30% operating
fuel loss

5–14%
off-cycle loss

50–90% useful
heat out

0–6% operating
jacket loss

100% ENERGYIN
(FUEL)

two types of efficiency. Combustion efficiency tells you the system's efficiency while it is running. Combustion efficiency is like the miles per gallon your car gets cruising along at 55 miles per hour on the highway. A more accurate estimation of actual fuel use, though, is the annual fuel utilization efficiency, or AFUE. This is a measure of the system's efficiency that accounts for start-up and cool-down and other operating losses that occur in real operating conditions. AFUE is like your car mileage between fill-ups, including both highway driving and stop-and-go traffic.

Electric Heat

There are two common types of electric heat: electric resistance heat and electric heat pumps. Electric resistance heat works by directly converting electric current into heat. Almost all of the energy in the electric current ends up as usable heat, but it is still pretty inefficient when the inefficiency of electricity generation by the power company and transmission losses are taken into account. Roughly one-third of the heating value of the fuel burned in a power plant will be delivered as useful heat in the house by a resistive system.

Alternative, portable (plug-in) electric heaters are inexpensive to buy, but costly to use. Often referred to as "oil-filled" or "Quartz-Infrared" heaters, these are basically just resistive heaters. A 1,500 watt plug-in heater will use almost the entire capacity of a 15-amp branch circuit, so adding much additional load will trip the circuit breaker or blow the fuse. The cost to operate a 1,500 watt unit for an hour is simple to compute: it is 1.5 times your electricity cost in cents per kilowatt-hour. In California, with a cost of $0.16 for electricity, that heater would cost $0.25/hr to run—and quickly cost more than its purchase price. On the other hand, for intermittent use, it is the "least-bad" solution when alternatives would require major investments to improve ductwork for a specific area, for example. Just remember, electric resistance heat is usually the most expensive form of heat and it is, therefore, seldom recommended.

In contrast, electric heat pumps operate on a quite different principle. Instead of directly producing heat from the electric current, they use electricity to move heat from one place to another. They work in the same basic way as a refrigerator, using a special refrigerant fluid (HCFC-22 or newer HFC alternatives) that changes back and forth between liquid and vapor. In the heating mode, a heat pump extracts heat from outside the house and delivers it to the house. Like furnaces, most heat pumps work with forced warm-air delivery systems.

Cool Air
Outside

Heat
Inside

HEATING CYCLE

Heat
Outside

Cool Air
Inside

COOLING CYCLE

Heat pumps can work in two different modes: heating and cooling.

Air-source heat pumps use the outside air as the heat source. Ground-source or "GeoExchange" heat pumps get their heat from underground, where temperatures are more constant year-round. Air-source heat pumps are far more common than ground-source heat pumps.

Because electricity in a heat pump is used to move heat rather than to generate it, the heat pump can deliver more energy than it consumes. The ratio of delivered energy to consumed energy is called the *coefficient of performance*, or COP, with typical values ranging from 1.5 to 3.5. A better measure for comparing air-source heat pump performance is the heating season performance factor, or HSPF. This is a ratio of the estimated seasonal heating output (Btus) divided by the seasonal power input (watt-hours).

One of the advantages of heat pumps is that they can be used for cooling during the summer months. In the cooling mode, the cycle is reversed: heat is taken from the house and dumped into the outside air or the ground. There will be more discussion of heat pumps in the section on selecting new heating systems.

If possible, provide a combustion air source for wood stoves.

Wood Heat

Wood heating can make a great deal of sense in rural areas if you enjoy stacking wood and stoking the stove or furnace. Wood prices are generally lower than gas, oil, or electricity. If you cut your own wood, the savings can be large. Pollutants from wood burning have been a problem in some parts of the country, causing the U.S. Environmental Protection Agency (EPA) to implement regulations that govern pollution emissions from wood stoves. As a result, new models are quite clean-burning. This edition of the *Consumer Guide to Home Energy Savings* does not include detailed information on wood stoves.

Fireplaces

Gas (and most wood) fireplaces are basically part of a room's décor, not a heating source. With customary installations that rely on air drawn from the room into the fireplace for combustion and dilution, the fireplace will generally lose more heat than it provides, because so much warm air is drawn through the unit and must be replaced by cold outside air. On the other hand, if the fireplace is provided with a tight-sealing glass door, a source of outside air, and a good chimney damper, it can provide useful heat.

UNVENTED FUEL-BURNING HEATERS: A BAD IDEA

Unvented gas space heaters have been sold for decades, but we strongly discourage their use for health and safety reasons. Known as "vent-free" gas heating appliances by manufacturers, they include wall-mounted and free-standing heaters as well as open-flame gas fireplaces with ceramic logs.

Manufacturers claim that because the products' combustion efficiency is very high, they are safe for building occupants. However, these efficiency claims are valid only under certain conditions, including keeping a nearby window open "an inch or two" for adequate fresh air—which defeats the purpose of supplemental heat. Kerosene heaters, which were popular in the 1970s, are similar except the fuel is liquid kerosene instead of natural gas. Most states have banned unvented kerosene heaters from residential use because of the same dangers discussed here for vent-free gas appliances. Combustion by-products, unavoidable indoors from unvented heaters, include nitrogen oxides (eye, nose, and throat irritants), carbon monoxide (an asphyxiant), and a lot of water vapor, which can cause condensation, mildew, or rot in wall and ceiling cavities.

Another problem is oxygen depletion. In the absence of a flame, air is 21% oxygen. Since flames consume oxygen much more strongly than human lungs, unvented gas heaters must be equipped with oxygen depletion sensors, which automatically shut off the gas to the heaters if oxygen falls below 18% of room air. Because of the hazards posed by vent-free appliances, five states (California, Minnesota, Massachusetts, Montana, and Alaska) prohibit their use in homes, and many cities in the United States and Canada have banned them as well.

Rather than purchasing an unvented gas heater, we recommend consumers stay warm and healthy by reducing heat loss from their home as described in Chapter 2, and improving their central heating system as described in this chapter.

SHOULD I REPLACE MY EXISTING HEATING SYSTEM?

This can be a difficult question. If you heat with electric resistance heat, rising electricity prices may force you to switch to a gas, oil, or heat pump system that is more affordable. If you currently have a gas- or oil-fired furnace or boiler, the decision to replace it depends on its age, condition, and performance.

If your furnace or boiler is old, worn out, inefficient, or significantly oversized, the simplest solution is to replace it with a modern high-efficiency model. Old coal burners that were switched over to oil or gas are prime candidates for replacement, as are gas furnaces without electronic (pilotless) ignition or a way to limit the flow of heated air up the chimney when the heating system is off (vent dampers or induced draft fan).

A typical heating system will last about 25 years, though some boilers can last twice that long. Your heating system technician or energy auditor may be able to help you evaluate your existing system and decide whether replacement is a good idea. If you're not going to replace it, see the sections on maintenance and modifications for ways to boost its efficiency and performance.

If you know how efficient your existing heating system is (AFUE), it's pretty easy to calculate the savings you will get by replacing it. The chart below will help you determine potential savings resulting from replacement of your existing system. Your heating service technician or energy auditor may be able to help determine the AFUE of your present system. If you were only provided with the combustion efficiency, you can estimate the AFUE by multiplying the combustion efficiency by 0.85. The numbers in the chart assume that both the old and new systems are sized properly; savings will be greater than indicated if the old system is too large.

DOLLAR SAVINGS PER $100 OF ANNUAL FUEL COST

		AFUE of new system				
		75%	80%	85%	90%	95%
AFUE	50%	$33	$37	$41	$44	$47
of	55%	26	31	35	38	42
existing	60%	20	25	29	33	37
system	65%	13	18	23	27	32
	70%	6	12	17	22	26
	75%		6	11	16	21
	80%			5	11	16
	85%				5	11

To determine savings, find the horizontal row corresponding to the old system's AFUE, then choose the number from that row that is in the vertical column corresponding to the new system's AFUE. That number is the projected dollar savings per hundred dollars of existing fuel bills. For example, if your present AFUE is 65% and you plan to install a high-efficiency natural gas system with an AFUE of 90%, then the projected saving is $27 per $100. If, say, your annual fuel bill is $1,300, then the total yearly savings should be about $27 x 13 = $351.

That's a lot of money to save each year, especially when you consider the expected lifetime of a heating system, but it still doesn't answer the question of whether replacing the system is a good investment. To answer that, you can calculate the first year return on investment (ROI). The equation is as follows:

ROI = first year savings ÷ installed cost

ROI = $351 ÷ $2,500 = 0.14 = 14%

A 14% return is pretty good—much higher than what you receive from a savings account or certificate of deposit. Plus, unlike most other investments, energy conservation investments are tax free. If fuel prices go up, the annual savings and return on investment also go up. For example, if fuel prices increase 30%, the annual savings in this example increases to $456, and the return on investment increases to 18%.

SELECTING A NEW HEATING SYSTEM

Fuel Options

If you're going to replace your existing heating system, you have a number of decisions to make. The first is what type of fuel to use. It usually makes sense to stick with the fuel your old system used, because the storage tank and necessary fuel supply piping will already be in place. But sometimes it makes sense to switch fuels. If you currently have electric resistance heat, for example, switching to gas or oil will probably save you money. Even electric heat pumps are more expensive than oil or gas heat in most of the country, though in warmer areas the use of a heat pump for cooling can help justify its use.

Switching from oil to gas or vice-versa based on current prices in your area, though, can be risky. Even though gas is usually cheaper today doesn't mean it will stay cheaper now that the gas industry is deregulated. Similarly, fuel oil prices fluctuate widely, as we have seen in recent years.

Switching from One Distribution System to Another

In some cases when replacing a heating system, you might want to change from one type of distribution system to another. If you have steam heat, for example, switching to hot water may make sense. Some steam piping systems can be retrofitted for hot-water heat. Discuss this possibility with the heating technicians you talk with. If you have a forced warm-air or hot-water system, though, it rarely makes sense to switch to something else. The cost of adding either new ducts or new piping will probably make the project prohibitively expensive.

Sizing the System

Before you actually start shopping for a new furnace or boiler, it pays to figure out how large a system you need. A system that is too large wastes fuel and money because it keeps cycling on and off. It only runs at peak efficiency for short periods of time and spends most of the time either warming up or cooling down. Many existing systems that were installed in the 1950s and 1960s are much too large. It is not uncommon for a heating system to be two or three times larger than necessary.

To be most efficient, your heating system should have to run almost continuously on the coldest day of the year to keep your house at 70°F. Never figure out how big a system you need by checking the size of the old system. If your heating contractor wants to do this, take your business elsewhere. A heat loss analysis is the only way to determine the proper size of a new heating system. (Steam systems are an exception: the boiler should be sized to the radiators.) A heat loss analysis can be done by your heating contractor or energy auditor; it should include measurements of wall, ceiling, floor, and window areas and account for insulation levels and weatherization features, including any energy improvements you have made. From the heat loss analysis, you need to know the peak hourly heating demand in Btu/hr on the coldest expected

Too large
a furnace or
boiler will
waste energy.

day of the year in your area (British thermal units or Btus are a measure of heat; one Btu is approximately the amount of heat released by burning a wooden kitchen match).

Furnaces and boilers are rated according to their Btu/hr output or heating capacity. A new heating system should be sized no more than 25% over the peak hourly heating demand. For example, if your home's peak hourly heating demand is calculated to be 60,000 Btu/hr, you should select a heating system with a heating output between 60,000 and 72,000 Btu/hr. The minimum acceptable heat loss calculation is called an "ACCA Manual J." Contractors with the technical capability to properly install modern systems should routinely perform this calculation. Ask to see a copy of the heat loss and system sizing calculations so that you can make sure they were thoroughly done.

Several manufacturers have combined water heating and space heating functions in one integrated piece of equipment. If you are considering replacing both your furnace and your water heater, such a combination system may be advantageous to you. These are discussed in more detail in Chapter 6, under **Indirect Water Heaters and Advanced Heating Systems with Integrated Water Heaters**.

Shopping for Gas- and Oil-Fired Heating Systems

Because a new system will cost $1,000 or more, you should shop carefully. You will need to decide on a fuel, and you will need to balance cost, efficiency, contractor reliability, warranty, and other considerations.

If you live in a cold climate, it usually makes sense to invest the extra few hundred dollars for the highest efficiency system available. In milder climates with lower annual heating costs, the extra investment required to go from 80% to 90–95% efficiency may be hard to justify.

When shopping for high-efficiency furnaces and boilers, look for dependability. Buy a system with a good warranty and a reputable company to back it up. Most quality furnaces have a limited lifetime warranty on the heat exchanger, and most hot-water boilers come with a 20-year warranty. The controls should have at least a one-year warranty. If the manufacturer is a relatively new company, ask the dealer about the company's reputation. Ask for the names of several homeowners in your area with their systems in place, and call to see if the homeowners are satisfied with performance and service.

With gas and oil systems, specify sealed combustion. Sealed combustion appliances bring outside air directly into the burner and exhaust flue gases directly to the outside, without the need for a draft hood or damper. They generally burn more efficiently, and they pose no risk of introducing dangerous combustion gases into your house. With non-sealed-combustion appliances, back-drafting of combustion gases can be a big problem.

High-efficiency systems—over about 85%—generally achieve that high efficiency in part by reclaiming most of the heat in the exhaust gases, including water vapor, that would otherwise escape up the chimney. The temperature of exhaust gases from a condensing gas furnace may be as low as 100°F—compared with 400°F or so for a conventional model. By sending less heat up the chimney, you deliver more heat to your house and keep more money in your pocket.

When exhaust gases cool below 212°F, water vapor in the exhaust condenses into water. The good news is that this releases additional heat, further boosting efficiency. The bad news is that the water is somewhat acidic and can corrode a conventional chimney. If the system will vent into an existing chimney that isn't lined, consider having a lining installed. Or better still, don't use a chimney at all; most of these very high-efficiency systems vent the exhaust gases to the outside through a plastic or stainless steel pipe that is installed through the basement wall. To handle the water produced, most condensing systems have condensate drains as well as exhaust drains.

In most climates, a "variable speed fan" or "ECM" circulating fan motor should be cost-effective. These motors are more efficient than conventional furnace fan motors, particularly at the lower speeds generally used for heating and air circulation (the highest fan speed is generally only used for air conditioning). Variable speed motors also allow finer control and some premium features such as enhanced dehumidification in the cooling season and quieter air circulation when neither the heating nor the air conditioning is on.

Choosing a Heating System Contractor

You'll be spending a lot of money to have a new furnace or boiler installed—anywhere from about $1,500 for a simple furnace installation to over $4,500 for a very complicated boiler installation. Any modifications to the distribution system will add significantly to the cost. To get the best deal, you should get bids for the price of equipment and installation from several contractors. It isn't unusual for bids to differ as much as $1,000, so get at least two or three bids.

When evaluating bids, look at prices, but also look at what you get for the price: quality, energy savings, and warranty. If you are not familiar with the contractor, ask for customer references and follow up on them. Make sure the contractor is fully bonded and insured. If you are putting in a very high-efficiency furnace or boiler, ask the contractor if he or she has had

Make sure your heating system installer has experience with high-efficiency systems.

any special training in this type of installation. If you think your old heating system is covered with asbestos insulation, make sure the contractor knows about it and will follow the proper procedures to deal with the asbestos. See Appendix 5 for more information on selecting a contractor.

Installation and Quality Control

A new heating system must be installed properly to ensure safe and efficient operation. With oil-fired furnaces and boilers, the system should be tuned and a combustion efficiency test performed after installation. Make sure the combustion efficiency meets the specifications (a calculation to convert from combustion efficiency to AFUE may need to be made). Gas furnaces and boilers come pre-adjusted from the factory and don't require a combustion efficiency test.

With both oil and gas systems, look for a neat installation. Mistakes are more likely if an installation is sloppy. If the furnace or boiler is very efficient (AFUE over about 85%), make sure that a plastic or stainless steel exhaust pipe for flue gases and a condensate drain have both been installed. The drain tube should run into a floor drain or sanitary sewer line.

THE MOST EFFICIENT FURNACES AND BOILERS

The most efficient furnaces and boilers on the market are listed in Part II of this book. The efficiency ranges vary according to the type of system. Gas furnaces generally have the highest efficiencies of any systems available. All the models listed in Part II have AFUE ratings over 93%, and the best exceed 96%. The best gas boilers achieve efficiencies in the upper-80% range, and two manufacturers, Burnham and Dunkirk, have introduced boilers attaining a 95% efficiency and higher. The best oil furnaces and boilers have efficiencies in the mid- to upper-80% range. In general, steam boilers are somewhat less efficient than hot-water boilers, although the best systems still have efficiencies over 80%. Products are listed in several different heating capacity groupings for convenience in finding what's best for your situation.

To qualify for an ENERGY STAR label, a furnace (oil or gas) must have an AFUE of 90% or higher, and a boiler (oil or gas) must have an AFUE of at least 85%. For more information about ENERGY STAR heating equipment, including special ENERGY STAR financing options, call the toll-free ENERGY STAR hotline (1-888-782-7937) or visit the ENERGY STAR website (www.energystar.gov).

The amount of electricity drawn by a furnace to power its motors and blow air through the house is often overlooked, since we focus on the natural gas or fuel oil burned to make heat. However, the electric energy demand by the furnace can be considerable—over 1,200 kWh/year for some models, adding up to $100 to your yearly electric bill. How much electricity a furnace uses depends on the design and configuration of the unit, and the efficiency of the motors and fans.

In addition to the AFUE ratings for the most efficient furnaces, we list in Part II the estimated amount of electricity each will use in an average year. This power consumption is not factored into the AFUE ratings, so it is another item for consideration when choosing a new furnace. The actual amount of electricity used by any furnace will vary with your local weather and house characteristics, such as the efficiency of your ducts. As noted above, the most important variable is the fan motor type. Most units today use "permanent split capacitor" motors, but premium units are often equipped with variable speed, ECM, or permanent magnet DC motors. These can be very cost-effective where the furnace or central air conditioner runs many hours, or where the homeowner uses the fan to circulate air through the house and filter, regardless of whether the system is calling for heating or cooling.

MOST EFFICIENT HEAT PUMPS

Heat pumps are far more energy efficient than electric resistance heat, including electric furnaces, and they can be used both for heating and air conditioning. But before deciding to replace your present system with a conventional heat pump, you should carefully look into whether it makes sense in your climate. Air-source heat pumps rely on the outside air as the heat source in the wintertime. The colder that air, the worse the energy performance (the lower the coefficient of performance, or COP). In fact, if the outside temperature falls below about 20°F or 30°F, most air-source heat pumps become no more efficient than electric resistance heating. For this reason, air-source heat pumps are much more common in warmer climates, where winter temperatures seldom fall below 30°F and where summer cooling loads are considerable. On the other hand, geothermal (or ground-source) heat pumps use the ground as a source of heat in the winter and also as a sink for heat in the summer, and they are more efficient than conventional, air-source heat pumps. Geothermal heat pumps are described further in their own section below.

Heat pumps are rated for heating and cooling—both in terms of capacity and efficiency. Capacity ratings are generally in Btu/ hr, as they are with other heating systems. Heating efficiency for air-source heat pumps is indicated by the heating season performance factor, or HSPF, which tells you the ratio of the seasonal heating output in Btu divided by the seasonal power consumption in watts. The seasonal energy efficiency rating, or SEER, tells you the seasonal cooling performance. Cooling will be addressed in Chapter 5.

The most efficient air-source heat pumps on the market are listed in Part II. Today's most efficient models range from HSPF 8.0 to 9.85, with smaller capacity heat pumps typically at the lower end of the efficiency range. To qualify for an ENERGY STAR label, an air-source heat pump must have an HSPF of 8.0 or higher, a SEER of 13 or higher, and an EER of 13 or higher. There are many more ENERGY STAR heat pumps than the models we list; the listings in Part II highlight only the very most efficient.

GROUND-SOURCE HEAT PUMPS OR "GEOEXCHANGE"

Ground-source heat pumps (also called "geothermal, GeoExchange," or "GX" units) use the earth or groundwater as the heat source, instead of outside air. Because temperatures underground are nearly constant year-round—warmer than the outside air during the winter and cooler than the outside air during the summer—a GeoExchange unit will be more efficient than an air-source unit. The stable underground temperature allows geothermal systems to be rated for heating efficiency in terms of coefficient of performance, or COP, and cooling efficiency in terms of energy efficiency ratio, or EER. GeoExchange heat pumps are easily 25–45% more efficient than new air-source heat pumps. For guidance on high-performance products, visit ENERGY STAR (www.energystar.gov) or the Federal Energy Management Program listings (www.eere.energy. gov/femp/procurement/groundsource_heatpumps.html). For the **most** efficient equipment, ACEEE recommends an EER rating of at least 18 for units less than 2 tons or greater than 3 tons and an EER of at least 22 for units in the 2 to 3 ton range.

GeoExchange heat pumps are less common than air-source heat pumps, and are often more expensive and difficult to install. But the dramatic improvement in efficiency yields attractive lifecycle cost savings through low energy bills, compared to conventional heat pumps. In addition, since the heat exchange pipes are underground and protected from the elements, GeoExchange units require less maintenance than conventional heat pumps, and there is no outside noise typically associated with conventional heat pumps and air conditioners. As an added bonus, most GeoExchange heat pumps are installed with a "desuperheater" that uses waste heat to heat water. As a result, a GeoExchange system can provide inexpensive water heating when the compressor unit is operating for cooling or heating.

Most GeoExchange "loops" are buried in the ground, usually in long, shallow (3–6' deep) trenches or in one or more vertical boreholes. The particular method used will depend on the experience of the installer, the size of your lot, the subsoil, and the landscape. An experienced loop installer will be able to design a pipe system that is appropriate to your lot and landscape. As an alternative, some systems draw in groundwater and pass it through the heat exchanger instead of refrigerant. The groundwater is then returned to the aquifer.

Several utilities, in cooperation with government agencies and other groups, have begun marketing GeoExchange systems as a superior alternative to air-source heat pumps, especially for new housing, where the cost and disruption of burying heat exchange coils is not as great as in replacement installations. New construction also provides the opportunity to combine GeoExchange heat pumps with other efficiency measures, such as extra wall and ceiling insulation, and high-efficiency windows. A more efficient building shell allows for a smaller and less costly GeoExchange system, and can lead to substantial home energy bill reductions compared to conventional new housing.

Utilities and the GeoExchange industry have been very active in the past few years to train installers, reduce system costs, and further improve system performance, reliability, and efficiencies. Table 4.1 provides contact information for the leading manufacturers. For more information on GeoExchange heat pumps, including manufacturers, installation, and related issues, please contact the following groups:

International Ground Source
Heat Pump Association
499 Cordell South
Oklahoma State University
Stillwater, OK 74078-8010
800-626-4747
405-744-5175
www.igshpa.okstate.edu

Geothermal Heat Pump
Consortium
701 Pennsylvania Avenue, NW
Washington, DC 20004-2696
888-255-4436
202-508-5500
www.ghpc.org

TABLE 4.1

MANUFACTURERS OF GROUND-SOURCE HEAT PUMPS

Addison Products Company
7050 Overland Road
Orlando, FL 32810
407-292-4400
www.addison-hvac.com

ECR Technologies
3536 DMG Drive
Lakeland, FL 33811
863-701-0096
www.ecrtech.com

American Geothermal, Inc.
1037 Old Salem Road
Murfreesboro, TN 37129
800-776-8039 615-890-6985
www.amgeo.com

FHP Manufacturing
601 NW 65th Court
Ft. Lauderdale, FL 33309
954-776-5471
www.fhp-mfg.com

Carrier Corporation
Carrier Parkway, A&R Building
P.O. Box 4808
Syracuse, NY 13221
315-432-6029
www.carrier.com

Loop Group Inc.
114 West Collins Rd.
Ft. Wayne, IN 46825
260-484-3631
www.loop-group.com

ClimateMaster
7300 SW 44th Street
P.O. Box 25788
Oklahoma City, OK 73125
405-745-6000
www.climatemaster.com

The Trane Company
182 Cotton Belt Parkway
McGregor, TX 76657
254-299-6329
www.trane.com

Econar Energy Systems Corp.
19230 Evans Street
Elk River, MN 55330
800-4-ECONAR 612-241-3110
www.econar.com

WaterFurnace International
9000 Conservation Way
Fort Wayne, IN 46809
800-222-5667 260-478-5667
www.waterfurnace.com

UPGRADING YOUR EXISTING HEATING SYSTEM

Even if you aren't about to go out and buy a state-of-the-art, high-efficiency heating system, you can still probably realize substantial savings by boosting the efficiency and performance of your present system. Measures described here fall into two categories: maintenance and modifications.

Regular Maintenance and Tune-Ups

Proper maintenance can have a big effect on fuel bills and should be performed on a routine basis. Maintenance operations are separated into two groups: those that can be performed by the homeowner or renter, and those that should be performed by a heating system service technician.

Maintenance by the Resident

When performing maintenance on hot-water and steam heating systems, you may come in contact with dangerously hot water and steam. Use caution. If you're uncertain about how to do something, call a service technician (or your landlord, if you rent).

■ *Clean or replace air filters.* Standard 1" deep fiberglass filters on warm-air furnaces and heat pumps should be checked once a month during the heating season and cleaned or replaced as necessary. Dust blocks the air flow and forces the blower to work harder, which raises electric bills and can lead to blower failure. These filters cost about $1 apiece and can usually be purchased at hardware stores. Some more expensive filters, generally much deeper and pleated, can run for 6–12 months before replacement.

Replace furnace air filter monthly during the heating season.

■ *Clean registers.* Warm-air registers (particularly the return registers) should be kept clean and should not be blocked by furniture, carpets, or drapes.

Clean warm-air registers.

■ *Keep baseboards and radiators clean and unrestricted* by furniture, carpets, or drapes. Air needs to freely circulate through them from underneath. Also, do not cover tops of radiators.

■ *Bleed trapped air from hot water radiators.* Trapped air keeps radiators from performing properly. Use a radiator key to bleed air out of hot-water radiators once or twice a season. Hold a pan under the valve and open it until all the air has escaped and only water comes out. If you are not mechanically inclined, you may want to have the technician show you how to do it the first time.

■ *Follow prescribed maintenance* for steam heat systems, such as maintaining water level, removing sediment, and making sure air vents are working. Check with your heating system technician for specifics on these measures and use caution: steam boilers produce high-temperature steam under pressure.

Baseboard radiator.

Bleeding hot-water radiator.

Maintenance and Tune-Ups by Heating System Technicians

Oil-fired systems should be tuned up and cleaned every year, gas-fired systems every two years, and heat pumps every two or three years. Regular tune-ups not only cut heating costs, but they also increase the lifetime of the system, reduce breakdowns and repair costs, and cut the amount of carbon monoxide, smoke, and other pollutants pumped into the atmosphere by fossil-fueled systems. System modifications to improve energy efficiency can be made when the service technician is there for the annual tune-up (see the next section).

The company that sells oil or gas usually has trained technicians who can test your furnace or boiler, clean it, and tune it for optimum efficiency. Independent contractors provide this service as well. A complete tune-up may cost $100 or so, and can reduce your heating bill from 3–10%. Some companies perform these services as part of a regular

Steam boilers take a considerable amount of regular maintenance to keep them operating properly. Your heating system technician can show you what needs to be done.

service contract. Check to make sure that all of the services listed below are included.

Tests the Technician Should Perform During a Tune-Up. The service technician will perform a number of tests to determine the system's performance and efficiency. Incomplete combustion of fuel and excessively high flue gas temperatures are the two main contributors to low efficiency. If the technician cannot get the combustion efficiency up to at least 75% after tuning it up, you should consider installing a new system or at least modifying your present system to increase its efficiency. Note that the combustion efficiency is different from annual fuel utilization efficiency (AFUE). For older burners, the AFUE can be estimated by multiplying the combustion efficiency by 0.85. Thus, if the combustion efficiency is 75%, the AFUE is around 0.75 x 0.85 = 64%.

The technician should measure the efficiency of your system both before and after tuning it up and provide you with a copy of the results. Combustion efficiency is determined indirectly, based on some of the following tests: 1) flue temperature; 2) percent carbon dioxide or oxygen; 3) smoke number; 4) carbon monoxide; and 5) draft. These are discussed below:

■ *Flue temperature.* High flue gas temperatures mean that a lot of heat (and money) is being lost up the chimney. Typical flue temperatures are:

Gas	300–600°F
Gas (condensing system)	100–140°F
Oil	400–600°F
Oil (flame retention burner)	300–500°F

■ *Carbon dioxide.* Carbon dioxide is the primary end-product of fossil fuel combustion. Too little carbon dioxide indicates incomplete combustion. For an oil burner, the CO_2 concentration should measure between 10 and 12%. For gas, it should be between 7 and 9%. If an oxygen reading is taken instead, it should be between 3 and 6% for oil systems, or between 5 and 7% for non-condensing gas systems.

■ *Smoke.* Smoke indicates lack of complete combustion and is usually not present in gas systems. For an oil system, on a scale of 0 to 10, the smoke number should be no higher than 1.

■ *Carbon monoxide (gas only).* Carbon monoxide (CO) indicates incomplete combustion. For safety reasons, recommended CO levels in the flue gas should not exceed 400 parts per million.

■ *Draft.* Correct draft promotes complete combustion and reduces net loss up the chimney. A pressure gauge measures the overfire draft through the combustion chamber, and the breach draft through the flue pipe. Overfire draft pressure should be between 0.01 and 0.02 inches of water, and breach draft should be between 0.02 and 0.04 inches higher than the overfire draft. If you have a sealed combustion or induced draft system (a fan pulling or pushing exhaust gases out), this is not relevant.

Cleaning. Parts to be cleaned include the burner (nozzle, electrodes, filters), combustion chamber, heat exchanger surfaces, oil line filter, and flue pipe. (Oil nozzles and filters are often replaced rather than cleaned.) Sediment should be removed from the boiler and steam lines; corrosion inhibitors may be added to the boiler.

Adjustments. Air and fuel flow adjustments will be made based on the results of the efficiency testing. The internal thermostat on the furnace or boiler (aquastat or fan thermostat) should be calibrated to turn on and off at the appropriate temperatures.

Pumps and Fans. Pumps and fans should be inspected and lubricated if necessary.

HEATING SYSTEM MODIFICATIONS

Even if your heating system is fairly efficient, there are probably still some modifications that could be made to further increase efficiency. Often, it makes more economic sense to modify your existing system than to replace it, at least if it's in pretty good shape and less than 15 or 20 years old. A service technician or energy auditor should be able to help you decide which approach makes the most sense. Common heating system modifications are described in the following few pages, divided into those that can be made by the homeowner and those that should be done by a technician.

Modifications You Can Do Yourself

All of these modifications deal with heat distribution—getting the most heat from your furnace or boiler to the rooms in your house. These should be done regardless of the tested combustion efficiency of the heating system.

■ *Pipe insulation.* All hot-water and steam pipes passing through unheated areas should be wrapped with insulation. Use specially made foam or fiberglass pipe insulation, which can cost $0.30–0.80 per foot and saves about $0.50 per foot per year. Try to use insulation with a wall thickness of at least ¾" for fiberglass, and ½" for foam. Do not wrap steam pipes with foam as it could melt. Most steam pipes will be wrapped already with asbestos, which should not present a health hazard as long as it is well-sealed, not flaky, and not in a living space. If some of the white protective sheathing is missing, contact an asbestos abatement contractor.

■ *Duct insulation.* First, seal all joints and seams with mastic (a special paste) or UL-181 certified duct tape to keep hot air from leaking out of the ducts. Duct tape is that strong, silver or grey tape most of us know for its other applications, such as repairing broom handles and car

Insulate hot-water pipes that run though unheated spaces. Be sure to use insulation that can withstand high temperatures.

parts. Unfortunately, non-UL-181 duct tape can dry up and lose its adhesion over time, especially in unheated spaces. Mastic, on the other hand, spreads easily and dries permanently, and is the preferred material for sealing joints and seams in metal ductwork. (See section on **Modifications by Heating System Technicians** below for more on duct sealing.)

Duct insulation is very important for ducts that pass through unheated spaces.

Secondly, all hot-air ducts passing through unheated spaces should be wrapped with insulation. You can use standard foil-faced fiberglass insulation, keeping the foil facing out and visible; vinyl-faced insulation made especially for ducts; or rigid foam insulation. At least R-5 is recommended in cold climates; R-8 is preferred. Then, seal all joints or seams in the insulation. Use UL-181 duct tape with standard fiberglass batts and rigid foam; with vinyl-faced duct insulation, use duct tape or double-over and staple the seams.

■ *Radiator reflectors.* Radiators are designed to heat the living space, but they can lose a lot of heat into the exterior walls they are installed against. You can reduce this loss by placing reflectors between the wall and the radiator. You can make

Installing reflectors behind your radiators can improve heat transfer into the room.

reflectors from foil-covered cardboard, available from many building supply stores. The reflector should be the same size or slightly larger than the radiator. The foil should be periodically cleaned for maximum heat reflection.

Modifications by Heating System Technicians

All these measures for boosting the efficiency of your furnace or boiler require a professional with the proper training and tools.

■ *Duct sealing.* In homes heated with warm-air heating, ducts should be inspected and sealed to ensure adequate airflow and eliminate loss of heated air. It is not uncommon for ducts to leak as much as 15–20% of the air passing through them. And, leaky ducts can bring additional dust and humidity into living spaces. Thorough duct sealing costs several hundred dollars but can cut heating and cooling costs in many homes by 20%.

A contractor can test your ducts to determine the extent and location of leaks. Traditionally, ducts are sealed using mastic, which is applied to the outside of duct joints and other leak sites. A new alternative to mastic is aerosol-based duct sealing ("Aeroseal"). A machine connected to the ductwork blows a latex aerosol throughout ducts to seal leaks from the inside. This system can reach leaks in hard to reach or inaccessible spaces and effectively seals leaks up to $\frac{1}{4}$" in diameter. Contractors around the country are receiving training in this new technology; see www.aeroseal.com to find franchises in your area.

■ *Reducing system size.* If you have an older gas or oil system, and if you've added insulation, upgraded your windows, or tightened your house, chances are that your burner runs for only a fraction of the time, even in the coldest weather. Having your heating system constantly turn on and off is like driving in stop-and-go traffic: you don't get very good mileage. A simple way to reduce this waste is by decreasing the rate at which oil or gas is fed into the burner. In some cases, however, derating of gas systems could damage the equipment or the venting systems and may violate local building codes and void manufacturers' warranties. Have a knowledgeable contractor check with the equipment manufacturer and local code officials before proceeding.

With oil systems, the service technician can install a smaller nozzle, which costs just a few dollars and can cut fuel bills by 5–10%. Nozzles are sized according to fuel flow rates. The specification plate on your burner should include an acceptable flow range; an average range would be from 0.50 to 1.25 gallons per hour (GPH). Nozzle size should not be reduced more than 25–30% below the lowest firing range on the specification plate.

With gas systems, reducing the nozzle (or orifice) size is tricky; costs and savings will vary widely depending on the system. On a unit that is highly oversized, both the nozzle orifice and the baffles could be changed at a cost of $60–80, with possible savings of 10–15%. The orifice size should not be reduced more than 30%. Again, consult a knowledgeable service technician to find out if size reduction is possible or practical for your system.

Oil burner nozzle.

Burners for steam systems should not be downsized.

Barometric damper on oil-fired furnace or boiler.

■ *Draft reduction (oil only).* The draft test will determine whether excess heat is being lost up the chimney. This problem is particularly common in systems that were converted from coal to oil. If the draft is too high, your service technician should install a barometric damper in the flue pipe. This may cost from $20–100, but can reduce fuel use by 5% or more. If a barometric damper is already there, it may simply need adjustment.

■ *New oil burner installation.* If you have an old, inefficient oil burner but are not ready to replace the whole thing, have a flame-retention burner installed. It will mix oil and air more thoroughly, operate with less air flow, and send less heat up the chimney. In addition, a flame-retention burner will block airflow through the burner when the system is not running, reducing heat loss up the chimney. Flame-retention burners cost $400–600, depending on whether a new combustion chamber and controls are needed. A properly sized flame-retention burner with reduced nozzle size should save 10–20%. You'll do even better, though, replacing the whole furnace or boiler with a state-of-the-art high-efficiency model.

Replacement oil burner.

■ *Modulating aquastats (hot-water boilers only).* An aquastat regulates boiler temperatures, keeping the water within a prescribed temperature range, usually around 180°F. Unfortunately, it will keep the water just as hot even when there is little need for heat, such as during spring and fall months. A modulating aquastat (or outdoor reset) senses outdoor temperature and keeps the boiler water only as hot as needed. Brand-name aquastats sell for $150–350 and reduce fuel consumption by 5–10%. You can control an aquastat manually as well (see the section below on operating your system). Aquastats must be installed with condensing boilers to gain benefits from the condensing feature.

■ *Time delay relay (hot water boilers only).* Another strategy for controlling boiler water temperature is the time delay relay. When the room thermostat signals a need for heat, water heated earlier is circulated through the radiators without the boiler turning on. If circulation of warm water is not sufficient to heat the home within a specified time, the boiler burner fires to further heat the boiler water. With a time delay relay, circulation of lower temperature boiler water can provide adequate heating during milder weather. A time delay relay can be installed by a contractor for $50–75 and yield savings of 10%.

■ *Pilotless ignition (gas only).* Electronic ignition eliminates the pilot light that ordinarily burns constantly. It costs from $100–250 and has a three- to eight-year payback. Electronic ignition is difficult to install on existing systems and should be undertaken only by someone who is very experienced in this type of work to avoid dangers from an improper installation.

■ *Automatic vent damper.* The automatic damper is a metal flap that closes off the flue when the burner shuts off. In practice, the electric vent damper is operated by the thermostat. In turn, opening the vent damper signals the boiler to turn on. This prevents the possibility of spilling combustion gases into the house if the damper malfunctions. Vent dampers cost from $125–400 installed and can cut fuel consumption by 3–15%. Savings are highest with steam boilers, large hot-water boilers, and warm-air furnaces that are located in heated spaces, where heated room air can escape up the chimney. If the heating system is located in an unheated basement or if it has a flame retention oil burner, savings will probably be less than 5%. If you have an older oil burner, converting it to a flame retention type is generally a better investment (see *New oil burner installation* above). Caution: vent dampers are not suitable for all gas heating systems. Ask your service technician whether a vent damper is appropriate for your system.

Automatic flue damper.

■ *Flue economizer.* Flue economizers are devices that recover heat from the hot gases going up the flue. They are expensive, costing $200–800, and generally not recommended. It is almost always better to replace or modify inefficient systems. If you install a flame retention burner instead, for example, you will improve combustion efficiency and reduce the amount of heat going up the chimney rather than trying to recover that heat as an afterthought. Flue economizers also frequently have corrosion problems.

■ *Adjustable radiator vents and valves.* To reduce heat flow to unused rooms, valves on some hot-water radiators may be turned down. Valves on steam radiators should always be completely on or off, not in-between. An alternative for steam radiators is to install an adjustable air vent, typically costing about $10–15 at hardware and heating supply stores. These vents are screwed onto the radiator in place of existing vents, and they control how much steam gets into the radiator to heat it up.

You can get even greater control with either steam or hot-water radiators by installing thermostatic radiator valves. These valves allow you to select the temperature of each room. When the designed temperature is reached, the valve shuts the radiator off. These valves cost

Adjustable radiator valve.

$50–125 each installed, and can be a less expensive way to create separate heating zones, compared to repiping the whole house.

■ *Clock (or "programmable") thermostats.* Setting the thermostat manually works well but is inconvenient. More convenient is a clock thermostat that will turn on the heat a half-hour before your alarm goes off in the morning. Some clock thermostats have several different set-back periods, helping you save energy when you go off to work and the kids leave for school. Clock thermostats cost from about $40 for simpler models, which allow one or two set-back periods each day, to $150 for models that allow separate programming for each day of the week. Most clock thermostats will pay for themselves in about a year, if they are used for several degrees of setback in winter and "set-up" in the air conditioning season.

Clock thermostat.

■ *Tankless coil water heaters.* If domestic hot water is provided by your heating system boiler with a tankless coil, then during the summer the boiler must operate constantly just to provide hot water for showers, washing dishes, etc. There are several ways to avoid this waste. The simplest but least convenient is to install a timer switch so that you can turn your whole heating system off at night and when you are away during the summer months. Another option is to install a stand-alone, gas-fired (or propane) water heater to use in the summer when your heating system is off. A third option is to install an indirect water heater that draws heat from the boiler (like a tankless coil), but stores the hot water so that the boiler does not need to run as frequently. This option is usually the most cost-effective alternative to tankless coils in cold climates.

A fourth solution may be to buy a solar water heater. In most areas of the country, solar water heaters can provide nearly 100% of summertime hot water needs, thus complementing your wintertime boiler-produced hot water perfectly. Although this system requires a large capital investment, it is the best solution from an environmental standpoint, because solar energy produces virtually no pollutants, in contrast to fossil fuels and electricity. (See Chapter 6 for more information on water heating.) If you are building a new house, planning for a south-facing roof and installing "rough-in" plumbing to support a solar water heater later are very inexpensive.

OPERATING YOUR HEATING SYSTEM
FOR MAXIMUM EFFICIENCY

How you operate the controls of your heating system can have a large effect on your heating bills. People living in identical houses can have utility bills that vary widely, with some families paying 50% or even up to 100% more than others.

■ *Thermostats.* Turn down thermostats in unused rooms and when you don't need the heat. In most homes, you can save about 2% of your heating bill for each degree that you lower the thermostat. Turning down the thermostat from 70°F to 65°F, for example, saves about 10% ($100 saved per $1,000 of heating cost). Setting your thermostat back 10°F for eight hours at night can save about 7% ($70 saved per $1,000 of heating cost). Clock thermostats, which automatically adjust the temperature setting one or more times per day, are widely available (see previous section on modifications).

You might also be able to turn the thermostats down somewhat when you're in the room if you do a little buttoning up of the house (see Chapter 2). Turning down thermostats even

Setting the thermostat back at night will save a lot of energy and money.

when you are in a room doesn't mean being uncomfortable. In fact, you can actually be more comfortable at a lower temperature setting under the right conditions. Eliminating temperature stratification in a room where the floor is a lot colder than the ceiling will help the most, and getting rid of air infiltration and cold drafts is the best way to do it. Covering windows at night with blinds or drapes also helps, as does higher humidity. Buy some house plants or a humidifier, but don't add so much moisture that you start seeing condensation on your windows.

■ *Aquastat (hot-water boilers).* This is the thermostat that regulates the temperature of the hot-water boiler. Normally, the aquastat keeps water in the boiler around 160–180°F. In milder weather, however, you don't need boiler water that hot. The aquastat can be set manually to 120–140°F, reducing fuel consumption by 5–10%. (If your boiler has a tankless coil for domestic hot water, you may not be able to turn the aquastat down this far.) The aquastat control is usually located in a metal box connected to the boiler. If you cannot locate it, ask your service technician for assistance. See the modifications section for information about modulating aquastats.

■ *Fan thermostat (warm-air furnaces).* Modern gas furnaces use timers to control furnace fan operation. They control the fan that blows warm air through the ducts. Some of these timers cannot be adjusted by service technicians. If the timer is adjustable, it should be adjusted according to the manufacturer's instructions. In contrast, older furnaces may have a thermostatically controlled circulating fan. If the fan's thermostat is set too high, the circulating fan comes on too late and shuts off too soon, leaving heat in the furnace to escape up the flue. If you can't find the fan thermostat, have the technician point it out. If it has two settings, set it to come on at 100–110°F and to shut off at 80–90°F. If it has one setting, set it at 100–110°F. Thermostats with a single setpoint may have a variable deadband that determines the maximum temperature fluctuation from the setpoint. In this case, the variable deadband should be set to 20°F. If you feel cold air blowing out of your registers at the end of a heating cycle, the shut-off temperature is set too low. Raise it enough to eliminate those cold drafts. Since common practice is to set the fan thermostat too high, adjustment can reduce energy use by 5–10% in most homes.

■ *Duct dampers (warm-air furnaces).* Often, air ducts have dampers (adjustable metal flaps) in them to control flow. Shut off or turn down dampers and registers that heat the basement. Other dampers and registers can be turned down or off to control heat flow to various rooms.

Damper Open

Duct damper.

Unused rooms should be kept cooler than occupied rooms to save energy. Don't close off too much airflow, though, because it may cause trouble for the fan.

RECOMMENDATIONS

1. Try to button up your house as much as possible before installing new heating equipment, because you might be able to buy a smaller, less expensive system. Energy conservation is cheaper than burning expensive fossil fuels. Have an energy auditor help you to decide which measures are cost-effective. The auditor can also help you size a new heating system properly. But even if you aren't going to insulate further or weatherstrip, go ahead with the heating system replacement or improvements.

2. Electric resistance heating is not recommended because electricity is much more expensive than gas or oil. Electric heat pumps may be appropriate in your area; conventional air-source heat pumps can be economical in areas with mild winters and substantial cooling loads, but they are not much better than electric resistance heating in very cold climates. Choose an air-source heat pump with an HSPF above 8.0, or look into GeoExchange heat pump options

3. When buying a new furnace or boiler, look for the ENERGY STAR label. *Condensing gas* furnaces and boilers (AFUE at least 90%) with sealed combustion make good sense in moderate to cold climates. Condensing oil equipment is not widely available, so look for units with the highest AFUE that fits your application. With boilers, there are also many "mid-efficiency" systems (AFUE of 85% or higher) that may be a good option.

4. Older heating systems that are still in good shape can often be upgraded. Most older burners are oversized, especially in homes that have been weatherized, and they don't burn fuel as efficiently as the new models. With oil systems, you can downsize by installing a smaller nozzle. Installing a new flame retention burner downsizes and otherwise improves the efficiency of the burner at the same time. With some older gas systems, you can downsize by modifying the orifice and installing new baffles. You can downsize and improve the efficiency of a gas burner by installing a high-efficiency power burner. Be sure to hire a knowledgeable, experienced technician.

5. Other modifications that can improve efficiency on older systems include barometric dampers in the flue vent (oil only), modulating aquastats or time delay relays (boilers only), automatic vent dampers, adjustable radiator vents and valves, and clock thermostats.

6. If your boiler provides domestic hot water with a tankless coil, its efficiency is quite low in the summer. The best solution is to install an indirect water heater, which operates off your boiler. You might also want to consider gas/propane or a solar water heater for summertime use, keeping the tankless coil for backup use when the heating system is on.

7. All heating systems must have regular maintenance. Residents should change filters on warm air furnaces, make sure radiators and registers are not blocked, check steam boiler water levels, and maintain radiators. A heating system technician should clean and tune oil burners each year and gas burners every two to three years. The technician should measure efficiency before and after the tune-up. Duct sealing can improve the efficiency of an older warm-air furnace or ensure that a new system operates optimally.

8. Keep your thermostat set at the lowest comfortable level. Don't heat unused rooms. Turn the thermostat down at night and when no one is home. Increase comfort levels at lower thermostat settings by maintaining humidity, stopping cold air leaks, and covering windows at night. Set aquastats to lower temperatures in milder weather. Set back the fan thermostat on warm air furnaces.

CHAPTER 5
Cooling Systems

More than two-thirds of all U.S. households have air conditioners, whose energy consumption amounts to almost 5% of all the electricity produced in the U.S. for all purposes, at a cost to homeowners of over $10 billion. That amount of electricity results in the release of roughly 100 million tons of carbon dioxide (CO_2) per year, or an average for homes with air conditioning of one and a half tons per year. Furthermore, air conditioning use in the U.S. has more than doubled just since 1981. Seventy-five percent of new homes are being outfitted with central air conditioning systems, including over 50% of new homes in the Northeast.

A switch to high-efficiency air conditioners and implementation of measures to reduce cooling loads in homes can reduce this energy use by 20–50%.

After briefly describing how air conditioners work, this chapter covers selection of a new system, upgrading existing air conditioners, operating air conditioners for maximum efficiency, and, finally, strategies to reduce the need for air conditioning. The information on reducing cooling loads can be valuable to you whether or not you use an air conditioner. By following the strategies outlined, many homes will be able to eliminate the need for air conditioning on all but the hottest days and with no sacrifice in comfort.

AIR CONDITIONING BASICS

Air conditioning, or cooling, is more complicated than heating. Instead of using energy to create heat, air conditioners use energy to take heat away. The most common air conditioning system uses a compressor cycle (similar to the one used by your refrigerator) to transfer heat from your house to the outdoors.

Picture your house as a refrigerator. There is a compressor on the outside filled with a special fluid called a refrigerant. This fluid can change back and forth between liquid and gas. As it changes, it absorbs or releases heat, so it is used to "carry" heat from one place to another, such as from the inside of the refrigerator to the outside, or from inside the house to the outside. Simple, right?

Well, no. And the process gets quite a bit more complicated with all the controls and valves involved. But its effect is quite remarkable. An air conditioner takes heat from a cooler place and dumps that heat in a warmer place, seemingly working against the laws of physics. What drives the process, of course, is electricity—quite a lot of it, in fact.

TYPE OF AIR CONDITIONERS

The most common types of air conditioners are room air conditioners, ducted central air conditioners, and ducted electric heat pumps. Room air conditioners are available for mounting in windows or direct mounting in walls, but in each case they work the same way, with the compressor located outside. Room air conditioners are sized to cool just that one room, so a number of them may be required for a whole house. Individual units cost less to buy than central systems.

Central air conditioners are designed to cool the entire house. The large compressor unit is located outside, and the indoor coils cool air that is distributed throughout the house via ducts. Generally, the same duct system is used for forced warm air heating systems and central air conditioners. Heat pumps are like central air conditioners, except that the cycle can be reversed and used for heating during the winter months. Using heat pumps for heating is described in Chapter 4.

Outside Unit

Inside Unit

Compressor Coils

Air conditioners take heat from your house and dump it outside.

Cool Indoor Air In

Hot Outdoor Air Out

Window air conditioners can be removed during the winter months.

Warm Outdoor Air In

Warm Indoor Air In

Central air conditioners have separate inside and outside units. The inside unit generally cools air that flows through your ducts.

OTHER TECHNOLOGIES

In addition to these common types of air conditioners, there are several other types used very successfully in certain parts of the country. Evaporative coolers are practical in very dry areas, such as the Southwest. Sometimes called swamp coolers, they work by blowing house air over a damp pad or by spraying a fine mist of water into the house air. The dry air evaporates moisture and cools off. You've experienced this process—it's why a breeze makes you feel cold when you get out of a swimming pool. A direct evaporative cooler adds moisture to a house.

An indirect evaporative cooler is a little different in that the evaporation of water takes place on one side of a heat exchanger. House air is forced across the other side of the heat exchanger where it cools off but does not pick up moisture. Like the direct evaporative cooler, though, this system depends on very dry air to operate.

"Mini-splits," which are more popular in some other countries, use an outside condenser with an individual unducted evaporator for each room being conditioned. They are typically wall- or ceiling-mounted, and do not use ductwork. Thus, they are particularly attractive as retrofits for houses with hydronic heat (see Chapter 4).

SELECTING A NEW AIR CONDITIONER

Choosing an air conditioner (or heat pump) is an important decision. Buying an inefficient model will lock you into high electric bills for years to come. The same issues apply whether you're buying your first air conditioner or replacing an existing one, though your choices may not be as numerous with replacement systems.

If you live in a hot, arid region, such as the Southwest, look into evaporative coolers. For the rest of the country, compressor-driven air conditioning systems are about the only choice, other than natural cooling (see discussion later in this chapter). This discussion will focus on conventional compressor-type air conditioners.

Choosing the Right Type of Air Conditioner

The type of air conditioner you need depends in large part on your climate and cooling loads. In small homes and those with modest cooling needs, room air conditioners often make the most sense. In fact, in a small, highly insulated house, even the smallest central air conditioner may be too large. If you are considering room air conditioners, you will need to decide between units that mount in the window and those that are built into the wall. Wall-mounted units are often a better choice, both for aesthetic and practical reasons, though they will cost more to install, because an opening has to be cut through the wall. Window air conditioners are harder to seal, they block views and light, and they prevent the use of the window for natural or forced ventilation.

Central air conditioners have a number of advantages. They are out of the way, quiet, and convenient. If you already have a forced-air heating system, you may be able to tie into the existing duct work. Whether or not your existing ducting will work for air conditioning depends on its size and your relative heating and cooling loads. Ask your air conditioning service technician. Plus, central air conditioners are more efficient (see **Efficiency** below).

Heat pumps, though more expensive, provide heat in addition to air conditioning all in one unit. If you already have a satisfactory gas or oil heating system and have decided to add air conditioning, it usually doesn't make sense to consider a heat pump, because even a high-efficiency heat pump will probably be more expensive to operate than your gas or oil heating system (see the discussion on heat pumps in Chapter 4). There are also situations where heat pumps can be beneficial. If you currently have electric resistance heat and you live in a relatively warm climate (winter temperatures seldom dropping below 30°F), a heat pump may be a good choice.

If you're unsure about which type of air conditioner makes the most sense for your house, ask for opinions and bids from several local air conditioning installers.

Sizing the System

No matter what type of system you choose, make sure that it is sized properly. Most air conditioners are rated in Btu/hour, but central air conditioners and heat pumps may also list cooling capacity by the ton. One ton is equivalent to 12,000 Btu/hour. With air conditioning systems, equipment cost is much more proportional to size than it is with heating equipment. Don't let a salesperson convince you to buy an oversized system. In addition to the higher cost for an oversized system, it will run only for short periods, cycling on and off, which will increase electricity use and decrease the unit's overall efficiency. If it just runs for short periods of time, it also won't do as good a job dehumidifying the air (see **Dehumidification** below).

Find a qualified air conditioning technician or energy auditor to determine your cooling load. Do not rely on simple rules-of-thumb by air conditioner salespeople, but insist on thorough analysis, including local climate information and calculations of heat gain through windows and walls. Insist on an "ACCA Manual J" load calculation to size the equipment, and do not allow oversizing relative to the load calculation.

You can save a lot of money by reducing your cooling loads as much as possible before buying the system. (See **Reducing the Need for Air**

Conditioning later in this chapter.) Make sure conservation efforts are taken into account when the technician is figuring out how large a system you need.

With heat pumps, proper sizing can be especially difficult, because the same unit is used for both cooling and heating. A heat pump sized for heating loads in a cold climate will be considerably oversized when it comes to cooling, and a heat pump that is sized for cooling loads in a warm climate will tend to be oversized when it comes to heating. If the heating load is larger than the cooling load, some heat pump salespeople will recommend sizing the heat pump for cooling and then adding enough electric resistance heat to make up the difference in the winter. In such a situation, it generally makes more sense to size the heat pump to provide all of the heating requirements in average winter conditions, even though it will mean a larger and somewhat more expensive model. In this situation, a 2-speed or modulating compressor may be a worthwhile investment. A good heat pump technician should be able to help you choose the best compromise between cooling and heating capacity.

Efficiency

Efficiency is just as important with air conditioning systems as it is with heating systems. Central air conditioners and heat pumps operating in the cooling mode are rated according to their seasonal energy efficiency ratio (SEER), which is the seasonal cooling output in Btu divided by the seasonal energy input in watt-hours for an average U.S. climate. Many older central air conditioners have SEER ratings of only 6 or 7. The average central air conditioner sold in 1988 had a SEER of about 9; by 2002 it had risen to 11.1. The national efficiency standard for central air conditioners now requires a minimum SEER of 10, and to qualify for an ENERGY STAR label requires a SEER of 13 or higher. In 2006, minimum standards will rise to 12 or 13. Besides SEER, there are two other factors to check. The first is high temperature performance. Although it is not a federally rated number, EER at 95°F is available. Look for at least EER 11. In addition, a small device called a "thermal expansion device" (TXV), preferably factory-installed, should be specified. The TXV improves high-temperature performance, and helps the unit deliver its rated efficiency even under adverse conditions (such as inaccurate or low refrigerant levels). The device costs much less than the service call or inefficiency it guards against.

The efficiency of room air conditioners is measured by the energy efficiency ratio (EER), which is the ratio of the cooling output (in Btu) divided by the power consumption (in watt-hours). A typical new room air conditioner has an EER of about 9.8. The national appliance efficiency standards for room air conditioners now require a minimum EER of about 9.7 or 9.8 for the most common units. The minimum efficiency varies depending on the design and cooling capacity of each unit. The ENERGY STAR criteria for room air conditioners is 10.7 or 10.8 for units of less than 20,000 Btu/hr.

When you're shopping for air conditioners, look for SEER ratings over 13 (14 in warm climates) for central air conditioners and EER ratings of 11 or higher for room air condi-

EnergyGuide labels for room air conditioners list the Energy Efficiency Ratio or EER.

tioners. High-efficiency units generally cost more, but in hot climates more efficient units pay for themselves over a few years through reduced electricity bills. Central air conditioners are usually more efficient than room air conditioners, and in general, larger capacity air conditioners have higher efficiency. However, don't buy a larger system than you need just because it has higher efficiency (see discussion on sizing above).

Other energy-saving features to look for include a fan-only switch, which will enable you to use the unit for nighttime ventilation (see discussion on ventilation below). A filter check light to remind you to check the filter after a pre-determined number of operating hours is helpful. With central air conditioners and heat pumps, a variable speed fan will allow efficient air circulation for ventilation and filtering.

It is difficult to verify quiet operation for central air conditioner and heat pump models (sound ratings are generally not listed by manufacturers). If you are shopping for a room air conditioner, ask the sales staff if you can listen to different models in operation.

Dehumidification

Air conditioners remove moisture from the air because the room air is forced past cold coils. Water vapor from the air condenses out on the coils the same way moisture from the air condenses on a glass of ice water on a hot, humid day. This water drains outside through a condensate drain.

Lowering the humidity in this way is both good and bad. You feel more comfortable at lower humidity levels, so the dehumidification contributes to cooling. But when water vapor condenses into liquid, it releases stored heat, reducing the apparent efficiency of the air conditioner. One of the ways manufacturers can boost the rated efficiencies of air conditioners is by keeping the condenser coils somewhat warmer, thus reducing condensation. Some new air conditioners may not dehumidify air as effectively. This could be a problem, especially in humid climates

High-efficiency air conditioning systems can get around the dehumidification problem by including variable-speed or multispeed blowers. High-speed operation leads to high efficiencies but low dehumidification. Lower speeds reduce efficiency somewhat, but increase dehumidification. Lower speeds are used during very humid weather; the rest of the time a more efficient higher speed is used.

If you live in a humid climate, look for air conditioner models that are effective at removing moisture. Although there is no industry standard for rating the effectiveness at removing moisture, most literature does list water removal in pints per hour, which will help you compare one model to another. Choose a model with a variable-speed fan to aid in dehumidification if you're buying a very high-efficiency air conditioner, even though you might have to pay more for it. Several manufacturers have models with a variable-speed blower controlled by a humidistat, automatically reducing fan speed at high humidities. Also try to keep moisture out of the house (see **Operation and Maintenance** below).

THE MOST ENERGY-EFFICIENT
AIR CONDITIONERS

Part II includes lists of the most energy-efficient air conditioners on the market today. These are divided into room air conditioners, central air conditioners, and heat pumps.

The most efficient room air conditioners have EERs ranging from 10.8 to 11.7. Most of these models are available for either window mounting or through-the-wall mounting. All of the models listed exceed the new minimum standards for room air conditioners, which took effect in October, 2000.

Manufacturers now offer a large number of very efficient central air conditioning systems. The models listed in Part II are representative of manufacturers' top model lines. Bear in mind that a SEER of 14 or higher identifies a very efficient system, and a SEER of 13 or better earns the ENERGY STAR distinction.

BUYING AND INSTALLING
AN AIR CONDITIONING SYSTEM

Room air conditioners can be purchased for as little as a few hundred dollars, while large central air conditioners and heat pumps can cost as much as $5,000. If any modifications need to be made in the ducting system for a central air conditioner, that can add substantially to the cost. It pays to shop around and get bids from a number of different contractors. There is substantially more variation among contractors in the quality of their work than there is among manufacturers, and a significant fraction of "equipment problems" can be tracked to improper sizing or installation.

When evaluating bids, be sure to consider what you are getting for the price. Does the system come with a warranty? If so, how long is it? Air conditioner warranties range from one year for complete parts and labor to five years for the compressor. Some manufacturers are now offering ten-year warranties on the compressors. If an existing system is being replaced, will the old unit be hauled away? Does the air conditioning contractor offer a service plan, and is it affordable? Make sure the contractor has been in business for a while and is fully bonded and insured. If you are not familiar with the company, ask for some local references and follow them up.

To maximize efficiency, the outside part of a central air conditioner, the compressor, should be located in a cool, shaded place. The best place is usually on the north side of the house under a canopy of trees or tall shrubs. However, it shouldn't be choked by vegetation; the compressor needs unimpeded air flow around it to dump waste heat effectively. Never place the compressor on the roof or on the east or west side unless it is completely shielded from the summer sun, because sunlight shining on it will heat it up and reduce its efficiency at dumping heat.

Also, the compressor may be somewhat noisy. Try to keep it some distance from a patio or bedroom window. If you're concerned about noise, ask to see (and hear) one in operation before buying it.

With heat pumps, location of the outside unit is more complicated. Because a heat pump is used for both cooling and heating, it usually makes more sense to locate the compressor on the south side—especially in colder climates, and shade it with a sunscreen or tall

If possible, locate room air conditioners on a north wall or a wall that is shaded.

The outside compressor for a central air conditioner should be shaded from direct sun.

annuals during the summer. In the winter, when the compressor is trying to extract heat, a southern location will allow it to absorb solar energy, which will boost its heating efficiency.

The location of room air conditioners is constrained by available walls and windows. To perform most efficiently, these units should be out of direct sunlight; if you have a choice of walls, the north is best and the south is second best; avoid east or west walls if at all possible.

UPGRADING EXISTING AIR CONDITIONERS

The compressor units of most air conditioners have an average lifetime of only around 10 to 12 years. By carefully following proper maintenance procedures, a quality model may hold up twenty years, but don't expect the kind of lifetime you get with boilers and furnaces.

If you have an old air conditioner—more than ten years old—chances are pretty good that it's also inefficient. A ten-year-old central air conditioner probably has a SEER rating between 7 and 8, compared with the best new models that are up to twice as efficient. It will definitely pay to replace it, but you may not have to replace the entire air conditioner. Sometimes just the outdoor compressor component needs to be replaced, though it may be hard to find high-efficiency parts for low-efficiency models.

If you're replacing just the compressor, though, make sure that the new outdoor unit is compatible with the indoor blower coil. The highly efficient outdoor unit will not reach its rated efficiency if it is not properly matched to the indoor unit. An air conditioning service technician should be able to help you match units effectively.

OPERATION AND MAINTENANCE

Using natural or forced ventilation at night, while keeping the house closed up tight during hot days, is less expensive than operating your air conditioner (see **Reducing the Need for Air Conditioning** below). Use air conditioning only when ventilation is inadequate. Don't cool unoccupied rooms, but don't shut off too many registers with a central system either, or the increased system pressure may harm the compressor. If your room air conditioner has an outside air option, use it sparingly. It is far more economical to recirculate and cool the indoor air than to cool the hot outdoor air down to comfortable temperatures. Always keep all doors and windows closed when operating an air conditioner. Do not operate a whole-house fan or window fans while using the air conditioner.

You will probably be comfortable with the thermostat set at about 78°F, but ceiling fans can increase your comfort range. You will save 3–5% on air conditioning costs for each degree that you raise the thermostat. You can also increase comfort at warmer temperatures by reducing humidity; use a bathroom exhaust fan when you shower, run your dishwasher during the cooler evening or early morning hours, don't dry firewood in your basement, and don't vent your clothes dryer inside.

Air conditioners and heat pumps need regular maintenance in order to perform at peak efficiency. Clean the air filters on room air conditioners monthly. They should never be allowed to get dirty enough to impede air flow, as this could cause damage to the unit. The condenser should be cleaned by a professional every other year, or even yearly in dusty locations.

Central air conditioning units should be inspected, cleaned, and tuned by a professional once every two to three years. This will extend the life of the unit and reduce electricity consumption. Check with your service technician about the proper maintenance schedule for your unit.

During service of your unit, its refrigerant may need recharging. It needs to be charged correctly. A 20% undercharged system can operate at 20% lower efficiency, and field studies show that the majority of central air conditioners are undercharged enough to affect performance.

**Clean air conditioner
air filters regularly.**

However, an overcharged system not only reduces operating efficiency, it can cause damage to the unit and reduce the lifetime of the system. Also, because refrigerants damage the ozone layer, federal law requires that the refrigerant be recovered and recycled.

The service technician should also measure airflow over the indoor coil. Recent studies show that inadequate airflow is a common problem and average airflow rates tend to degrade over time due to poor maintenance. Correction of airflow rates can improve efficiency by 5–10%.

Even if an air conditioner or heat pump is installed and maintained with adequate airflow and the appropriate level of refrigerant, the unit will not operate efficiently if the duct system is in poor condition. Duct sealing can reduce cooling energy use by 10–15%. (See **Modifications by Heating Service Technicians** in Chapter 4 for more on duct sealing.)

The power to a central unit should be shut off when the cooling season ends, otherwise the heating elements in the unit could consume energy all winter long. Flip the circuit breaker to turn it off if the unit doesn't have a separate switch. Turn the power back on at least one day before starting up the unit in order to prevent damage to the compressor.

REDUCING THE NEED FOR AIR CONDITIONING

Even with the most efficient air conditioners, it makes a great deal of sense to do everything you can to reduce air conditioning loads. The following conservation measures are often so effective that houses in the northern third of the country and in mountainous regions can get by without air conditioning on all but the very hottest days. If you're planning to buy a new system, reducing the cooling load will save you a lot of money right away be letting you buy a smaller, less expensive system.

Human Comfort

In looking at how air conditioning costs can be reduced, it helps to understand human comfort. The standard human comfort range for light clothing in the summer is between 72°F and 78°F and between 35% and 60% relative humidity, according to the American Society for Heating, Refrigerating and Air-Conditioning Engineers (ASHRAE). The comfort range can be extended to 82°F with modest air movement, as might be provided by ceiling fans, for example. Often the house can be kept within this range using little or no mechanical air conditioning.

To extend the comfort range to 82°F, you need a breeze of about 2.5 ft/sec or 1.7 mph. A slow-turning ceiling-mounted paddle fan can easily provide this airflow. The following table gives the necessary fan blade diameters for various size rooms. Fans should have multiple speed settings so that airflow can be reduced at lower temperatures.

TABLE 5.1

CEILING FAN SIZING

Room area (sq ft)	Minimum fan diameter (inches)
100+	36
150+	42
225+	48
375+	52
400+	2 fans

Source: Don Abrams, *Low Energy Cooling.*

Common heat sources in a house.

Sources of Unwanted Heat

There are three major sources of unwanted heat in your house during the summer: heat that conducts through your walls and ceiling from the outside air, waste heat that is given off inside your house by lights and appliances, and sunlight that shines through your windows. These are described below, along with techniques to reduce them.

1. *Heat gain through your walls and ceiling.* Whenever the outdoor temperature is higher than the indoor temperature, heat will conduct through the walls and ceiling of the house to the interior. Warm air will blow into the house through cracks.

To reduce these gains, you can insulate and tighten your house. One of the most cost-effective energy conservation measures, for both heating and cooling, is to add extra ceiling insulation. Increase its depth to a full 12". If you don't have wall insulation,

Compact fluorescent lights
add less heat to the house than
incandescent lights.

have cellulose or fiberglass blown into the walls by a qualified insulation contractor. Tighten up your house to reduce infiltration. You might also want to install a radiant barrier in the attic to cut down on summer heat gain. If properly installed, a radiant barrier can reduce cooling costs to some extent, particularly in the South. New light-colored roofing materials and roof coatings can also reduce cooling loads. An energy auditor can help you decide which measures make the most sense for your house and how much they will cost (see Chapter 2).

2. *Waste heat from appliances and lights.* Most of the energy used for lights, refrigerators, stoves, washers and dryers, dishwashers, and other household appliances eventually ends up as waste heat that will raise the interior temperature of your house.

The best solution is to buy energy-efficient products. Energy-efficient appliances and lights produce far less waste heat. Standard incandescent light bulbs, for example, emit 90% of their energy as heat—only 10% as light. Compact fluorescent lights produce only a fraction of the heat (see Chapter 11). In some cases, you can delay heat-producing tasks, such as dishwashing, until the cooler evening hours. You might

Attic ventilation is a very important way to get rid of unwanted summer heat.

Trees are a very
effective way to shade
a house on the
east and west.

Sometimes it's possible to channel
summer breezes through the house
by planting hedges.

PREVAILING WINDS

also consider relocating a freezer to the basement or garage, where it won't contribute its waste heat to your living space. And by planning your meals carefully, you can minimize use of the oven on the hottest days.

3. *Solar gain through windows.* Sunlight shining in windows, particularly those on the east and west sides of the house, usually adds the largest amount of unwanted summertime heat. In addition, the sun heats up the roof and walls of the house, increasing heat conduction to the interior. With no shading of east and west windows, the interior temperature of a typical house could rise as much as 20°F on a hot day, either making your air conditioner work a lot harder, or making you a lot less comfortable.

The best way to eliminate solar gain is to provide effective shading. Use horizontal trellises above east- and west-facing windows, which collect more summer sun than the others. Plant tall trees (prune lower branches so as not impede summer breezes), or use awnings wider than the windows to provide shade. If you have a choice, place porches, sheds, and garages on east and west walls to provide further shading. Unless you have extensive areas of south glass, the south wall should not require summer shading because the summer sun is at too high an angle to cause much of a problem. Planting evergreen trees in front of south windows will block beneficial winter gains.

If you're replacing windows, put in high-performance windows with low-e glazings that look perfectly clear yet block out a large percentage of unwanted heat gain (see Chapter 3). It makes sense to install windows with low solar heat gain coefficients (SHGC) on west and east walls, where heat gain from the sun is the greatest in the summer. Windows with high SHGC make more sense on the south, especially when you want to benefit from passive solar heating during the winter months. Another way to reduce solar gain through windows is to install drapes with light-colored linings or operable blinds that will reflect sunlight back outside. Vertical blinds are particularly effective on east- and west-facing windows. Also choose lighter colors for roofs and walls to reflect sunlight and reduce conductive heat gain.

Getting Rid of Unwanted Heat through Ventilation

Natural or mechanical ventilation can help reduce air conditioning costs in every area of the country. In the northern United States and in mountainous areas, ventilation can often totally eliminate the need for air conditioning. In the rest of the country, ventilation can provide comfort over much of the cooling season, especially during the spring and fall months.

In order for ventilation to be most effective, the temperature of the incoming air should be 77°F or lower, making this strategy most effective at night and on cooler days. Keep the house closed up tight on hot days and try to limit unwanted heat gains as outlined above, then ventilate the house at night. In breezy locations, natural ventilation can be provided simply by opening screened windows. Plantings and fences can be used to help funnel breezes towards your house. If there isn't much wind, you'll need to provide mechanical ventilation with either window fans or a whole-house fan.

Window Fans. Window fans for ventilation are a reasonable option if they are used properly. They should be located on the leeward (downwind) side of the house facing out. A window should be open in each room. Interior doors must remain open to allow airflow. Window fans will not work as well in houses with long, narrow hallways or those with small rooms and many interior partitions. Window fans can be noisy, especially on high settings, but they are inexpensive.

Window fan.

Whole-House Fans. A whole-house fan is a more convenient option than window fans and may cost no more than three or four window fans. Mounted in a hallway ceiling on the top floor, the fan sucks air from the house and blows it into the attic. The fan is usually covered on the bottom by a louvered vent. (To reduce heat loss through the fan during the wintertime, the entire assembly should be installed within an insulated, weather-stripped box with a removable or hinged lid.)

The fan should have at least two speeds, with the highest one capable of changing the entire volume of air in the house very quickly. Because the fan blows air into the attic, the attic must have sufficient outlet vents. The attic free vent area, including soffit vents, ridge vents, and gable-end vents, should be twice the free vent area of the fan opening. (Free vent area is a measure of the area of the vent opening minus the area blocked by screening and louvers.)

Before turning on the fan, be sure to open several windows in various areas of the house. If just one or two windows are open, the airflow through them will be intolerably high. For safety reasons, the fan should have manual controls (either in addition to or instead of automatic controls). A *fusible*

Whole-house fan.

link, which automatically shuts the fan down in case of fire, should be included for safety (the controls should be installed by a licensed electrician). The fan should be installed carefully; a loose installation can cause vibrations and excessive noise. Units with low-speed motors (700 rpm or less) will usually be less noisy. Ask for a demonstration.

The whole-house fan can be turned on as soon as the outdoor temperature drops about three degrees below the indoor temperature. The fan speed should be adjusted according to how quickly you want to cool the house down. Mechanical ventilation uses far less electricity than mechanical air conditioning.

RECOMMENDATIONS

1. Reduce the cooling load by employing cost-effective conservation measures. Provide effective shade for east and west windows. When possible, delay heat-generating activities such as dishwashing until evening on hot days.

2. Over most of the cooling season, keep the house closed tight during the day. Don't let in unwanted heat and humidity. Ventilate at night either naturally or with fans.

3. Use ceiling fans to increase comfort levels at higher thermostat settings. It takes much less energy to move air than to cool it.

4. In hot climates, plant shade trees around the house. Don't plant evergreen trees on the south if you want to benefit from passive solar heating in the winter.

5. If you have an older central air conditioner, consider replacing the outdoor compressor with a modern, high-efficiency unit. Make sure that it is properly matched to the indoor unit.

6. If buying a new air conditioner, be sure that it is properly sized. Get assistance from an energy auditor or air conditioning contractor.

7. Buy a high-efficiency air conditioner: for room air conditioners, the EER should be above 10.8; for central air conditioners, look for a SEER of 13 or higher (14 in warm climates), with an EER of at least 11 (preferably 11.6). Look for the ENERGY STAR label or ask your contractor about ENERGY STAR models.

8. In hot, humid climates, make sure that the air conditioner you buy will adequately get rid of high humidity. Models with variable or multi-speed blowers are generally best. Try to keep moisture sources out of the house.

9. Particularly for newer houses in humid climates (and especially during the spring and fall), it can be hard to obtain acceptable humidity and temperature levels with "conventional" central air conditioners, even premium models. If you are considering a new central air conditioner, consider a unit with independent humidity control ("humidistat") functions. Until then, usually the most feasible way to reduce humidity without over-cooling is to install an ENERGY STAR dehumidifier.

10. Seal all air conditioner ducts with mastic, and insulate ducts that run through unheated basements, crawl spaces, and attics.

11. Keep the thermostat set at 78°F—or higher if using ceiling fans. Don't air-condition unused rooms.

12. Maintain your air conditioners properly to maximize efficiency. In particular, check your air filter monthly or as recommended by the manufacturer. Dirty air filters affect performance.

CHAPTER 6
Water Heating

Next to heating or cooling, water heating is typically the largest energy user in the home. As homes have become more and more energy efficient during the past 20 years, the percentage of energy used for water heating has steadily increased. This chapter takes a look at the high-efficiency water heaters available and how you can reduce water heating costs with your present water heater.

TYPES OF WATER HEATERS
Storage Water Heaters

Storage water heaters are by far the most common type of water heater used today in this country. Ranging in size from 20 to 80 gallons (or larger) and fueled by electricity, natural gas, propane, or oil, storage water heaters work by heating up water in an insulated tank. When you turn on the hot water tap, hot water is pulled out of the top of the water heater and cold water flows into the bottom to replace it. The hot water is always there, ready for use. Because heat is lost through the walls of the storage tank (this is called standby heat loss), energy is consumed even when no hot water is being used. New energy-efficient storage water heaters contain higher levels of insulation around the tank, substantially reducing standby heat loss.

Storage water heater.

Demand Water Heaters

Demand or instantaneous water heaters do not contain a storage tank. A gas burner or electric element heats water only when there is a demand for hot water. Hot water never runs out, but the flow rate (gallons of hot water per minute [gpm]) may be limited. By eliminating standby losses from the tank, energy consumption can be reduced by

10–15%. Before rushing out to buy a demand water heater, though, be aware that they aren't appropriate for every situation, and they may not even save that much energy and money.

The largest readily available gas-fired demand water heaters can supply only four gallons of hot water per minute with a temperature rise of 90°F (50° to 140°F, for example). However, such a sharp temperature rise may only be needed in commercial applications, where the hot water is mixed with cold. For home use, a rise of 60°–70°F is suffi-

Demand water heater.

cient, bringing water from 50°F to 110°–120°F. Gas demand water heaters can provide five to six gpm at this temperature. If you've installed a low-flow showerhead (see **Conserve Water** below) and won't need to be doing a load of laundry or dishes while someone is taking a shower, then four to five gpm might be fine. But if you have a couple of teenagers in the house, or if you need hot water for several tasks at the same time, a demand water heater might not be adequate. Newer instantaneous gas water heaters modulate their output over a broad range; typical outputs might range from 15,000 to 180,000 Btuh—a 12:1 range in hot water output, depending on demand (hand washing vs. washing machine, for example). This is an improvement over earlier models.

Electric demand water heaters provide even less hot water. The largest models require 18 kilowatts at 240 volts yet provide less than 2 gpm at a 70°F temperature rise. Then again, an electric demand unit might make good sense in an addition or remote area of the house, thereby eliminating the heat losses through the hot water pipes to that area. Small electric demand water heaters can be placed under sinks to boost the temperature of incoming warm water. If you want to consider an electric unit, make sure your electrical wiring can handle the job before you make a purchase.

Demand water heaters make the most sense in homes with one or two occupants, and in households with small and easily coordinated hot water requirements. Without modulating temperature control (above), you and your family may find yourselves unhappy with fluctuating water temperatures—particularly if you have your own water system with varying pressure.

With gas-fired demand water heaters, keep in mind that the pilot light can waste a lot of energy. In gas storage water heaters, energy from the pilot light is not all wasted because it heats the water in the tank. This is not the case with demand water heaters. A 500 Btu/hour pilot light can consume 20 therms of gas per year, offsetting some of the savings you achieve by eliminating standby losses of a storage water heater. To solve this problem, you can keep the pilot light off most of the time, and turn it on when you need hot water—a routine that should work fine in a vacation home, but not in a regular household. A growing number of demand water heater models have electronic ignition, eliminating the need for a continuously burning pilot. Table 6.2 lists manufacturers and distributors of leading demand water heaters.

Heat Pump Water Heaters

Heat pump water heaters are more efficient than electric resistance models because the electricity is used for moving heat from one place to another rather than for generating the heat directly (see discussion on heat pumps in Chapters 4 and 5). The heat source is the outside

Heat pump water heater.

air or air in the basement where the unit is located. Refrigerant fluid and compressors are used to transfer heat into an insulated storage tank. While the efficiency is higher, so is the cost to purchase and maintain these units. Heat pump water heaters are available with built-in water tanks called integral units, or as add-ons to existing hot water tanks. A heat pump water heater uses one-third to one-half as much electricity as a conventional electric resistance water heater. In warm climates they may do even better. Table 6.3 lists manufacturers of heat pump water heaters.

Tankless Coil Water Heaters

Tankless coil water heaters use the home's main heating system as the heat source for water heating. They are common in older oil-fired boilers, although gas-fired boilers are also sometimes fitted with tankless coil water heaters. They operate directly off the house boiler; there is no separate storage tank. When hot water is drawn from the tap, the water circulates through a heat exchanger in the boiler. As long as the boiler is being used regularly (during the winter months), a tank-less coil works very well because the boiler is usually hot. During the summer, spring,

Tankless coil water heater.

and fall months, however, the boiler has to cycle on and off frequently just for water heating, wasting energy the same way your car wastes gas in stop-and-go traffic. Tankless coils can consume 3 Btu of fuel for every 1 Btu of hot water they provide, making them more expensive to operate than most other types of water heaters. In general, tankless coil water heaters are not recommended. There are other integrated space and water heating systems that are far more effective.

Indirect Water Heaters

Indirect water heater.

Indirect water heaters use the home's boiler or furnace as the heat source, but in a very different way than a tankless coil. In boiler systems, hot water from the boiler is circulated through a heat exchanger in a separate insulated tank. In the less common furnace-based systems, water in a heat exchanger coil circulates through the furnace to be heated, then through the water storage tank. Since hot water is stored in an insulated storage tank, the boiler or funace does not have to turn on and off as frequently, improving its fuel economy. Electronic controls determine when water in the tank falls below a preset temperature and trigger the boiler or furnace to provide heat as long as needed. The more sophisticated of these systems rely on a heat purge cycle to circulate leftover heat remaining in the heat exchanger into the water storage tank after the boiler shuts down, thereby further improving overall system efficiency.

Indirect water heaters, when used in combination with new, high-efficiency boilers or furnaces, are usually the least expensive way to provide hot water (see **COMPARING THE TRUE COSTS OF WATER HEATERS** below). These systems can be purchased in an integrated form, incorporating the boiler or furnace and water heater with controls, or as separate components. Gas, oil, and propane-fired systems are available. Any form of hydronic space heating—hydronic baseboards, radiators, or radiant heat—can be provided by boiler systems.

Advanced Heating Systems
With Integrated Water Heaters

If you're building a new home or upgrading your heating system at the same time you're choosing a new water heater, you might consider a combination water heater and space heating system. These systems, also called dual integrated appliances, put water heating and space heating functions in one package. Space heating is provided via warm-air distribution.

Integrated gas heaters feature a powerful water heater, with space heating provided as the supplemental end-use. Heated water from the water heater tank passes through a heat exchanger in a fan-coil unit to heat air. The fan blows this heated air into the ducts to heat the home. Many combination systems of this type are available at low initial costs, but space and water heating efficiency is often less than that of conventional systems. Models incorporating a high-efficiency condensing water heater, such as the American Water Heater and Lennox CompleteHeat, are exceptions. These models realize efficiency gains over traditional equipment.

Households using electric water heating and a heat pump for space conditioning can reduce water heating costs by installing a multi-function heat pump system. Fully integrated, single-unit systems are available, or an existing heat pump and storage water heater can be retrofitted with a specially designed add-on heat pump water heater module. Multi-function air- and ground-source heat pump systems are available.

As you may have guessed, proper sizing of a dual integrated appliance is very important for economical performance, since both space heating and water heating are given from one "box." The manufacturers listed in Table 6.4 should be able to identify your local distributors and contractors who are familiar with these products and their installation.

Solar Water Heaters

As the name implies, these use energy from the sun to heat water. While the initial cost of a solar water heater is high, it can save a lot of money over the long term (see **COMPARING THE TRUE COSTS OF WATER HEATING** below). Solar water heaters are much less common than they were during the 1970s and early 1980s when they were supported by tax credits, but the units available today tend to be considerably less expensive and more reliable. For example, in New England, it is now possible to have a complete system that will provide approximately two-thirds of a typical family's hot water requirements installed for less than $3,000. At that price, solar water heaters compete very well with electric and propane water heaters on a life-cycle cost basis, though they are still usually more expensive than natural gas.

Solar water heaters are designed to serve as preheaters for conventional storage or demand water heaters (either gas or electric). They work quite well with demand water heaters that have modulating temperature controls. Because the solar system preheats the water, the extra temperature boost required by the demand water heater is relatively low, and a high flow rate can be achieved.

If you are building a new house, it is to your advantage to have a south-sloping roof for easier installation of a solar water heater. At low cost, you can have the best place "pre-plumbed" or "roughed in" so the pipes are in place if you later want to install a solar water heater. If you have extra money to invest now and want to do more for the environment, a solar water heater can be a good choice in most areas today. But make sure you find a

Solar water heater.

qualified installer who can properly design and size the back-up water heating system. Solar water heaters can be particularly effective if they are designed for three-season use, with your heating system providing hot water during the winter months. If you heat with wood, the solar water heater installer may be able to fit your wood stove with a water heating coil to take over in the winter months.

This edition of the Consumer Guide does not list individual solar water heating equipment; a list of manufacturers is provided in Table 6.5.

SELECTING A NEW WATER HEATER

Whether you're replacing a worn-out existing water heater or looking for the best model for a new house you're building, it pays to choose carefully. Look for a water heater that satisfies your hot water needs and uses as little energy as possible. Often you can substantially reduce your hot water needs through water conservation efforts (see **Conserve Water** below).

Think About a Replacement Now

If you're like most people, you're unlikely to go out looking for a water heater until your existing one fails. That will happen at the worst possible time—like just after your in-laws arrive for a week-long visit. You'll have to rush out and put in whatever is available, without taking the time to look for a water heater that most appropriately fits your needs and offers the highest level of energy efficiency.

A much better approach is to do some research now. Figure out what type of water heater you want—gas or electric, storage or demand, stand-alone or integrated with your heating system, etc. Figure out the proper size for your household (not just gallon capacity, but first-hour rating as well—see **Sizing a Water Heater** below). And then use the listings here to identify your most energy-efficient options.

If possible, replace your existing water heater before it fails. Most water heaters have a lifespan of about 10–15 years. If yours is up there in age, have your plumber take a look at it and advise you on how much useful life it has left. If it's in bad shape, replace it now before it starts leaking or the burner stops working. In fact, it often makes sense to replace an inefficient water heater even if it's in good shape. The energy savings alone could pay for the new water heater after just a few years, and you'll be happy knowing that you are dumping fewer pollutants into the air and less money down the drain.

Sizing a Water Heater

To determine how big a storage water heater you need, you should first estimate your family's peak-hour demand. To do this, estimate what time of day (morning or evening) your family is likely to require the greatest amount of hot water. Then calculate the maximum expected hot water demand using Table 6.1. Note that this does not provide an estimate of your family's total daily use, only the peak hourly use. Also, the values in this table do not consider water conservation measures, like low-flow showerheads and faucet aerators, that can reduce hot water use for each activity.

The ability of a water heater to meet peak demands for hot water is indicated by its first-hour rating. This rating accounts for the effects of tank size and how quickly cold water is heated. In some cases, a water heater with a small tank but powerful burner can have a higher first-hour rating than one with a large tank and less powerful burner. First-hour ratings are provided in the listings that follow, along with tank size and efficiency (given as estimated energy use). You can also ask appliance dealers for the first-hour ratings of appliances they sell.

Buying too large a storage water heater will reduce energy performance by increasing the standby losses. If gas- or oil-fired, larger systems will also lose more heat up the flue.

Demand water heaters should be sized according to the required gpm flow rate and temperature rise required for your largest expected hot water fixture (usually a shower). (See discussion on demand water heaters above.)

TABLE 6.1

PEAK HOURLY HOT WATER DEMAND

	Avg. gallons hot water per usage		Times used in hour		Gal. used in hour
Showering	20	×	_____	=	_____
Bathing	20	×	_____	=	_____
Shaving	2	×	_____	=	_____
Washing hands and face	2	×	_____	=	_____
Shampooing hair	4	×	_____	=	_____
Hand dishwashing	4	×	_____	=	_____
Automatic dishwashing	12	×	_____	=	_____
Preparing food	5	×	_____	=	_____
Automatic clothes washing	32	×	_____	=	_____

For example, if your family's expected greatest hot water use is in the morning, the total might be:

3 showers	20	×	3	=	60 gallons/hr.
1 shave	2	×	1	=	2 gallons/hr.
Hand-wash dishes	4	×	1	=	4 gallons/hr.
Peak hour demand				=	66 gallons/hr.

Source: Gas Appliance Manufacturers Association and ACEEE estimates.

With solar water heaters, you should discuss your requirements carefully with the solar water heating salesperson. You will need to size both the solar hot water system itself and the back-up electric or gas water heater. It generally makes the most sense to size a solar water heater to provide two-thirds to three-fourths of your total demand, and provide the rest with a back-up system.

Fuel Options

What type of fuel makes the most sense for your water heater? If you currently have an electric water heater and natural gas is available in your area, a switch might save you a lot of money. Oil- and propane-fired water heaters are also usually less expensive to operate than electric models.

Before you rule out electricity, though, check with your utility company. It may offer special off-peak rates that make electricity a more attractive option. With off-peak electricity for water heating, the utility company puts in a separate meter with a timer in it. You can only draw electricity through that meter during off-peak periods, when the utility company has more capacity than it needs and is willing to sell it less expensively.

Look for Sealed Combustion or Power-Vented Systems

For safety as well as energy efficiency reasons with gas- and oil-fired water heaters, look for units with sealed combustion or power venting. Sealed combustion means that outside air is brought in directly to the water heater and exhaust gases are vented directly outside. The combustion is totally separated from the house air. Power-vented equipment can use house air for combustion, but flue gases are vented to the outside with the aid of a fan.

Sealed combustion gas water heater.

In very tight houses, drawing combustion air from the house and passively venting flue gases up the chimney can sometimes result in back-drafting of dangerous combustion gases into the house.

WATER HEATER EFFICIENCY

The energy efficiency of a storage water heater is indicated by its *energy factor* (EF), an overall efficiency based on the use of 64 gallons of hot water per day. The first national appliance efficiency standards for water heaters took effect in 1990. New standards scheduled to take effect January 20, 2004 will require the energy factors listed on the next page, based on storage tank size.

All other things being equal, the smaller the water heater tank, the higher the efficiency. Compared to small tanks, large tanks have a greater surface area, which increases heat loss from the tank and decreases the energy efficiency somewhat, as mentioned above. If your utility company offers off-peak electric rates and you'd like to use them,

MINIMUM ENERGY FACTORS (EF)

Tank size	Gas	Oil	Electric
30 gallons	0.61	0.53	0.93
40 gallons	0.59	0.51	0.92
50 gallons	0.57	0.50	0.90
60 gallons	0.56	0.48	0.89

you may need to buy a larger water heater to provide carry-over hot water for periods when electricity is not available.

THE MOST EFFICIENT WATER HEATERS

The tables in Part II list the most efficient gas- and oil-fired water heaters on the market today. For storage water heaters, the first-hour ratings, energy factors, storage capacities, and estimated annual energy use are listed. The most efficient gas-fired storage water heaters have energy factors ranging from 0.60 to 0.65, corresponding to estimated gas use below 250 therms/year. Condensing water heaters have energy factors as high as 0.86.

The efficiency of a combination water heater with integrated space heating is given by its combined annual efficiency, which is based on the AFUE of the space heating component and the energy factor of the water heating component. We list the most efficient combination units, only including those with combined annual efficiencies of 0.75 (75%) or higher.

There is little difference between the most efficient electric resistance storage water heaters and the minimum-efficiency standard for this product that will take effect in January 2004. As a result, we no longer list specific electric resistance models. Fortunately, heat pump water heaters using less than half as much electricity as conventional electric resistance water heaters are becoming commercially available. If you use electricity for water heating, consider installing a heat pump water heater. Otherwise, look for the most efficient electric resistance unit in your size range. The most efficient electric storage water heaters have energy factors between 0.93 and 0.95, resulting in estimated annual energy use below 4,725 kWh/year.

With demand water heaters, the manufacturers provide different specifications: the energy input (Btu/hour for gas, kilowatts [kW] for electric); the temperature rise achievable at the rated flow; the flow rate at the listed temperature rise; the minimum flow rate required to fire the heating elements; whether or not the unit is available with a modulating temperature control to automatically adjust the amount of heating required to maintain the desired delivery temperature; and the maximum water pressure. In comparing the different models, be aware that you aren't always looking at direct comparisons, especially with temperature rise and flow rate. For example, while one model might list the flow rate at a 100°F temperature rise, another might list the flow rate at 70°. Until there are industry-standard ratings for temperature rise and flow rates, it will be difficult to compare the performance of products from different companies. Some companies are beginning to publish energy factor ratings for these products and this information should make for easier comparisons.

TABLE 6.2

MANUFACTURERS OF INSTANTANEOUS ("TANKLESS") GAS WATER HEATERS

Aquastar by Bosch
Controlled Energy Corporation
  (Distributor)
340 Mad River Park
Waitsfield, VT 05673
866-330-2725
www.cechot.com

Infinion
Low Energy Systems (Distributor)
2916 S. Fox St.
Englewood, CO 80110
800-873-3507
www.tanklesswaterheaters.com

Paloma Industries, Inc.
2151 Eastman Avenue
Oxnard, CA 93830
805-278-5499
www.palomaindustries.com

Rinnai Corporation
103 International Drive
Peachtree City, GA 30269
866-746-6241
www.rinnaina.com

Takagi Industrial Co. USA, Inc.
3 Goodyear, Suite B
Irvine, CA 92618
888-882-5244
www.takagi-usa.com

TABLE 6.3

MANUFACTURERS OF HEAT PUMP WATER HEATERS

Applied Energy Recovery Systems (E-Tech)
3285 Saturn Court
Norcross, GA 30092
770-734-9696
www.aeretech.com

ECR International
2201 Dwyer Avenue
Utica, NY 13504-4729
315-797-1310
www.ecrinternational.com

Nyle International
P.O. Box 1107
Bangor, ME 04402
207-942-2865
www.nyletherm.com

TABLE 6.4

MANUFACTURERS OF COMBINATION WATER HEATERS/SPACE HEATERS

American Water Heater
P.O. Box 1597
Johnson City, TN 37605
800-456-9805
www.americanwaterheater.com

Lennox (CompleteHeat)
P.O. Box 799900
Dallas, TX 75379-9900
800-953-6669
www.lennox.com

COMPARING THE TRUE COSTS OF WATER HEATERS

There are a number of important considerations when deciding what type of water heater you should buy: fuel type, efficiency, configuration (storage, demand, integrated), size, and cost. The information above covers most of these issues. Cost, however, needs some additional discussion. There are really two types of cost you need to look at: purchase cost and operating cost.

It may be tempting when you're buying a water heater simply to look for a model that is inexpensive to buy, and ignore the operating cost. This is a poor strategy. Often, the least expensive water heaters to buy are the most expensive to operate. Life-cycle costs, which take into account both the initial costs and operating costs of different water heaters, provide a much more accurate representation of the true costs

TABLE 6.5

NORTH AMERICAN SOLAR WATER HEATING SYSTEMS

Alternate Energy Technologies
P.O. Box 61326
Jacksonville, FL 32236
904-781-8305
www.aetsolar.com

Radco
2877 Industrial Parkway
Santa Maria, CA 93455
800-927-2326

Solar Development Incorporated
3634 Reese Ave.
Riviera Beach, FL 33404
561-842-8935
www.solardev.com

Thermo Dynamics, Ltd.
101 Frazee Ave.
Dartmouth, Nova Scotia B3B 1Z4
Canada
902-468-1001
www.thermo-dynamics.com

of the water heater. Life-cycle costs for the most common types of water heaters under typical operating conditions are shown in Table 6.6.

From the table, we see that when both purchase and operating costs are taken into account, one of the least expensive systems to buy (conventional electric storage) is one of the most costly to operate over a 13-year period. An electric heat pump water heater, though expensive to

Even though a standard electric water heater is probably the least expensive type to buy, it costs the most to operate.

purchase, has a much lower cost over the long term. A solar water heating system, which costs the most to buy, has the lowest yearly operating cost among electric systems.

TABLE 6.6

LIFE-CYCLE COSTS FOR 13-YEAR OPERATION OF DIFFERENT TYPES OF WATER HEATERS

Water heater type	Efficiency	Cost[1]	Yearly energy cost[2]	Life (years)	Cost over 13 years[3]
Conventional gas storage	57%	$380	$179	13	$2,707
High-eff. gas storage	65%	$525	$157	13	$2,566
Conventional oil storage	55%	$950	$220	8	$4,760
High-eff. oil storage	66%	$1,400	$180	8	$5,140
Conventional electric storage	90%	$350	$410	13	$5,680
High-eff. electric storage	95%	$440	$380	13	$5,380
Demand gas	70%	$650	$160	20	$2,730
High-eff., pilotless demand gas	84%	$1,200	$90	20	$2,370
Demand electric (2 units)	100%	$600	$414	20	$5,982
Electric heat pump	220%	$1,200	$140	13	$3,220
Indirect water heater with efficient gas or oil boiler	79%	$600	$100	30	$1,900
Solar with electric back-up	n/a	$2,500	$125	20	$4,125

1. Approximate. Includes installation.
2. Energy costs based on hot water needs for typical family of four and energy costs of 8.28¢/kWh for electricity, 68.8¢/therm for gas, $1.09/gallon for oil.
3. Future operation costs are neither discounted nor adjusted for inflation.
Source: American Council for an Energy-Efficient Economy.

INSTALLING A WATER HEATER

Select an installation contractor carefully. Make sure that he or she has experience with the type of system you want to put in. If the system is integrated with your heating system, have your heating contractor put in the water heater.

To get a good price, ask for bids from several contractors and evaluate the bids carefully. Consider warranties, service, and reputation as well as the price.

Storage water heaters will lose less heat if they are located in a relatively warm area. Don't install the water heater in an unheated basement if at all possible. Also try to minimize the length of piping runs to your kitchen and bathrooms. The best location is a centralized one, not too far from any of your hot water taps.

When the water heater is being installed, make sure heat traps or one-way valves are installed on both the hot and cold water lines to cut down on losses through the pipes. Without heat traps, hot water rises and cold water falls within the pipes, allowing heat from the water heater to be lost to the surroundings. Heat traps cost around $30 and will save $15–30 per year. Some new water heaters have built-in heat traps. If heat traps are not installed, you should insulate several feet of cold water pipe closest to the water heater in addition to the hot water pipes. Even with heat traps, insulate the cold water line between the water tank and heat trap.

Also follow general energy conservation tips when you are installing a new water heater (see **UPGRADING YOUR EXISTING WATER HEATER** below). Just because it's a new water heater, for example, doesn't mean it won't benefit from an added insulation blanket.

UPGRADING YOUR EXISTING WATER HEATER

Even if you aren't going to buy a new water heater, you can save a lot of energy and money with your existing system by following a few simple suggestions.

Conserve Water

Your biggest opportunity for savings is to use less hot water. In addition to saving energy (and money), cutting down on hot water use helps conserve dwindling water supplies, which in some parts of the country is a critical problem. A family of four each showering five minutes a day can use about 700 gallons per week—a three-year drinking water supply for one person! Water-conserving showerheads and faucet aerators can cut hot water use in half. That family of four can save 14,000 gallons of water a year and the energy required to heat it.

If you aren't sure how much water your shower currently uses, you can find out with

Low-flow showerheads and faucet aerators reduce your hot water use, saving energy and money.

a bucket that holds at least a gallon and with a watch with a second hand. Turn on the shower to the usual pressure you use, hold the bucket under it and time how many seconds it takes to fill to the one-gallon mark. If it takes less than 20 seconds, your flow rate is over 3 gpm, and your shower is a good candidate for a low-flow showerhead. Many older showerheads typically deliver 4–5 gpm.

In fact, federal efficiency standards now require that all new showerheads perform at no more than 2.5 gallons per minute. A variety of high-quality showerheads meet this standard while providing very satisfactory performance, including some of the shower massage products that have become more popular.

New faucets are also subject to the 2.5 gpm standard, but there are opportunities to save even more. Look for faucet aerators that deliver ½–1 gpm, especially if you tend to run the water when rinsing dishes. Some models are sold with a convenient shut-off valve at the aerator that allows you to temporarily turn off the water without changing the hot/cold mix. Sink aerators cost just a few dollars apiece. Repair leaky faucets right away. Even a relatively small hot water drip can dump a lot of energy and money down the drain.

Also, refer to Chapters 9 and 10 for water-saving tips with dishwashers and washing machines. In addition to saving money, any measure to conserve water will also reduce your water and sewer bills.

Insulate Your Existing Water Heater

Installing an insulating jacket on your existing water heater is one of the most effective do-it-yourself energy-saving projects, especially if your water heater is in an unheated basement or space. The insulating jacket will reduce standby heat loss—heat lost through the walls of the tank—by 25–40%, saving 4–9% on your water heating bills. Water heater insulation jackets are widely available for around $10. An insulating jacket will pay for itself through energy savings in less than a year. Add at least an additional R-8 to the sides and top of the tank.

Some newer water heaters come with fairly high insulation levels, reducing (though

Even with new water heaters, it is usually a good idea to wrap them with insulation.

not eliminating) the economic advantages of adding additional insulation. In fact, some manufacturers recommend against installing insulating jackets on their energy-efficient models. Always follow directions carefully when installing an insulation jacket. Leave the thermostat(s) accessible. With conventional gas- and oil-fired water heaters, you need to be careful not to restrict the air inlet(s) at the bottom or the draft hood at the top.

Insulate Hot Water Pipes and Install Heat Traps

Insulating your hot water pipes will reduce losses as the hot water is flowing to your faucet and, more importantly, it will reduce standby losses when the tap is turned off and then back on within an hour or so. A great deal of energy and water is wasted waiting for the hot water to reach the tap. Even when pipes are insulated, the water in the pipes will eventually cool, but it stays warmer much longer than it would if the pipes weren't insulated.

Also have heat traps installed, as described above, if they are not already in place (see **INSTALLING A WATER HEATER** above).

Install heat traps on cold and hot water lines to cut losses.

Lower the Water Heater Temperature

Keep your water heater thermostat set at the lowest temperature that provides you with sufficient hot water. For most house-holds, 120°F water is fine (about midway between the "low" and "medium" setting. Each 10°F reduction in water temper-ature will generally save 3–5% on your water heating costs. If you have a dishwasher without a booster heater, you should prob-ably keep the water temperature up to 140°F (the "medium" setting) or buy a new, more efficient, dishwasher (see Chapter 9). Not only will lowering the ther-mostat save a lot of energy, but it will also increase the life of

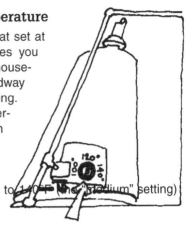

You will save a lot of energy and money by lowering the thermostat setting on your water heater.

your water heater and reduce the risk of children scalding themselves with the hot water.

Electric water heaters often have two thermostats—one for the upper heating element and one for the lower heating element. These should be adjusted to the same level to prevent one element from doing all the work and wearing out prematurely. Be sure to turn off the electricity at the circuit breaker before removing the access panels on an electric water heater.

When you are going away on vacation, you can turn the thermostat down to the lowest possible setting, or turn the water heater off alto-gether for additional savings. With a gas water heater, make sure you know how to relight the pilot if you're going to turn it off while away.

RECOMMENDATIONS

1. Plan ahead. Don't wait until your existing water heater fails before you look into replacement. It often makes very good economic sense to replace an old, inefficient model with a high-efficiency one even before the old one fails.

2. Take into account life-cycle costs when you're choosing a water heater. Don't be tempted to simply buy the lowest price model available.

3. With storage water heaters, buy an efficient model, such as the ones listed in this chapter.

4. Implement water conservation strategies. You'll save energy and money whether you're buying a new system or not. Install low-flow showerheads and faucet aerators. Refer to Chapters 9 and 10 for water-saving tips with other appliances.

5. Insulate your water heater if it's a storage model. Even new energy-efficient models should generally be insulated.

6. Insulate hot water pipes.

7. Lower the temperature setting on your water heater to about 120°F.

CHAPTER 7
Food Storage

The energy use of refrigerators and freezers has improved dramatically in the past 20 years, but they are still among the largest energy consumers in the home. A typical new refrigerator today uses less than 500 kWh per year, while the typical model sold in 1973 used more than three times as much. Moreover, the typical unit today is larger and has better controls. This increase in efficiency has been achieved through more insulation, tighter door seals, larger coil surface area, and improved compressors and motors.

Much of the increase in efficiency is due to national energy efficiency standards for new refrigerators. The current refrigerator standards took effect July 1, 2001. In some states, utilities offer rebates for the purchase of models that exceed the minimum standards.

BUYING A NEW REFRIGERATOR

All refrigerators are much more efficient today, but your choices when buying equipment still lead to large variations in the amount of energy your refrigerator will use. So, it pays to shop for an energy-efficient model. For full-size refrigerators, ENERGY STAR units will use at least 10% less electricity than conventional units, sometimes at no additional first cost. And some models will use 15% and even 20% less electricity. In 2003, the ENERGY STAR program was expanded to cover both compact and full-size refrigerators. Compact refrigerators less than 7.75 ft^3 must be 20% more efficient than the minimum federal standard.

More important, consider what style and features you want, and what the energy penalties can be. For example, side-by-side refrigerator/ freezers use more energy than similarly sized models with the freezer on top. Built-in designer refrigerators may also consume more energy than store models, but are less wasteful than they used to be since the national appliance energy standards took effect. If maintained well (to minimize frost build-up), manual defrost models use less electricity than automatic defrost models. However, they are not widely available. Features such as automatic icemakers and through-the-door cold water dispensers will increase energy consumption by 10% to 20%.

Size matters, too. Generally, the larger the unit, the greater the energy consumption. Too large a model will result in wasted space and energy; too small a model could mean extra trips to the supermarket. However, some refrigerator sizes tend to be more efficient. You may find that a more efficient 18 ft³ model costs less to run than a 15 ft³ model with similar features.

If you are thinking of buying a second refrigerator, you might want to reconsider. It is generally much less expensive to buy and operate one big refrigerator than two small ones. If the extra refrigerator is an old model, it's probably an energy guzzler. If you only need a second refrigerator a few days a year or to hold a few six-packs of beer, why spend an extra $50–150 per year in electricity? If you need a second refrigerator for convenient beverage and snack storage in a family room, buy the smallest ENERGY STAR model available.

BUYING A NEW FREEZER

There are two basic freezer styles: upright (front loading) and chest (top loading). Chest freezers are 10–25% more efficient than uprights because they are better insulated and air doesn't spill out when the door is opened. However, you should also consider convenience when selecting a freezer—chest models can be more difficult to organize. A new standard for freezers also went into effect in July 2001. To help consumers identify the most efficient freezer, an ENERGY STAR labeling program for freezers was launched. To qualify for the label, full-size freezers must use at least 10% less electricity than the federal minimum standard and compact freezers must use 20% less electricity.

Manual defrost freezers are more common than automatic defrost models, and they tend to do a better job at storing food. (Automatic defrost freezers may dehydrate frozen foods, causing freezer burn.) Because a freezer is opened less frequently than a refrigerator, frost will generally not build up as quickly as it might in manual defrost refrigerators.

THE MOST EFFICIENT REFRIGERATORS AND FREEZERS

The most energy-efficient refrigerator and freezer models are listed in Part II. The listings are organized according to configuration and size. Models are listed within each group in order of increasing electricity use (although technically, a larger refrigerator that uses only slightly more electricity than a smaller model may be considered more efficient on the basis of cubic feet per kWh consumed). All of the full-sized refrigerators listed exceed the ENERGY STAR level and are at least 11% more efficient than the minimum efficiency required by law. The compact refrigerator and freezer listings include all models that comply with the new ENERGY STAR specifications. Check with your electric utility to see if a rebate is available for a high-efficiency model, and look for the ENERGY STAR label or visit the ENERGY STAR website (www.energystar.gov) for an updated listing of qualified models.

INSTALLATION

If possible, locate refrigerators and freezers away from heat sources and direct sunlight. In the kitchen, try to keep your refrigerator away from the dishwasher and oven. Allow at least 1" space on each side of a refrigerator or freezer to allow good air circulation. Freezers can be installed in an attached garage or basement, which will boost energy performance somewhat during cooler months and reduce cooling loads in your house somewhat during the warmer months. However, don't put a refrigerator or freezer in a space that frequently goes below 45°—the refrigerant will not work properly.

BOOSTING THE EFFICIENCY
OF YOUR EXISTING REFRIGERATOR OR FREEZER

From an energy standpoint, you will save the most by replacing your existing refrigerator or freezer with a new, more efficient model. If it is more than about 15 years old, it may be so inefficient that a new one would pay for itself in energy savings in just a few years. Unfortunately, that is often not practical. Refrigerators cost a lot. If your present one is working fine, it's hard to justify running out to buy a new one. So here are a number of ways to boost energy efficiency and performance of refrigerators and freezers.

Check Door Seals

Check the door seals or gaskets on your refrigerator/freezer. These can deteriorate over time, greatly increasing heat gain and decreasing energy performance. Put a dollar bill in the door as you close it; if it is not held firmly in place, the seals are probably defective. With newer magnetic door seals, this test may not work. Instead, put a bright flashlight inside the refrigerator and direct the light toward a section of the door seal. With the door closed and the room darkened, inspect for light through the crack. You will have to reposition the light as you move along the perimeter of the seal. Use a mirror to check the seal at the bottom of the door. If you don't see light, the seals should be in good shape.

The dealer you purchased the refrigerator or freezer from should be able to install new seals. New seals aren't cheap, though. If the seals are bad, you might want to evaluate whether it's time to buy a new, high-efficiency model.

Check the Temperature

Check the temperature inside your refrigerator and freezer with an accurate thermometer. The refrigerator compartment should be kept between 36°F and 38°F, and the freezer compartment between 0°F and 5°F. If the temperature is outside these ranges, adjust the thermostat control. Keeping temperatures 10°F lower than these recommended levels can increase energy use by as much as 25%.

Inspect your refrigerator door gaskets for tightness with a piece of paper or a light.

Move the Refrigerator to a Cooler Location

Take a look at where the refrigerator is located. If it's in the sunlight or next to your stove or dishwasher, it has to work harder to maintain cool temperatures. If you can move it to a cooler location, you'll boost energy performance. Also, make sure that air can freely circulate around the condenser coils. If that air flow is blocked, energy performance will drop (see **INSTALLATION** above).

Check Power-Saver Switch

Many refrigerators have small heaters built into the walls to prevent moisture from condensing on the outer surface—as if the refrigerator doesn't have to work hard enough already! On some newer units, this feature can be turned off with an energy-saver or power-saver switch. Unless you have noticeable condensation, keep this switch on the energy-saving setting.

Defrost as Necessary

Manual defrost and partial automatic defrost refrigerators and freezers should be defrosted on a regular basis. The buildup of ice on the coils inside the unit means that the compressor has to run longer to maintain cold temperatures, wasting energy. If you live in a very hot, humid climate and don't use air conditioning, defrosting may be required quite frequently with a manual defrost model. After defrosting, you might be able to adjust the thermostat to a warmer setting, further saving energy.

RECOMMENDATIONS

1. When shopping for a new refrigerator or freezer, look for the ENERGY STAR label.

2. Avoid putting hot foods directly in the refrigerator or freezer. Let them cool in the room first.

3. Cover foods, especially liquids. Otherwise they will release moisture into the refrigerator compartment, increasing energy use by the refrigerator.

4. A full freezer will perform better than a nearly empty freezer. This can be especially true in the event of a power outage. If your freezer isn't full, fill plastic containers with water and freeze them.

5. If you have a freezer or second refrigerator that's nearly empty, turn it off. You'll do no harm to your refrigerator or freezer by turning it on and off periodically. If you won't be using it at all, unplug it and remove the door to be sure that children can't accidently get trapped inside.

6. Mark items in the freezer for quick identification so that you don't have to stand there with the door open.

CHAPTER 8
Cooking

COOKING APPLIANCES

Choosing cooking appliances is a lot more complex and confusing today than it was 20 years ago. Along with the standard range with four top burners and an oven or two, we now have down-vented ranges with pop-out grills, fancy cooktops, separate ovens, microwave ovens, convection ovens, and a host of other smaller cooking appliances from slow-cook crockpots and bread ovens to high-tech toaster ovens.

Cooking patterns have also changed considerably. During the past two decades, many Americans have dined out more, cooked less, and used a microwave oven instead of a stove for preparing and heating many dishes. If you don't cook much, more efficient cooking appliances won't save much energy! On the other hand, these appliances tend to have long lives, so it is worth using efficiency as one guide when you purchase a new cooktop, stove, or oven. At the same time, common accessories can make a big difference (details are discussed under each type of equipment).

Cooktops

This discussion applies equally well to standard kitchen ranges and separate cooktops, which are gaining in popularity. Ovens will be addressed separately.

Cooktops are widely available for either electric or gas cooking. Gas burners are often preferred by people who like to cook because gas offers a greater level of control in the speed of cooking. All new gas ranges are now required to have electric ignition instead of energy-wasting pilot lights. A downside to gas cooking appliances is that gas combustion products are introduced into the house. Operate a ventilation fan that vents to the outside when using a gas cooktop or oven.

With electric cooktops, there are a number of new types of burners on the market, some of which offer energy savings and greater cooking control. The most common electric burners in this country are exposed coils, but you can also buy models with solid disk elements, radiant elements under glass, or high-tech halogen or induction elements.

Solid Disk Elements. These have been very popular in Europe. They are more attractive than coils and they are easier to clean up, but they heat up even more slowly than electric coils. Furthermore, because solid disk elements take longer to heat up and because higher-wattage elements are generally used, energy consumption will be higher. Good contact between the pan and the burner is especially important with solid disk elements. Slightly rounded pots and pans will significantly reduce cooking performance and correspondingly increase energy usage.

Radiant Elements Under Ceramic Glass. Ceramic glass units offer excellent cleanability and they heat up faster than solid disk elements—though not as quickly as conventional coil elements. The energy efficiency of ceramic glass cook-tops is higher than coil or disk element cook-tops. As with solid disk elements, flat pans are important with this type of cooking surface.

Halogen Elements. Fairly new in this country, halogen elements use halogen lamps as the heat source under a glass surface. The lamp delivers instant heat and responds very quickly to changes in the temperature setting. However, the main mode of heating a pan with halogen lamps still comes from contact of the pan with the hot ceramic glass surface. Therefore, the heating efficiency of halogen units may not be better than with ceramic glass units, and halogen elements will provide only marginally faster speed. Improvements in heating speed will not generate enough energy savings to justify the higher cost of halogen cook-tops.

Induction Elements. This is the newest and most innovative type of cook-top to come along. The induction elements transfer electromagnetic energy directly to the pan where the heat is needed. As a result, they are very energy efficient—using less than half as much energy as standard electric coil elements. One catch is that they work only with ferrous metal cookware (cast iron, stainless steel, enameled iron, etc.). Aluminum cookware will not work. When the pan is removed, there is almost no lingering heat on the cook-top. Currently, induction elements are available only with the highest-priced cook-tops. The extra cost is difficult to justify on the basis of energy savings alone.

Range Hoods and Downdraft Ventilation

Proper ventilation for cooking appliances is very important. The range hood should ventilate to the outside and not simply recirculate and attempt to filter the cooking fumes. This is especially important with gas ranges. Whether you choose a conventional updraft hood or a downdraft hood can make a large difference in the amount of air that

Downdraft ventilation.

has to be heated or cooled to maintain comfort in the house: downdraft fans require several times more air than conventional ones.

Also be careful about the size of the fan—too large a fan can waste energy and possibly even pose a safety risk. When a ventilation fan is operated, it depressurizes, or creates a slight vacuum in the house. To balance that pressure difference, cold air is sucked in through cracks in the walls and around windows (infiltration). That makes your heating system work harder, wasting energy. In some situations, that negative pressure can even prevent an oil or gas heating system from venting properly, causing backdrafting of dangerous combustion gases into the house. This latter concern is especially serious with the large downdraft ventilation fans used with some cooktops and ranges. Ask about make-up air ducts for these ventilation systems. Some manufacturers, such as Jenn Air, are beginning to introduce such an option. Clearly, down-draft range hoods require many extra steps to work safely because of the large airflow required. This makes them both less efficient and more expensive.

OVENS

In addition to the standard electric and gas oven, there are now convection ovens, microwave ovens, and combination models that work in one or more modes.

Conventional Ovens. With standard gas or electric ovens, self-cleaning models are more energy efficient because they have more insulation. But if you use the self-cleaning feature more than about once a month, you'll end up using more energy with the feature than you save from the extra insulation. If you're the type of cook who needs to peek into the oven all the time, buy a model with a window in the door, so you won't have to open the door all the time.

Convection Ovens. These can be more energy efficient than standard ovens because the heated air is continuously circulated around the food being cooked. You get more even heat distribution, and for many foods, temperatures and cooking time can be decreased. In some cases, you can cook multiple batches at the same time, cutting the additional energy consumption required for cooking each batch separately in a conventional oven. On average, you'll cut energy use by about 20 percent.

Microwave Ovens. Microwaves are very high-frequency radio waves. In these ovens, the energetic waves penetrate the food surface and heat up water molecules inside. Energy consumption and cooking times for certain foods are greatly reduced, especially small portions and leftovers to be rewarmed. Overall, energy use is reduced by about two-thirds. Because less heat is generated in the kitchen, you also save on air conditioning costs during the summer. Some microwave ovens include sophisticated features to further boost energy efficiency and cooking performance, such as temperature probes, controls to turn off the microwave when food is cooked, and variable power settings. New "rapid-cook" ovens combining microwaves with other cooking technologies—notably halogen lights or convection—are designed to cut cooking time and improve the quality of foods prepared in standard microwaves.

ENERGY-SAVING TIPS FOR COOKING

Whether or not you plan to buy a new range or other cooking appliances, you can probably save a lot of energy just by modifying your cooking habits. A few tips for energy-efficient cooking are listed below:

■ Full-size ovens are not very efficient when cooking small quantities of food. When cooking small- to medium-sized meals, it generally pays to use smaller microwave ovens, toaster ovens, or slow-cook crockpots (an insulated ceramic pot with an electric heating element). Some new oven models are equipped with large and small oven compartments so it's easier to match the oven space to the size of your dish. Several ways of cooking the same casserole are compared in the following table:

Frying Pan

Crockpot

Gas Oven

Toaster Oven

Convection Oven

Microwave

Deciding how to cook a meal is not as easy as it used to be. Some options result in significant energy savings.

ENERGY COSTS OF VARIOUS METHODS OF COOKING

Appliance	Temp.	Time	Energy	Cost[1]
Electric oven	350°F	1 hr.	2.0 kWh	16¢
Convection oven (elec.)	325°	45 min.	1.39 kWh	11¢
Gas oven	350°	1 hr.	.112 therm	7¢
Frying pan	420°	1 hr.	.9 kWh	7¢
Toaster oven	425°	50 min.	.95 kWh	8¢
Crockpot	200°	7 hrs.	.7 kWh	6¢
Microwave oven	"High"	15 min.	.36 kWh	3¢

1. Assumes 8¢/kWh for electricity and 60¢/therm for gas.

■ If you have two ovens, use the smaller one whenever you can.

■ For soups and stews that require long cooking periods, using a crockpot will save a substantial amount of energy.

■ For stove-top cooking, consider using a pressure-cooker. By building up steam pressure, it cooks at a higher temperature, reducing cooking time and energy use considerably.

■ Use the smallest pan necessary to do the job. Smaller pans require less energy.

■ With electric cook-tops, match the pan size to the element size. For example, a 6" pan on an 8" burner will waste over 40% of the heat produced by the burner.

■ Consider copper-bottom pans. These heat up faster than regular pans.

■ Keep the burner pans (the metal pans under the burners that catch grease) clean and shiny so they'll be more effective at reflecting heat up to the cookware. Blackened burner pans absorb a lot of heat, reducing burner efficiency.

■ With electric burners, solid disk elements, and radiant elements under ceramic glass, use flat-bottomed cookware that rests evenly on the burner surface. The ideal pan has a slightly concave bottom—when it heats up, the metal expands and the bottom flattens out. An electric element is significantly less efficient if the pan does not have good contact with the element.

■ With electric burners, you can turn off the burner just before the cooking is finished. The burner will continue radiating heat for a short while.

■ With gas burners, make sure you're getting a bluish flame. If the flame is yellow, the gas may not be burning efficiently. Have your gas company check it out.

■ To reduce cooking time, defrost frozen foods in the refrigerator before cooking.

■ With conventional ovens, keep preheat time to a minimum. Unless you're baking breads or pastries, you may not need to preheat the oven at all.

■ Try to avoid peeking into the oven a lot as you cook. Each time you open the door, a significant amount of heat escapes. Food takes longer to cook and you waste energy. Use your oven light and inspect through the window in the oven door instead.

■ Food cooks more quickly and more efficiently in ovens when air can circulate freely. Don't lay foil on the racks. If possible, stagger pans on upper and lower racks to improve airflow if you're baking more than one pan at a time.

■ Cook double portions when using your oven, and refrigerate or freeze half for another meal. It doesn't take as much energy to reheat the food as it does to cook it—not to mention the saved preparation time!

■ Use glass or ceramic pans in ovens. You can turn down the temperature about 25°F and cook foods just as quickly.

■ Use meat thermometers and timers to avoid overcooking. Overcooking not only spoils the taste and reduces nutritional value but also wastes energy.

■ If you have a self-cleaning oven, use the feature just after you've cooked a meal—that way, the oven will still be hot and the cleaning feature will require less energy. Try not to use the self-cleaning feature too often, and operate the ventilation fan when it's on.

■ With microwave ovens, keep the inside surface clean to allow more efficient microwave cooking. You can often cook foods right in their serving dishes, thus saving time and reducing the amount of hot water needed for dishwashing. (Always follow manufacturer's instruction on what type of cookware to use, which thermometers can be used, etc.)

CHAPTER 9
Dishwashing

AUTOMATIC DISHWASHERS

Most of the energy used by a dishwasher goes towards heating the water. In fact, water heating accounts for approximately 80% of total energy use by dishwashers. Models that use less water therefore use less energy. Older dishwashers use between 8 and 14 gallons of water for a complete wash cycle. Dishwashers built since mid-1994 only use 7–10 gallons per cycle, thanks to national efficiency standards. Look at the manufacturer's literature for total water use with different cycles. If the literature does not provide this information, ask the salesperson.

Along with water use, a number of important features affect the energy use of dishwashers. These should be considered when shopping.

Booster Heater

Since the early 1990s, most dishwashers in the U.S. have been sold with built-in heaters to boost water temperature up to 140–145°F, the temperature recommended by manufacturers for optimum dishwashing performance. Some models will automatically boost water

A dishwasher with a booster heater allows you to reduce your water heater temperature setting, saving a lot of energy.

temperature if it is not hot enough, while other models require preselecting the feature before starting the cycle. The advantage to the booster heater is that you can turn down your water heater thermostat, significantly reducing water heating costs. Each 10°F reduction in the water heater temperature setting cuts energy consumption from water heating by 3–5%. Check the dishwasher manufacturer's instructions for the minimum recommended water heater temperature setting (usually 120°F).

Energy-Saving Wash Cycles

Most dishwashers have several different wash cycle selections. If a load of dishes is only lightly soiled, a "light wash" cycle will save energy by using less water and operating for a shorter period of time. For example, the same dishwasher may use 7 gallons for a "light/china" cycle, 10 gallons for a normal wash cycle, and 13 gallons for the "pots/pans" cycle. Energy-saving cycles can save $5 to $15 per year.

Many of the dishwashers on the market today use "soil sensor" technology to automatically adjust water use depending on how dirty the dishes are in each load. Several reports on these dishwashers have found uneven performance; it appears that on dirty loads these dishwashers consume the same amount or even more energy and water than less sophisticated models. Furthermore, some units did not adjust water levels down for the first two or three lightly soiled loads washed after a heavily soiled load. Potential energy benefits from these models are hard to measure under the existing test procedure, which requires testing on clean loads. It is also important to note that the energy use estimates listed in Part II of this book and presented on EnergyGuide labels are based on this test procedure. As a result, the actual energy use of soil-sensing models may deviate significantly from these estimates, particularly for very dirty dishes. A new test procedure currently under development will better estimate the energy consumption of soil-sensing dishwashers. Until this new procedure is adopted, the data presented in Part II and on the EnergyGuide label may not allow for accurate comparison among available models.

Energy-Saving "No-Heat" Dry

An electric heating element is generally used to dry dishes at the end of the final rinse cycle. Most new dishwashers now offer an energy-saving no-heat drying feature. At the end of the rinse cycle, if the feature is selected, room air is circulated through the dishwasher by fans, rather than using an electric heating element to bake the dishes dry.

BUYING A NEW DISHWASHER

EnergyGuide labels must be displayed on all new dishwashers sold. This label tells you the estimated energy use by the dishwasher. However, you should understand some limitations to the EnergyGuide ratings for dishwashers. The rating is based on operating the dishwasher through 312 cycles annually on the normal setting. If you're considering a model with other setting options that you would use most of the time, your energy use could vary substantially.

Also, be aware that there are two dishwasher classifications: compact capacity and standard capacity. Compact models will use less energy, but they also hold fewer dishes. Compact models are usually 18 inches wide, compared to the 24 inch width of most standard capacity models. According to the U.S. Federal Trade Commission, to be considered "standard capacity," a dishwasher must be able to hold at least eight place settings of dishes. A compact dishwasher may actually result in more energy use if you have to run it more frequently.

Our list of most efficient dishwashers includes several models that are only 18 inches wide, yet they can accommodate eight full place settings of dishes, thanks to creative design of the dish racks. Since these models meet the FTC definition of standard capacity, they are included among the most efficient.

You should realize that manufacturers aren't required to test cleaning effectiveness on the same settings that they rate energy efficiency. Claims about performance may be based on a heavy-duty pot-scrubbing setting, while the energy ratings are based on the normal setting. Finally, some European machines may require frequent manual cleaning of the drain filters. In contrast, many domestic dishwashers use tiny grinders to dispose of food particles and keep filters clear automatically.

All of the dishwashers listed in Part II of this book qualify for the ENERGY STAR label and are at least 50% more efficient than the 1994 federal minimum-efficiency standard.

INSTALLING A DISHWASHER

When you install a dishwasher, try to position it away from the refrigerator. The dishwasher produces heat and will increase the energy consumption of your refrigerator. If it is a built-in dishwasher, you might be able to add extra insulation to the top, sides, and back when it's installed (check with the dealer first). This will both save energy and reduce noise levels. Use unfaced fiberglass batts.

USING A DISHWASHER FOR MAXIMUM ENERGY SAVINGS

Whether buying a new dishwasher or using an existing one, you may be able to save a considerable amount of energy by changing the way you operate it. Below are tips on how to save energy with dish washing.

■ Use energy-saving cycles whenever possible.

■ If your dishwasher has a booster heater, turn down your water heater thermostat. Most dishwasher booster heaters can raise the water temperature at least 20°F, so a setting of 120°F for your water heater should work fine. The washing cycle will take longer if the dishwasher has to boost the temperature, but unless you need to wash several loads in a row, this shouldn't be a problem.

■ Use the no-heat air-dry feature on your dishwasher if it has one. If you have an older dishwasher that doesn't include this feature, you can turn the dishwasher off after the final rinse cycle is completed and open the door to allow air drying. Using the no-heat dry feature or opening and air drying the dishes will increase the drying time, and it could lead to increased spotting, according to some in the industry. But try this method sometime to see how well it works with your machine.

■ Don't pre-rinse dishes before putting them in the dishwasher. Modern

Depending on how you wash dishes by hand, you might actually save energy by switching to a dishwasher—if you use it wisely.

dishwashers do a superb job of cleaning even heavily soiled dishes. Scrape off food and empty liquids—the dishwasher will do the rest. If you must rinse dishes first, at least use cold water.

■ Wash only full loads. The dishwasher uses the same amount of water whether it's half-full or completely full. Putting dishes in the dishwasher throughout the day and running it once in the evening will use less water and energy than washing the dishes by hand throughout the day.

If you currently wash dishes by hand and fill sinks or plastic tubs with water, it's pretty easy to figure out whether you would use less water with a dishwasher. Simply measure how much water it takes to fill the wash and rinse containers. If you wash dishes by hand two or three times a day, you might be surprised to find out how much water you're currently using. Whether or not you will save energy by switching from washing-by-hand to using a dishwasher depends on both the dishwasher and how you wash the dishes by hand.

■ Load dishes according to manufacturer's instructions. Completely fill the racks to optimize water and energy use, but allow proper water circulation for adequate cleaning.

CHAPTER 10
Laundry

CLOTHES WASHERS

Like dishwashers, most of the energy used by clothes washers is for heating the water. Water heating accounts for 85% to 90% of the energy use—even more than with dishwashers. The primary energy conservation strategies, therefore, involve using cooler wash and rinse cycles and reducing water use. Unlike dishwashers, clothes washers can use cooler temperature water with perfectly adequate results for most clothes.

New resource-efficient models use much less water and energy than conventional washers. Many perform well using only one-third as much water, and thereby reduce energy use by two-thirds. These resource-efficient models also use higher spin speeds to extract more water from each load of clothes, saving significant dryer energy as a result. In general, horizontal-axis (H-axis—usually front-loading) washers are much more efficient than conventional vertical-axis (V-axis—top-loading) washers with agitators. However, several new top-loading designs have been introduced with energy and water savings comparable to H-axis models.

Resource-Efficient Clothes Washers

The emergence of resource-efficient clothes washers on the American market is an exciting development for consumers interested in energy savings and environmental quality. In addition to attractive energy savings, the water savings from these machines is crucial in areas where water is scarce.

To understand how these washers use so much less water and energy, consider that in a conventional top-loader the tub must be filled with water so that all the clothes are kept wet. The agitator then swirls the water around to clean the clothes. In contrast, resource-efficient washers need less water because the tub never needs to be filled completely. In H-axis washers, the tub itself rotates, making the clothes tumble into the water. Re-designed V-axis washers use sprayers to wet the clothes from above or a moving plate in the bottom of the tub to lift and bounce clothes through the wash water.

Resource-efficient washers also reduce the energy required for clothes

Horizontal-axis washing machines are far more energy efficient than conventional top-loaders.

drying. After completing the rinse cycle, these washers spin clothes faster than conventional V-axis machines, so the remaining moisture content of the clothes is lower. This mean clothes need less time in the dryer. Since mechanical water extraction is more efficient than thermal extraction (heating clothes in a dryer), this yields additional energy savings.

At present, some resource-efficient clothes washers are more expensive to purchase than conventional washers; however, their substantial energy and water savings translates into big money savings and a quick return on your investment. Depending on your local energy and water rates and the amount of laundry you do each year, you may realize annual savings of $100 or more. If a resource-efficient washer costs $500 more to purchase than a conventional machine, your savings would be a tax-free return on your investment of 20%. Field studies have also shown that resource-efficient washers are gentler on clothes. Less dryer time also reduces wear-and-tear. With the average load of laundry valued up to $500, this can add up to substantial additional savings.

A growing number of energy and water utilities around the country recognize the benefits of efficient clothes washers, and are offering rebates to consumers who purchase qualifying machines. Call your energy and water utilities and ask if they provide rebates for high-efficiency clothes washers.

The Most Energy-Efficient Clothes Washers

All new clothes washers must display EnergyGuide labels to help consumers compare energy efficiency. The EnergyGuide label for clothes washers is based on estimated energy use for 416 loads of laundry per year. But this value does not tell you the whole story for washers because of variations in tub size and other factors. Conventional washers with smaller tubs may have better EnergyGuide ratings, but the smaller capacity may mean you have to run the machine more often, so it may actually cost more to operate. Although the tubs in horizontal-axis machines are often smaller than top-loading tubs, their capacity for clothes is often the same because there are no agitators in the H-axis models and their tumbling tubs can accommodate more clothes. Resource-efficient top-loaders typically have a very large tub capacity.

A better measure of a clothes washer's energy efficiency is given by its modified energy factor (MEF), which is a combination of tub capacity and energy consumption per cycle: ft^3/(kWh/cycle). Unlike the previously used energy factor ratings, MEF takes into account the remaining moisture content of the wash load and, thus, incoporates dryer energy use. The higher the MEF, the more efficient the washer. At present the MEF is not reported on EnergyGuide labels, but some manufacturers may provide this information upon request. MEF is included in our list of the most efficient washers (see Part II) and the list of ENERGY STAR-labeled washers found on the ENERGY STAR website (www.energystar.gov).

COST OF A LOAD OF LAUNDRY, VERTICAL-AXIS WASHER

Electric water heater			Gas water heater		
Wash/rince settings	kWh used	Avg. cost per load (cents)[1]	Wash/rinse settings	Therms used	Avg. cost per load (cents)[2]
Water heater thermostat set at 140°F					
Hot/Hot	8.3	66	Hot/Hot	.329	20
Hot/Warm	6.3	50	Hot/Warm	.247	15
Hot/Cold	4.3	34	Hot/Cold	.164	10
Warm/Warm	4.3	34	Warm/Warm	.164	10
Warm/Cold	2.3	18	Warm/Cold	.082	5
Cold/Cold	0.4	3	Cold/Cold	—	3
Water heater thermostat set at 120°F					
Hot/Hot	6.5	52	Hot/Hot	.248	15
Hot/Warm	4.9	39	Hot/Warm	.186	10
Hot/Cold	4.3	27	Hot/Cold	.124	7
Warm/Warm	3.4	27	Warm/Warm	.124	7
Warm/Cold	1.9	15	Warm/Cold	.062	4
Cold/Cold	0.4	3	Cold/Cold	—	3

1. Assumes 8 cents per kWh.
2. Assumes 60 cents per therm.

The current standard for clothes washers requires a minimum energy factor of 1.18—roughly equivalent to an MEF of .82. Stricter new federal standards will take effect in two stages beginning with an interim standard in January 2004 requiring a minimum MEF of 1.04. In January 2007, the standard will be further strengthened to require an MEF of 1.26 or higher. Currently, to qualify for the ENERGY STAR label, washers must have an MEF of at least 1.26. This requirement will increase to 1.42 on January 1, 2004.

Look for energy-saving features on washing machines, such as cold-water rinse and multiple water-level settings.

The most energy-efficient clothes washers are listed in Part II, in order of efficiency based on each model's MEF. All of the models listed exceed the 2007 federal minimum-efficiency standard. Bear in mind that all of the machines listed are at least twice as efficient—and some are four times as efficient—as an average new top-loading, vertical-axis machine.

Wash and Rinse Cycle Options

Choose a clothes washer that offers plenty of choices for energy-conserving wash and rinse cycles. The table below shows the average energy use for conventional washers with both electric and gas-fired water heating (water temperature set at 140°F and 120°F). The dramatic differences in energy use with these different wash/rinse cycles are obvious. Warm wash cycles generally clean clothes perfectly well, and, in many cases, cold water washing is fine. Note: With oily stains, hot water may be required for satisfactory cleaning. You should experiment with the different cycle options and find one that meets your needs. Cold water rinses are just as effective as hot or warm rinses.

Options to vary the cycle length have a very small effect on energy consumption, but some clothes washers feature a "suds-saver" option that stores the wash water from one load of lightly soiled clothes to use for the next load. A presoak cycle may allow you to get the same cleaning performance using a cold or warm water wash as you are used to getting with hot water—while using less total energy.

Water Level Controls

Most conventional clothes washers use from 30 to 40 gallons of water for a complete (large) wash cycle. Choose a machine that lets you select lower water levels when you are doing smaller loads. For a given temperature cycle, energy use is almost directly proportional to hot water use. The lowest setting may use just half as much water as the highest. In general, you'll save energy by running one large load instead of two medium loads. Many new models feature advanced electronic controls to adjust the water level automatically according to the size of the load. Unfortunately, most manufacturers do not publish the actual water use of their machines in different settings, so it is difficult to compare one brand to another.

Faster Spin Speed

Faster spin speeds can result in better water extraction and thus reduce the energy required for drying. Mechanical water extraction by spinning is much more efficient than thermal extraction (heating clothes in a dryer). Front-loading washers and re-designed efficient top-loading machines generally spin at a faster speed than conventional top-loaders.

DRYERS

Dryers work by heating and aerating clothes. Operation of both electric and gas-fired models is pretty straightforward. In terms of energy use, gas dryers are generally much less expensive to operate than electric models. There is no requirement to display the EnergyGuide label on clothes dryers, so it is not easy to compare the energy use of various dryer models. However, the energy use of dryers currently on the market does not vary widely. Other than fuel type, the major energy consideration is whether the dryer uses termination controls to sense dryness and turn off automatically and, if so, what the sensing mechanism is.

Automatic Shut-off

Dryers used to be controlled simply by setting a timer. You guessed how long it would take to dry a particular load of laundry and set the timer for 60 minutes or 75 minutes, etc. If the clothes came out dry, chances are you continued to use that setting. However, some types of clothes dry much more quickly than others. Overdrying can reduce the life of clothes. You can save a significant amount of energy by buying a model that senses dryness and automatically shuts off. Most of the better quality dryers today include this feature.

The best dryers have moisture sensors in the drum for sensing dryness, while most only infer dryness by sensing the temperature of the exhaust air. The lower-cost, thermostat-controlled models may overdry some types of clothes, but even these are much better than timed-dry machines. Compared with timed drying, you can save about 10% with a temperature-sensing control, and 15% with a moisture-sensing control.

Electric Ignition on Gas Dryers

Electric ignition, rather than pilot lights, is now required for all new gas dryers.

Features That Reduce the Need for Ironing

While the energy used for ironing clothes is not technically part of the energy used for washing or drying clothes, it is very related. If clothes are taken out of the dryer while still slightly damp and then hung up, they may not need ironing. Moisture-sensing automatic shut-off helps here—especially if the dryer includes a feature to adjust the level of dryness desired. Wrinkling can also be reduced with a cool-down (fluff) cycle and by a feature that tumbles the clothes periodically after the end of the cycle if the clothes are not removed right away. Look for these features when shopping for dryers.

Dryer Exhaust Vent Hood

Along with your dryer, buy a dryer vent hood that blocks air infiltration. Dryer vent hoods are available that seal very tightly when the dryer

(Additional) Heat/Humidity Diverter (Electric Only)

Put in a dryer vent hood that keeps out cold air.

blower is not on. Standard dryer vent hoods have a simpler flapper that is not as effective. Ask your appliance salesperson about dryer vent systems and spend the extra $15 to $20 to buy a tight-sealing one.

INSTALLING CLOTHES WASHERS AND DRYERS

Try to install your clothes washer as close to the water heater as reasonably possible and insulate the hot water pipes leading to it to minimize heat loss through the pipes. Also, if possible, locate the washer and dryer in a heated space. This is particularly important with dryers, which depend on heat to dry.

The most important part of the dryer installation is the exhaust system. In most cases—and always with gas dryers—the exhaust should vent to the outside, using as short and straight a section of smooth metal ducting as possible. Do not use flexible vinyl duct because it restricts air flow, can be crushed, and may not withstand high temperatures from the dryer. Use a vent hood on the outside that blocks air infiltration (see **Dryer Exhaust Vent Hood** above).

Electric dryers may be vented inside the home during the winter months if the house air is dry and if the air vent is properly filtered. Compact electric dryers in apartments and condos are sometimes installed for indoor venting. If the electric dryer is vented inside, watch for moisture on the windows, which would indicate that you're introducing too much moisture into the house.

LAUNDRY TIPS FOR MAXIMUM ENERGY SAVINGS

There are a number of easy ways to save energy with laundry, whether you're buying new appliances or not. Follow these suggestions whenever possible to keep energy use to a minimum.

■ Use lower temperature settings. Use warm or cold water for the wash cycle instead of hot (except for greasy stains), and only use cold for rinses. Experiment with different laundry detergents to find one that works well with cooler water. By presoaking heavily soiled clothes, a cooler wash temperature may be fine. The temperature of the rinse water does not affect cleaning, so always set the washer on cold water rinse.

■ Turn down the thermostat on your water heater. A setting of 120°F is adequate for most home needs. By reducing your hot water temperature, you will save energy with either hot or warm wash cycles.

■ Load the washer to capacity when possible. Most people tend to underload rather than overload their washers. Check your machine's load capacity in pounds, then weigh out a few loads of laundry to get a sense of how much laundry 10 or 18 or 20 pounds represents. Then use your eye to judge the volume of clothes for a load. Washing one large load will take less energy than washing two loads on a low or medium setting. Don't go to the other extreme and overload your machine, though. The clothes won't get clean and you may end up having to wash them again. When you don't have a full load, match the water level to the size of the load. Most clothes washers, even older ones, offer several different settings. Note: Permanent press fabrics should be washed on a "permanent press cycle" to minimize wrinkling.

■ If washing lightly soiled clothes, use the suds-saving feature if it's available on your machine. This saves the wash water to be reused in the next load. Only use this feature, though, if the second load is to be washed right away.

■ When drying, separate your clothes and dry similar types of clothes together. Lightweight synthetics, for example, dry much more quickly than bath towels and natural fiber clothes.

■ Don't overdry clothes. Take clothes out while they are still slightly damp to reduce the need for ironing. Overdrying also causes shrinkage, generates static electricity, and shortens fabric life. If your dryer has a setting for auto-dry, be sure to use it instead of the timer to avoid wasting energy.

■ Don't add wet items to a load that is already partially dried.

■ Dry two or more loads in a row, taking advantage of the heat still in the dryer from the first load.

■ Clean the dryer filter after each use. A clogged filter will restrict air flow and reduce dryer performance.

■ Dry full loads when possible, but be careful not to overfill the dryer. Drying small loads wastes energy. Overloading causes wrinkling and uneven drying. Air should be able to circulate freely around the drying clothes. If your washer and dryer are properly matched, a full washer load will be about the right size for the dryer as well.

■ Check the outside dryer exhaust vent. Make sure it is clean and that the flapper on the outside hood opens and closes freely. If the flapper stays open, cold air will blow into your house through the dryer and increase heating costs. Replace the outside dryer vent hood with one that seals tightly.

■ In good weather, consider hanging clothes outside and using totally free solar energy to do the drying.

CHAPTER 11
Lighting

Lighting accounts for 5–10% of total energy use in the average American home and costs $50 to $150 per year in electricity. That's not a huge amount, but it's enough to justify doing something about—especially when the advantages of energy-efficient alternatives are considered.

This chapter describes the most important new developments in energy-efficient lighting, includes listings of manufacturers and/or products, and provides recommendations on how to save energy with lighting around the home. One note on terminology: The lighting industry uses the term lamp to refer to the actual source of light—what the public usually calls the light bulb. In this chapter, we use the terms lamp and bulb interchangeably.

TYPES OF LIGHTING

Incandescent Lighting

Most lighting in the home today is incandescent lighting. In an incandescent lamp, electric current heats up a metal filament in the light bulb, making it glow white-hot and give off light. The problem is that only 10% of that electricity is actually used to produce light—the rest ends up as heat. During the winter months, incandescent lighting is an expensive form of electric heat; during the summer months, it makes your air conditioner work harder.

Compact Fluorescent Lamps

The introduction of compact fluorescent lamps in the early 1980s revolutionized lighting. Compact fluorescent lamps (often referred to as "CFLs") use just one-quarter to one-third as much electricity as incandescent lamps, and they last up to ten times longer. They work in the same way as standard tube-fluorescent lamps, only the tube is smaller and folded over to decrease the amount of space required. The compact design allows them to be used in place of incandescent light bulbs. In fact, circular fluorescent tubes ("circline" lamps) were an early application of

Compact fluorescent lights last, on average, ten times as long as incandescent lights.

fluorescents in incandescent fixtures. Today's compact fluorescent lamps continue this evolution in technology.

The environmental benefits of these lights are dramatic. A single 20-watt compact fluorescent lamp, for example, used in place of a 75-watt incandescent light bulb, will save about 550 kWh over its lifetime. If your electricity is produced from a coal-fired power plant, that savings represents about 500 pounds of coal that would release 1,300 pounds of carbon dioxide and 20 pounds of sulfur dioxide.

Better yet, compact fluorescents are a profitable investment, saving several times their purchase price through reduced electricity bills and fewer replacement bulbs.

Compact fluorescent lamps do contain a very small amount of mercury vapor that is needed to produce light. The amount is so small that it presents no danger during household use—even if the lamp breaks. At present the lamps can be safely disposed of along with household trash. However, as the number of compact fluorescent lamps in use grows, there is an increasing interest in recycling facilities that can properly dispose of the lamps and reduce the impact on landfills. The ENERGY STAR Lighting Program is working with manufacturers, retailers, and local communities to establish recycling programs for spent compact fluorescent lamps. Visit www.1800cleanup.org or call 1-800-CLEANUP for information on facilities in your area.

Integral vs. Modular Compact Fluorescent Lamps. All fluorescent lamps need ballasts to operate. The ballast is a device that alters the electric current flowing through the tube, which activates the gas inside, causing the tube to emit light. For this reason, compact fluorescent lamps are more complex to manufacture than standard incandescent light bulbs, and until recently they were a lot larger. Most compact fluorescent lamps today have electronic ballasts that are integral with the lamp. That is, the ballast and lamp are combined in a single unit, which screws into a standard light bulb socket.

Compact fluorescent lights are either integral with ballast and lamp combined (right) or modular, with separate ballast and lamp.

Because of the performance advantages of electronic ballasts, manufacturers of compact fluorescent lamps are switching their consumer product lines to integral units with electronic ballasts. Consumer acceptance of products with electronic ballasts is greater than those with magnetic ballasts.

Modular compact fluorescent lamps have separate ballasts and lamps. Some modular ballasts, or adapters, screw into standard light bulb sockets. Others are hard-wired into light fixtures—i.e., the ballast is built into the fixture. The advantage of modular compact fluorescent lamps is that you don't have to replace the ballast when the fluorescent tube fails. Compact fluorescent lamps generally last about 10,000 hours, while ballasts are expected to last 50,000 hours or longer. Replacement lamps cost just a few dollars apiece, so in the long term you can save a lot with modular units.

Major manufacturers of compact fluorescent lamps are listed in Table 11.1. The ENERGY STAR label can also help identify high-quality, energy-efficient compact fluorescent lamps. To qualify for the label, lamps must comply with specifications on energy use, light output, lamp life, and other operating characteristics. A full list of ENERGY STAR lamps is available at www.energystar.gov.

Using Compact Fluorescent Lamps in Standard Fixtures. New products from all the major manufacturers are both smaller and brighter than older models. Rather than two folded-over fluorescent tubes, most of these new products have three, and a new generation of 4-tube lights is now on the market. By using more and shorter tubes per lamp, the surface area of

TABLE 11.1

COMPACT FLUORESCENT LAMP MANUFACTURERS

American Power Products
5525 Brooks Street
Montclair, CA 91763
800-533-2929 or 909-988-0819
www.applighting.com

Feit Electric
4901 Gregg Road
Pico Rivera, CA 90660
800-543-3348 or 562-463-2852
www.feit.com

GE Lighting
4521 Highwoods Parkway
Glen Allen, VA 23060
800-435-4448
www.ge.com/lighting

Greenlite Lighting
115 Brunswick Blvd., Suite 102
Pointe Claire, PQ H9R 5N2
Canada
514-695-9090
www.greenlite.ca

Lights of America
611 Reyes Drive
Walnut, CA 91789
800-321-8100 x222
www.lightsofamerica.com

MaxLite
19 Chapin Road, Building B
Pine Brook, NJ 07058
973-244-7300
www.maxlite.com

Osram Sylavania, Inc.
100 Endicott Street
Danvers, MA 01923
800-255-5042 or 978-777-1900
www.sylvania.com

Panasonic Lighting
1 Panasonic Way 4A-6
Secaucus, NJ 07094
866-292-7292 or 201-348-5381
www.panasonic.com

Philips Lighting Company
200 Franklin Square Drive
P.O. Box 6800
Somerset, NJ 08875-6800
800-555-0050
www.lighting.philips.com

Technical Consumer Products
300 Lena Drive
Aurora, OH 44202
330-995-6111
www.tcpi.com

Westinghouse Lighting Corporation
12401 McNulty Road
Philadelphia, PA 19154-1004
888-417-6222 or 215-671-2078
www.westinghouselightbulbs.com

the lamp is increased, allowing for more light from a smaller lamp. While they still aren't quite as small as standard incandescent light bulbs, these compact fluorescents now fit in most household fixtures designed for incandescent light bulbs. The smallest folded-tube compact fluorescent lamps are now just 4" to 5" long and 2.3" in diameter.

Despite the smaller size, even these compact fluorescent lamps—and many older ones—won't fit in all light fixtures. Sometimes they are too tall or the bases too wide. You may want to buy just one or two initially and try them in various fixtures around your house to check where they do and do not fit.

The latest development in compact fluorescent lamps is the subcompact fluorescent lamp. These small, spiral-shaped lamps are significantly smaller than conventional compact fluorescent lamps, in fact several models are the same length as incandescent light bulbs.

Because they come in many shapes and sizes, it is likely that there is a compact fluorescent lamp that will fit your needs. Also, some compact fluorescents come as small, attractive globes, which can be installed in some ceiling sockets as attractive lamps by themselves, without any other fixture.

If a compact fluorescent lamp is too tall for your table lamp or standing lamp, you can buy a taller wire harp. If the compact fluorescent lamp is too wide, you can buy special adapters to spread the base of the harp. Be aware that compact fluorescent lamps can be somewhat heavier than standard light bulbs, although with electronic ballasts the extra weight is considerably less than with magnetic ballasts. The added weight could make some lightweight floor or table lamps unstable and easy to tip over.

For recessed downlights, spotlights, and track lights, some compact fluorescent lamps are too wide at the base to fit into the can or cone. Again, finding a product that fits may take some trial and error. Socket extenders are available and can help in some situations, although these may result in the tip of the lamp extending from the can or cone.

Never use compact fluorescent lamps in circuits that have dimmers unless the lights are specifically designed for that use.

Hard-wired fixture for compact fluorescent lamps.

Dimmable products are beginning to enter the market in greater numbers. Compact fluorescents can be used in 3-way fixtures. They will operate on two of the three "on" settings, but only provide one light level.

ENERGY STAR-labeled light fixtures suitable for use with compact fluorescent lamps are now available. A range of indoor and outdoor fixtures carry the ENERGY STAR label. Many indoor models incorporate dimmers or two-way switches; outdoor models automatically shut off during the day or come equipped with motion sensors. Look for ENERGY STAR for compact fluorescent fixtures that meet EPA's safety, reliability, and performance guidelines.

Economics. Compact fluorescent lights save a lot of money compared to incandescent lights. To figure out how, you have to look at both the purchase and operating costs to arrive at total life-cycle costs. It may surprise you to learn that the light bulbs you currently use cost a lot more to operate than they cost to buy. When you spend 75¢ for a 100-watt incandescent light bulb, for example, you're committing yourself to spending about $6.00 for electricity (at 8¢/kWh) over that bulb's expected 750-hour life—and almost twice as much in some parts of the country.

With a high-quality compact fluorescent lamp, you might spend $5–15 to buy it (unless your utility company offers a rebate), but you save money in the long run, because it uses a lot less electricity and lasts a lot longer. Most compact fluorescent lamps last about 8,000–10,000 hours. The longer a particular light fixture is used each day, the faster a compact fluorescent replacement will pay for itself. This is shown in Table 11.2. If the light is on just two hours a day, it won't pay for itself until after the third year. If it's on eight hours a day, though, you'll come out ahead during the first year. If modular compact fluorescent lamps are purchased, the savings will be even greater, because, as lamps fail, only the lamp itself and not the ballast has to be replaced.

Lower-cost compact fluorescents manufactured in China are now available in the U.S. While these products have historically been of questionable quality and limited life, recent joint ventures between major international manufacturers and Chinese lamp companies are leading to improved quality. The problem today is differentiating between the poor-quality and good-quality products. Before buying these lamps, ask the salesperson about any complaints and their return policy. Chinese-produced lamps continue to improve and, as a result, low-cost compact fluorescent lamps are becoming an attractive option. Also, check for the ENERGY STAR label. Lamps from

TABLE 11.2

SAVINGS ACHIEVED BY SWITCHING FROM INCANDESCENT TO COMPACT FLUORESCENT

Replace 75-watt incandescent with 20-watt integral compact fluorescent	Savings after 1st year	Savings after 2nd year	Savings after 3rd year	Savings after 5th year	Savings after 10th year
Lights on 2 hrs/day	($6.04)	($2.08)	$1.89	$9.81	$29.62
Lights on 4 hrs/day	($2.08)	$5.85	$13.77	$29.62	$59.24
Lights on 8 hrs/day	$5.85	$21.70	$37.54	$59.24	$127.73
Lights on12 hrs/day	$13.77	$37.54	$51.32	$88.11	$186.22

Assumptions:	75-watt incandescent	20-watt compact fluorescent
Lamp output (lumens)	1,220	1,200
Lamp life (hours)	750	10,000
Lamp cost ($)	0.75	10.00

Electricity cost: 8¢/kWh.
Numbers in parentheses are negative.

manufacturers in the U.S., China, and a number of other countries meet the energy efficiency and quality specifications required for the ENERGY STAR label.

Tube Fluorescent Lighting

When you think of standard tube fluorescent lighting, what probably comes to mind is the buzzing, flickering bluish-white lights in supermarkets or offices that make colors look washed out and give some employees headaches. That is hardly the kind of light you want in your house. Well, times have changed. Tube fluorescent lighting has improved dramatically over the past ten years. Fluorescent lighting is available today that almost matches incandescent lighting in quality—accurately illuminating colors and providing a pleasant warm-light atmosphere. Just as importantly, electronic ballasts that eliminate any noticeable hum or flicker are now available for tube fluorescent lighting. These newer tube fluorescent lights make a great deal of sense for indirect lighting around a room perimeter or above a bathroom mirror.

Tube fluorescent fixture
showing cut-away lamps and ballast.
You can buy quiet, flicker-free electronic
ballasts for these fixtures.

When shopping for tube fluorescent lighting fixtures and lamps, it helps to know what you want. Even at retail lighting stores, salespeople may not be familiar with some of the advanced products on the market. If you can't find what you want, go to a commercial lighting supplier.

For use in living areas, ask for electronic ballasts for tube fluorescent fixtures. These cost more than standard magnetic ballasts, but they are far more pleasant, and they save as much as 35% on energy use as well. Major manufacturers of electronic ballasts are listed in Table 11.3.

When selecting tube fluorescent lighting, don't be satisfied with standard cool-white or warm-white lamps. Look for products with high color rendition index (CRI). This is a measure of the ability of the light to illuminate colors accurately. Also, look for high efficiency (or efficacy, as it is called in the lighting industry). Lighting efficacy is measured in lumens (light output) per watt (electricity use). The best fluorescent lamps use special coatings ("trichromatic phosphors") to achieve both high CRI ratings and high efficacy. Some of the most energy-conserving fluorescent tube lamps are thinner in diameter and may require different fixtures and ballasts than standard fluorescents. Energy-saving, high-performance tube fluorescent lamps are listed by manufacturer in Table 11.4.

HID Lighting

High-intensity discharge, or HID, lighting is what you typically see along streets and in parking lots. HID lighting has advanced almost as

TABLE 11.3

ELECTRONIC BALLASTS MANUFACTURERS
(for tube fluorescent lamps)

Advance Transformer Co.
800-372-3331
www.advancetransformer.com

MagneTek
800-BALLAST
www.magnetek.com

Aromat Corp.
800-543-6204
www.aromat.com

Motorola Lighting
800-654-0089
www.motorola.com

L.G. Industrial Systems
888-544-7872
www.lgisusa.com

Osram Sylvania
800-842-7010
www.sylvania.com

TABLE 11.4

HIGH-PERFORMANCE TUBE FLUORESCENT LAMPS

Manufacturer	Lamp (48")	Watts	CRI	Efficacy*
Osram Sylvania 800-255-5042 www.sylvania.com	Octron (T-8)	32	75–85	87–93
General Electric 800-435-4448 www.ge.com/lighting	Watt-Miser (T-8)	30	82	95
Litetronics Int'l 800-860-3392 www.litetronics.com	(T-8)	32	75–85	85–95
Philips Lighting Co. 800-555-0050 www.lighting.philips.com	ALTO (T-8)	32	86	91
Panasonic 866-292-7292 www.panasonic.com	Tri-Color (T-10)	40	84	89

* Efficacy values are initial lumens/watt.

quickly as fluorescent lighting in recent years. There are three types commonly used: mercury vapor, high-pressure sodium, and metal halide. Like fluorescent lamps, they require ballasts to operate, and most HID lamps take several minutes to warm up.

Mercury vapor lamps are still used for outdoor lighting, but they are quickly becoming obsolete because of the higher efficacy of high-pressure sodium and metal halide lights. High-pressure sodium lamps are available with efficacies as high as 140 lumens per watt, though the light is somewhat yellowish. Metal halide lights produce a whiter light, closer to incandescent in quality, but the efficacy is lower than that of high-pressure sodium.

The primary place you will use HID lighting at home is outdoors: to light up the driveway, swimming pool, tennis court, etc. But a few manufacturers have introduced products designed for indoor lighting where very high lumens are needed, such as some commercial facilities.

Halogen Lighting

Halogen or tungsten-halogen lighting has improved somewhat over the past few years and remains the lighting option of choice where high light quality or precise light focusing is required. A halogen lamp is really a specialized type of incandescent lamp, often featuring a parabolic aluminized reflector (PAR) to improve light focus. Halogen lamps are slightly more energy-efficient than standard incandescent lamps, but not as energy-efficient as fluorescent lamps. In situations where light is needed on a precise area, halogen lights may be a more effective choice than fluorescent lights due to this tight focusing feature.

Torchiere Lamps

It is important to distinguish halogen torchiere floor lamps from the other halogen lighting discussed above. These fixtures, which have become quite popular in recent years, are actually quite inefficient, since they consume 300–600 watts of electricity yet direct the light to the ceiling. Even though a smooth white ceiling can reflect some light, bathing a ceiling with light from a halogen torchiere wastes much of the light quality and tight focusing benefits of halogen lamps. Halogen torchieres are particularly poor choices in rooms with non-white or textured ceilings. In addition, these low-cost light fixtures pose a fire hazard due to the extremely hot temperatures produced by their high-wattage bulbs.

Halogen torchieres are an example of a low-price technology that proves to be costly over the long term. For example, a 300-watt torchiere used just two hours per day will consume 219 kWh per year at an average cost of $18 per year. Many discount stores sell halogen floor lamps for about $15, so this floor lamp can easily cost more to operate each year than it cost to purchase in the first place! Put another way, halogen torchieres use so much power that using one can cancel the savings you would gain by replacing six 75-watt incandescent light bulbs with 18-watt compact fluorescent lamps.

Fortunately, several companies have begun making energy-efficient torchieres with compact fluorescent lamps. These new, attractive products feature full-dimming or three-stage dimming (three light levels) and are much safer than halogen floor lamps while using only a fraction of the electricity. Most of these products carry the ENERGY STAR label for easy identification. Visit www.energystar.gov for a full listing of ENERGY STAR-qualified torchieres and information on manufacturers and retailers.

Solar-Powered Walkway and Patio Lights

Another novel idea in lighting is the use of solar energy to power outdoor lights. During the daytime, a photovoltaic (PV) panel generates electricity, which is stored in a battery. At night, that stored electricity is used to energize the light. Some models are turned on manually, while others are turned on automatically by light-sensing controls or activated by motion-sensing devices. Most of these walkway or security lights require no wiring or installation other than pushing the stake into the ground, or screwing the fixture to a garage wall.

Solar walkway lights.

Most of the widely marketed solar walkway lights do not put out a whole lot of light—don't expect to read the newspaper under a $50 walkway light—but they are very useful for lighting the path to your door so your guests can find their way. Larger solar lights are available that do provide a lot of light, but these can be quite expensive.

Solar-powered outdoor

TABLE 11.5

CATALOG RETAILERS OFFERING PV-POWERED LIGHTING

Alternative Energy Engineering
P.O. Box 339
Redway, CA 95560
888-840-7191
www.alt-energy.com

Solar Webb, Inc.
136 East Santa Clara #6
Arcadia, CA 91006
888-786-9322
www.solarwebb.com

Backwoods Solar Electric Systems
1395 Rolling Thunder Ridge
Sandpoint, ID 83864
208-263-4290
www.backwoodssolar.com

Sunelco
P.O. Box 787
Hamilton, MT 59840
800-338-6844
www.sunelco.com

Kyocera
7812 Esat Acoma Dr.
Scottsdale, AZ 85267-4230
800-544-6466
www.kyocerasolar.com

Sunnyside Solar
1014 Green River Road
Guilford, VT 05301
802-257-1482
www.sunnysidesolar.com

Real Goods
360 Interlocken Blvd.
Broomfield, CO 80021-3440
800-762-7325
www.realgoods.com

lights can be found in many hardware and department stores, or purchased through catalog retailers of alternative energy and stand-alone power equipment (see Table 11.5).

Lighting Controls

In addition to saving energy by using more energy-efficient lamps, you can also save by having the lights on for a shorter period of time or at a lower output level. The simplest lighting control strategy, of course, is to turn lights off when you leave a room. Even if you are leaving for just a few minutes, it saves energy to turn the lights off. This applies to both incandescent and fluorescent lights.

With closets and cabinets, you can buy switches that turn the lights on when the door is opened and turn them off when the door is closed, thereby saving energy—as long as you remember to shut the door.

If you're the type of person who forgets to turn off lights when you leave a room, consider installing occupancy sensors that automatically turn lights off once a room is vacant. Most of these work by sensing heat or motion. While used primarily in commercial buildings, they can save energy in the home as well. Some models are available for as little as $20, while most are more expensive. However, inexpensive controls may be incompatible with electronic ballasts.

Light-sensing controls are increasingly being used to control outdoor lights. If you currently turn outdoor lights on at night, these controls are a great convenience, and they can save even more energy if connected to a timer to turn the lights off sometime late at night. Motion-sensing controls for outdoor security lighting both save energy and discourage potential intruders. A few of the manufacturers of the many lighting control products on the market are listed in Table 11.6.

Another control strategy is to reduce light level and energy use with dimmers. Tube fluorescent lamps are dimmable only if they have dimming ballasts. Dimmable compact fluorescents have been introduced—check the packaging to determine whether a compact fluorescent will work with a dimmer. Dimming will reduce the energy consumed by compact

An occupancy sensor will turn lights off automatically when you leave a room to save energy.

TABLE 11.6

LIGHTING CONTROLS MANUFACTURERS

Hubbell Building Automation
706 Brentwood Street
Austin, TX 78752
800-245-9135
www.hubbell.com

Novitas, Inc.
370 Amapola Avenue
Torrance, CA 90501
310-568-9600
www.novitas.com

Intermatic
7777 Winn Road
Spring Grove, IL 60081
815-675-2321 ext. 520
www.intermatic.com

Watt Stopper
4101 East Park Blvd., Suite 138
Plano, TX 75074
800-879-8585
www.wattstopper.com

Lightolier
631 Airport Road
Fall River, MA 02720
800-217-7722 or 508-679-8131
www.lightolier.com

---

fluorescent and tube fluorescent lamps, but does not improve the efficiency of incandescent lamps. Because of the way incandescent lights work, dimming to half the light output may still require three-quarters of the power!

TIPS FOR SAVING ENERGY AND MONEY WITH LIGHTING

Make Use of Natural Daylighting

Nothing's nicer than natural light, and in terms of energy use, nothing's more efficient. A single skylight or properly positioned window can provide as much light as dozens of light bulbs during the daylight hours. To benefit more from natural lighting you may need to rearrange your rooms somewhat—putting your favorite reading chair over by the south window, for example. Or you may want to go to more effort and install one or more skylights. To help get that light deeper into the room, you can paint your walls a light color and use reflective louvers or venetian blinds.

As you plan for natural lighting, don't forget that too much glass area

Natural daylighting is the least expensive light source of all.

on the east or west walls or on a south-facing roof can increase your air conditioning requirements. The best design balances passive solar heating, daylighting, and cooling considerations.

Reduce Background Light Levels and Rely More on Task Lighting

You can save a lot of energy by concentrating light just where it's needed and reducing background or ambient light levels. This strategy—called task lighting—is widely used in office buildings, but it makes just as much sense at home. Install track or recessed lights to illuminate your desk or the kitchen table where you do the crossword puzzle, and keep the ceiling lights off. Small compact fluorescent lamps can be used in many locations. Halogen lights can be focused precisely where you need the light.

Switch to Compact Fluorescent Lamps

Most of the lighting currently provided by incandescent lights can be provided just as well with compact fluorescent lamps. Replacing your incandescent lamps with compact fluorescents is the best way to save

Use task lighting
where you need
the light most and
reduce ambient light levels.

lighting energy in the average home. See the above discussion on compact fluorescent lighting and specific products that are available.

Where Design Permits, Use Tube Fluorescent Lighting

The best tube fluorescent lamps with new electronic ballasts are a far cry from what most of us think of as fluorescent lighting. They now make sense in places other than your garage or basement workshop. In fact, they can provide very satisfactory (and energy-efficient) recessed lighting around the perimeter of a living room, or overhead lighting in kitchens and bathrooms. You can now even buy dimming fluorescent fixtures to vary ambient light levels precisely for excellent mood lighting.

Use Incandescent Lights Wisely

Higher-wattage incandescent light bulbs are more efficient than lower-wattage bulbs. It takes two 60-watt bulbs or four 40-watt bulbs to provide as much light as a single 100-watt bulb. In a fixture that holds several bulbs, you'll save by using a single higher-wattage bulb instead of several smaller bulbs (be sure to follow precautions on the fixture about maximum wattage, though).

"Watt Miser," "Supersaver," or "Econo-Watt" bulbs, available from the major lamp manufacturers, use 5–13% less energy than standard bulbs. They sometimes cost a little more, but that extra cost is more than made up for through energy savings. Halogen lights offer even greater savings, and they last longer. Long-life and rough-service bulbs, on the other hand, are less efficient and not recommended except in locations where changing bulbs is difficult, or where rough conditions cause standard bulbs to fail prematurely. Also avoid the "energy-saver" buttons that are widely promoted for saving energy and extending bulb life. They reduce energy use, but they reduce light output even more.

Turn Lights Off
When You Leave the Room, or
Install Occupancy Sensors

Get in the habit of turning off lights when you leave a room. If you're forgetful, consider buying occupancy sensors that automatically turn lights off when you leave a room.

One 100-watt incandescent light bulb provides as much light as two 60-watt bulbs and uses less electricity.

Install Energy-Saving
Floodlights Outdoors

For outdoor lighting, use halogen, cold-start compact fluorescent, metal halide, or high-pressure sodium lights. Of these, halogen is the least energy efficient, and high-pressure sodium the most. If you generally leave outdoor lights on all night or (horrors) 24 hours a day, use light-sensing controls to turn the lights on at dusk and off at dawn.

Use Solar-Powered Accent Lights Outdoors

Solar walkway and patio lights are widely available in hardware and department stores or through catalogs. You can install them yourself in a few minutes without having to bury electric wires or hire an electrician.

Buying Energy-Efficient Lighting Equipment

Compact fluorescent lamps—and most of the other energy-efficient lighting products covered here—are still pretty new, although they are really catching on in some parts of the country. They sometimes aren't available in great variety on the shelf with light bulbs at the supermarket or local convenience store, but most large home hardware centers now carry a wider array of efficient lights. Also, as more people learn about the benefits of efficient lighting, the products should become more readily available.

When you're looking for compact fluorescent lamps, ask for them in the stores where you normally buy light bulbs. If the stores carry them, buy them there. This will reinforce the company's decision to stock this new item. If they don't carry compact fluorescents, see if they will order them for you, or encourage them to consider stocking them from a wholesaler. But don't give up on buying compact fluorescent lights just because you can't find them locally.

There are quite a few mail-order and Internet suppliers of energy-efficient lighting products that carry everything you might need. If you can't buy locally, contact one of these companies listed in Table 11.7 and ask for a catalog of lighting products. You can also contact the manufacturers of compact fluorescent lighting products, or a wholesale distributor specializing in energy-saving lighting products, to find out what stores near you carry these products. A lighting wholesaler is listed in Table 11.8.

Last, but certainly not least, you should check with your local electric utility company to find out if it either sells compact fluorescent products or offers rebates on their purchase. Some utilities are subsidizing customer purchases of compact fluorescents lamps as part of demand-side

---

TABLE 11.7

MAIL-ORDER LIGHTING EQUIPMENT RETAILERS

Energy Federation, Inc.	Real Goods
40 Washington Street	360 Interlocken Boulevard
West Boro, MA 01581	Broomfield, CO 80021
800-876-0660 or 508-653-4299	800-762-7325
www.efi.org	www.realgoods.com

TABLE 11.8

WHOLESALER OF ENERGY-CONSERVING LIGHTING PRODUCTS

Lighting Products
Fred Davis Corp.
93 West Street
Medfield, MA 02052
800-497-2970 or 508-359-3610

---

management programs. The basic idea is that it is less expensive for utility companies to invest in energy conservation than to invest in building new power plants, so many utility companies are interested in helping you reduce your electric bills.

CHAPTER 12
Other Energy Uses
In the Home

When we think about saving energy in the home, we generally focus on the obvious energy uses: heating, cooling, water heating, refrigerators, and so on—uses and products that the bulk of this book addresses. In many homes, though, there are miscellaneous uses of energy that are for the most part overlooked: such things as waterbed heaters, well-water pumps, pool filtering systems, engine block heaters, hot tubs, or even aquariums for tropical fish.

While the energy use of each of these products may be relatively small on a national level, it can be quite large in individual houses. In fact, it is not too uncommon to find that one or more of these miscellaneous products can account for more energy use than your refrigerator, water heater, or even heating system. Other common products, such as TVs, audio equipment, and computers, use relatively small amounts of energy on an individual basis but consume a lot of electricity overall due to their sheer numbers.And when these miscellaneous products are looked at collectively on a national level, the energy consumption is very significant: almost 20% of all electricity used in homes.

In many cases, the federal government's ENERGY STAR program has established criteria to recognize more energy-efficient products, from TVs to cordless telephones.For many miscellaneous products, looking for the ENERGY STAR label will help you find very cost-effective products with very high performance in other ways, too.

Let's take a look at these miscellaneous energy uses—both how they can affect energy use in an individual home and what the nationwide effect is. Table 12.1 lists the typical energy consumption of these household products and the saturation of these products nationwide. Table 12.2 looks at the nationwide energy consumption of these appliances.

One area of growing concern is electricity "vampires": the energy consumption from home electronics and small household appliances that require direct current (DC). These products (TVs, VCRs, answering machines, electric-powered portable tools, etc.) draw power not only when they are in use, but also when the power is supposedly "off."

TABLE 12.1

TYPICAL ENERGY CONSUMPTION AND PERCENT SATURATION OF MISCELLANEOUS ELECTRICITY USES IN THE HOME

Household product	Saturation	Typical energy consumption (kWh/yr)
Aquarium/terrarium	5–15%	200–1,000
Auto block heater	2–6%	150–800
Black & white television	20%	10–100
Bottled water dispenser	1–2%	200–400
Ceiling fan	100–140%	10–150
Clock (electric)	200%	17–50
Coffee maker	30–50%	20–300
Color television	210%	75–1,000
Computer	30%	25–400
Crankcase heater	5%	100–400
Dehumidifier	10–13%	200–1,000
Electric blanket	25–35%	75–200
Electric mower	5–8%	5–50
Furnace fan	50%	300–1,500
Garbage disposer	50%	20–50
Grow light & accessories	2–5%	200–1,500
Humidifier	8–15%	20–1,500
Instant hot water	1/2 –2%	100–400
Iron	20–40%	20–150
Pipe & gutter heater	2–5%	30–500
Pool pump	4–6%	500–4,000
Spa/hot tub (electric)	1–2%	1,500–4,000
Sumps/sewage pump	10–20%	20–200
Toaster/toaster oven	90–100%	25–120
VCR	80%	10–70
Ventilation fan	30–60%	2–70
Waterbed heater	12–20%	500–2,000
Well pump	10–15%	200–800
Whole-house fan	8–10%	20–500
Window fan	5–15%	5–100

Source: Leo Rainer (Davis Energy Group), Marla Sanchez, Steve Greenberg & Alan Meier (Lawrence Berkeley National Laboratory), and U.S. Department of Energy surveys.

TABLE 12.2

RESIDENTIAL ENERGY CONSUMPTION OF MISCELLANEOUS APPLIANCES IN THE UNITED STATES

Household product	Number in use (millions)	Energy use per unit (kWh/yr)	Total national consumption (TWh/yr)	Percent of total
Color television	210	250	52.5	5.20
Furnace fan	50	500	25.0	2.58
Waterbed heater	14	900	12.6	1.30
Pool pump	5	1500	7.5	0.77
Well pump	13	500	6.5	0.67
VCR	80	80	6.4	0.66
Aquarium/terrarium	10	600	6.0	0.62
Computer	60	130	7.8	0.77
DC wall-pack power supplies	200	25	5.0	0.52
Spa/hot tub (electric)	2	2300	4.6	0.47
Clock (electric)	180	25	4.5	0.46
Dehumidifier	11	400	4.4	0.45
Toaster/toaster-oven	86	45	3.9	0.40
Electric blanket	27	120	3.2	0.33
Cable TV boxes	40	80	3.2	0.33
Grow light & accessories	3	800	2.4	0.25
Ceiling fan	140	50	7.0	0.69
Coffee maker	40	50	2.0	0.21
Iron	32	50	1.6	0.16
Crankcase heater	5	250	1.3	0.13
Humidifier	11	100	1.1	0.11
Black & white television	20	40	0.8	0.08
Ventilation fan	54	15	0.8	0.08
Whole-house fan	8	80	0.6	0.07
Bottled water dispenser	2	300	0.6	0.06
Sumps/sewage pump	13	40	0.5	0.05
Garbage disposal	50	10	0.5	0.05
Pipe & gutter heater	3	100	0.3	0.03
Window fan	9	20	0.2	0.02
Electric yard tools	10	10	0.1	0.01
Total miscellaneous electric use	**1,011**	**16,782**	**172.9**	**17.10**
Total household electric use	**1,011**	**100,002**	**1010.0**	**100.00**

1. 101 million houses is the total number in the United States.

2. Average per house.

Source: Adapted by John Morrill from work by Leo Rainer (Davis Energy Group), Steve Greenberg & Alan Meier (Lawrence Berkeley National Laboratory), Jennifer Thorne & Margaret Suozzo (ACEEE), and data from U.S. Dept. of Energy surveys.

STANDBY AND OFF-MODE POWER

Home electronics and small household appliances that require direct current (e.g., TVs, VCRs, cordless phones, telephone answering machines, portable tools, rechargeable vacuums, etc.) draw energy not only when they are in use, but also when the power is apparently off. The average U.S. household consumes 50 watts of standby and off-mode power constantly, amounting to about 440 kWh per year. Nationwide, this electricity costs consumers over $3 billion per year.

TVs, VCRs, and cable boxes are responsible for more than half of this electricity. These appliances draw power when off to support features such as instant-on, remote control, channel memory, and LED clock displays. Digital satellite systems also contribute; these devices consume an average of 13 watts when not in use, and subscriptions are growing rapidly.

Considering that more than half of all American households have two or more color televisions (and over five million households have four or more color TVs), it is clear that home entertainment systems are becoming a major household energy use.

Fortunately, many manufacturers are working with the U.S. EPA to develop home electronics with low standby losses. Look for the ENERGY STAR label when purchasing a new TV, VCR, DVD, digital satellite, home stereo, cordless telephone, or answering machine. Also, ask your cable operator or satellite company about ENERGY STAR-labeled set-top boxes if you rent your box from them. Simply through improved circuitry and better power supplies, ENERGY STAR products will use much less electricity than conventional electronics—in some cases only 1 watt or less.

In addition to these products, DC power supplies for home alarm systems and rechargeable tools (even electric toothbrushes) also consume electricity when the product is not in use. These familiar "wall packs" each draw 2–6 watts of power as long as they are plugged in, even if the appliance is fully charged. The fact that these boxes are drawing power can be demonstrated simply by grasping a wall pack that has been plugged in for a while: it will be warm to the touch. That warmth is simply electrical energy wasted as heat.

Researchers are working with power supply manufacturers to improve the efficiency of DC power supplies to reduce these standby losses in new devices. Several manufacturers now offer high-efficiency power supplies (typically "switch-mode" power supplies) and a growing number of products including cellular phones are sold with these improved devices. These power supplies are much smaller and lighter than the wall-pack power supplies they replace. In the meantime, consumers should unplug wall packs for appliances that are not used often, such as hand-held vacuums, portable TVs, and rechargeable tools.

REMEMBER TO BOOST ENERGY EFFICIENCY WHENEVER POSSIBLE IN YOUR HOME— IT'S EASY ON THE POCKETBOOK AND THE PLANET

As you consider energy-saving opportunities in the home, look over this list. If you have a lot of these or other miscellaneous energy users in the home, there may be opportunities for savings. Recommendations are listed below for reducing energy use of a few of these household products.

■ *Furnace fans.* Refer back to Chapter 4 on heating systems. If your furnace is improperly sized, or if the fan thermostat is improperly set, the fan may operate longer than it needs to. If you're getting a lot of cold air out of the warm-air registers after the furnace turns off, this may be the case. Along with making you uncomfortable, the fan is wasting energy. On the other hand, if the fan shuts off too soon, heat from the furnace will be wasted. Have a service technician check the fan thermostat setting if you're unsure.

■ *Well pumps.* Well pumps are very common in rural areas. The amount of energy they use is dependent on how deep the well is, the

Make sure you use an
insulated cover on a hot tub or spa.

Home office equipment.

pump quality, and the pressure controls. If the pump seems to be switching on more often than it should, there may be a leak in the system somewhere, or the pressure switch may not be functioning properly. Have the system checked out. You can also save on well pumping electricity costs by reducing your water use (see discussion on water conservation in Chapter 6).

■ *Spas and hot tubs.* As you can see from the tables, spas and hot tubs can use a tremendous amount of energy. If you have one, keep it covered with a tight-fitting insulated cover when it's not in use. If installing a spa or hot tub, insulate it well around the sides and bottom.

■ *Computers and home office equipment.* More and more people are working at home or using computers in their leisure time. As home office use increases, so does energy use by such equipment as computers, printers, copiers, fax machines, and other computer peripherals. Some of this equipment (especially color monitors and laser printers) consumes a great deal of energy. So look for the ENERGY STAR label on any new computer equipment you purchase. The ENERGY STAR label identifies efficient PCs, printers, faxes, and copiers. Fortunately, any increase in household energy use when you work at home is usually made up for by reduced energy use for transportation. In fact, the trend toward more home offices could have a significant impact on energy use for commuting.

■ *Waterbeds.* As many as 20% of homes have waterbeds, and most are heated with electric coils underneath. Waterbeds can be the largest electricity user in the home—exceeding even the refrigerator and water heater! Simple habits can significantly reduce energy waste from waterbeds. Regularly making the bed with a comforter can save more than 30%; insulating the sides of the bed can save over 10%. You might also consider putting the waterbed heater on a timer so that it doesn't waste energy throughout the day.

■ *Electric blankets.* Each electric blanket in a house uses an average of 150 kWh per year. If you use an electric blanket and frequently forget to turn it off in the morning, you can save energy by buying a simple timer control. Putting a second blanket or quilt over the electric blanket also saves energy, but be sure to check the electric blanket instruction for possible precautions against this practice. Electric blankets may actually save energy by allowing you to turn your thermostat down further at night.

■ *Block heaters.* If you live in a cold area and use a block heater to help your car start on cold mornings, you might be surprised at how much energy it draws. A 5-amp block heater could be using 14 kWh per day if you leave the car plugged in all the time. That's over a dollar per day! You will probably find that using the block heater for just a half-hour or so before you start the car will warm it up perfectly well. If you don't want to go out to the cold garage a half-hour before you leave, install an extra circuit with a timer-controlled switch in the house, and plug in the car when you get home. Then set the timer about a half-hour before you need to leave in the morning.

■ *Rechargeables.* Many rechargeable products are sold with simple battery chargers and power supplies that continue to draw power even after the product is fully recharged. An easy way to cut this power use is to unplug rechargeable appliances and devices when the battery is recharged or the product is not in use. Also, consider whether it is necessary to keep continuously charging the batteries for all of the rechargeable products in your home.

USE YOUR COMMON SENSE

Saving energy with many of these incidental energy-consuming products—and with other products throughout the house—is very easy. Most of the time, it just takes some common sense. If we all become a little more aware of the energy we use, we might just begin to solve some of our major environmental problems, and we'll end up with a little more money in our pockets as well.

PART II

The Most
Energy-Efficient
Appliances

Introduction

THE IMPORTANCE OF
ENERGY-EFFICIENT APPLIANCES

The cost of using appliances and heating and cooling equipment averages more than $1,200 per year. You can sharply reduce your energy bill by using high-efficiency appliances and space conditioning equipment. While these may be more expensive to buy than comparable models with lower or average efficiency, your reduced energy bills will put that money back into your pocket long before the product wears out.

By purchasing energy-efficient appliances, you can also have a positive effect on national security, the economy, and the environment. The efficient use of oil, gas, and electricity cuts petroleum imports, improves U.S. economic competitiveness, and reduces the environmental pollution associated with energy production and use.

In fact, choosing energy-efficient appliances is one way you can immediately reduce your contribution to global climate change. Carbon dioxide (CO_2) is the primary gas affecting global warming and virtually all energy-using equipment results in CO_2 emissions either directly or indirectly. Since burning oil or gas in your furnace creates CO_2 directly, choosing a more efficient furnace will reduce this pollutant right from your home. Furthermore, coal or gas is burned in most power plants to create electricity and this produces emissions. By replacing a 20-year-old refrigerator with a new, energy-efficient model, not only will you save about 800 kWh per year, you will also reduce your home's CO_2 contribution by about one ton per year—all while saving about $65 per year through reduced electric bills.

NATIONAL APPLIANCE EFFICIENCY STANDARDS

The National Appliance Energy Conservation Act of 1987 established minimum-efficiency standards for major home appliances and heating and cooling equipment. Following is the timetable for when these standards took effect.

1990: the first standards for most appliances

1992: standards for central air conditioners, heat pumps, and furnaces

1993: revised standards for refrigerators and freezers

1994: revised standards for dishwashers, clothes washers, and dryers

2000: revised standards for room air conditioners

2001: revised standards for refrigerators and freezers

Following is the timetable for when new standards, published in 2001, will become effective.

2004: revised standards for clothes washers and water heaters

2006: revised standards for central air conditioners and heat pumps

Even though standards eliminate the production of the worst energy-guzzling appliances, many products are still available over a broad range of efficiencies and you will benefit from shopping carefully for highly efficient appliances that exceed the minimum-efficiency standards. After all, the air conditioner, furnace, or refrigerator you buy today will still be in use 15 or 20 years from now.

REBATE AND TAX INCENTIVE PROGRAMS

Some states and utilities offer rebates if you purchase energy-efficient appliances. Rebates reduce your initial purchase price of high-efficiency models, making them even more attractive.

Rebate programs are most common for high-efficiency refrigerators, air conditioning equipment, and clothes washers. Some gas utilities offer rebates for high-efficiency furnaces, while water utilities may offer rebates for water-saving clothes washers. If you plan to buy a major appliance soon, ask your utility if it offers rebates for efficient models.

A number of states have introduced tax incentives—typically income tax credits or elimination of state sales tax—for the purchase of high-efficiency appliances. Federal tax credits are also under consideration.

For more information on rebates and tax incentive programs, visit the ACEEE website for a state-by-state summary of programs (www.aceee.org/new/eedb.htm).

THE INFORMATION IN THIS GUIDE

This guide lists, to the best of our knowledge, the most energy-efficient residential appliances available in the United States as of January 2003. Because of space limitations, only the very highest-rated models are listed within each appliance category. You should be aware that the models listed here represent fewer than 5% of all the different models currently available. Many appliances are above average in efficiency, but space limitations prevent us from listing them all.

Our lists are based on information from the appliance industry associations' product directories, the U.S. Department of Energy and Environmental Protection Agency's ENERGY STAR program, and individual manufacturers. We only include models that are mass-produced and widely distributed in the United States. Also, we only include products for which there are standardized efficiency ratings. Therefore, this booklet does not cover ranges, ovens, clothes dryers, solar water heaters, wood stoves, tankless water heaters, portable space heaters, or air-to-air heat exchangers.

The efficiency ratings in this guide are the same test ratings shown on the yellow EnergyGuide labels required for most home appliances. The EnergyGuide labels show the estimated annual energy consumption in kilowatt-hours (kWh) for refrigerators, freezers, dishwashers, clothes washers, and electric water heaters. For gas water heaters, the EnergyGuide labels show the estimated annual energy consumption in therms (1 therm = 100 cubic feet of gas). The label also provides the estimated annual energy cost for operating these appliances.

For furnaces, boilers, air conditioners, and heat pumps, the lists in this guide (and the EnergyGuide labels) feature the equipment's efficiency rating rather than estimated consumption. The operating cost for this equipment varies widely from house to house depending on climate, house size, and other factors. Nonetheless, the efficiency ratings are good indicators of relative energy use—the higher the efficiency rating, the lower the operating cost.

HOW TO USE THIS INFORMATION

When you buy an appliance, you pay more than just the sales price—you commit yourself to paying the cost of running the appliance for as long as you own it. This energy cost adds up. The sum of the purchase price and the energy cost of running an appliance over its lifetime is called its lifecycle cost. The lifecycle cost of an energy-efficient appliance is typically lower than the lifecycle cost of an average model.

The model numbers in this guide are those used by manufacturers in their product directories. In some cases, appliance dealers use abbreviated model numbers. An asterisk (*) appearing in a model number indicates a digit or letter that varies with features of the appliance not affecting efficiency or capacity (for example, color).

If you cannot find some of the models listed in this guide, you can still use the information to your advantage: compare the efficiencies of the models you can find to those listed here. The models listed in this guide represent a very small fraction of all the new appliances available. Manufacturers constantly introduce new models, and very efficient models may have become available after this guide was compiled. Also, **you can ensure you are purchasing a relatively efficient product by looking for the ENERGY STAR label** on refrigerators, freezers, dishwashers, clothes washers, central and room air conditioners, heat pumps, furnaces, and boilers.

When shopping for major appliances, you may want to call several stores or dealers to check the price and availability of different models. Ask the salesperson for information about the efficiency of each model.

The yellow EnergyGuide labels can help you compare similar models.

We realize that energy performance is only one of several important criteria for selecting home appliances. We do not collect information on product reliability or other concerns. However, energy-efficient appliances are generally high-quality products due to better materials and components used in their construction.

The Lists of the Most Energy-Efficient Appliances

REFRIGERATORS AND FREEZERS

The energy efficiency of refrigerators and freezers has improved dramatically over the past three decades. A typical new refrigerator with automatic defrost and a top-mounted freezer uses less than 500 kWh per year, whereas a typical model sold in 1973 used over 1,800 kWh per year. Federal efficiency standards first took effect in 1993, requiring new refrigerators and freezers to be more efficient than ever before. A new set of stricter standards took effect July 1, 2001. Full-size products that exceed the federal standard by 10% or more qualify for the ENERGY STAR label. Compact refrigerators and freezers must exceed the standard by 20% to qualify for ENERGY STAR. All of the models listed here exceed the level required by the 2001 standard by 10% or more.

When purchasing a new refrigerator, seriously consider getting rid of your existing refrigerator rather than moving it to the basement or garage. By sending the older unit for recycling, you will reap all the savings from your new high-efficiency refrigerator.

The models list below are grouped by cabinet style and volume. Models are listed within each group in order of increasing electricity use (although if two different-sized refrigerators or freezers use the same amount of electricity per year, the larger model can be considered more efficient because it keeps more space cold with the same amount of electricity).

MOST EFFICIENT REFRIGERATORS AND FREEZERS				
Brand	Model	Volume	Energy Use (kWh/yr)	Annual Energy Cost ($)[†]
Top freezer, automatic defrost, less than 18 cubic feet				
Sun Frost[††]	RF-16	14.31	254	21
Whirlpool	ET5WSE*K*0*	14.54	372	31
Magic Chef	CTL1511GEW	14.96	386	32
Magic Chef	CTN1511GEW	14.96	386	32
Kenmore	3140*20*	14.4	394	33
Kenmore	3141*20*	14.4	394	33
Roper	RT14HD*K*0*	14.4	394	33
Whirlpool	ET4CSE*K*0*	14.4	394	33

[†] Annual energy cost based on U.S. national average electricity cost of 8.28 cents per kWh.
[††] This unit has partial automatic defrost.

MOST EFFICIENT REFRIGERATORS AND FREEZERS (cont.)

Brand	Model	Volume	Energy Use (kWh/yr)	Annual Energy Cost ($)†

Top freezer, automatic defrost, 18 to 21 cubic feet

Brand	Model	Volume	Energy Use (kWh/yr)	Annual Energy Cost ($)†
Kenmore	6397*30*	18.79	392	32
Kenmore	6398*30*	18.79	392	32
Kenmore	7397*30*	18.79	392	32
Kenmore	7398*30*	18.79	392	32
Kenmore	7290*20*	18.75	416	34
Kenmore	6199*10*	18.79	416	34
Kenmore	6399*20*	18.79	416	34
Kenmore	7299*20*	18.79	416	34
Whirlpool	GT9SHK*M*0*	18.81	416	34
Kenmore	6197*10*	18.79	417	35
Kenmore	6198*10*	18.79	417	35
Kenmore	7197*10*	18.79	417	35
Kenmore	7198*10*	18.79	417	35
LG Electronics	LRT*(C)18##**	18.01	431	36
Estate	TT18HP*L*0*	18.2	434	36
Roper	RT18HD*K*0*	18.2	434	36
Whirlpool	ET8MTE*K*0*	18.2	434	36
Whirlpool	ET8WTE*K*0*	18.2	434	36
LG Electronics	LRT*(C)20##**	20.02	450	37
Maytag Performa	PTB2153GE*	20.82	463	38

Top freezer, automatic defrost, greater than 21 cubic feet

Brand	Model	Volume	Energy Use (kWh/yr)	Annual Energy Cost ($)†
Kenmore	7328*30*	21.55	437	36
Kenmore	7329*30*	21.55	437	36
Kenmore	6328*30*	21.59	437	36
Kenmore	6329*30*	21.59	437	36
Kenmore	6125*10*	21.59	457	38
Kenmore	7125*10*	21.59	457	38
Kenmore	7120*10*	21.61	457	38
Kenmore	7129*10*	21.61	457	38
Kenmore	7220*20*	21.61	457	38
Kenmore	6128*10*	21.65	457	38
Kenmore	7128*10*	21.65	457	38
Kenmore	7229*20*	21.65	457	38
LG Electronics	7325#	22.1	468	39
LG Electronics	7326#	22.1	468	39
LG Electronics	LRT*223##**	22.1	468	39
Whirlpool	GR2SHM*K*0*	21.65	472	39
Whirlpool	GT2SHM*L*0*	21.65	472	39
Whirlpool	GT2SHK*L*0*	21.65	472	39
General Electric	PTC22MFML**	21.7	550	46
General Electric	PTC22MFMR**	21.7	550	46

MOST EFFICIENT REFRIGERATORS AND FREEZERS (cont.)

Brand	Model	Volume	Energy Use (kWh/yr)	Annual Energy Cost ($)[†]
Top freezer, automatic defrost, greater than 21 cubic feet (cont.)				
General Electric	PTC22SFMLBS	21.7	550	46
General Electric	PTC22SFMRBS	21.7	550	46
General Electric	PTI22MFML**	21.7	550	46
General Electric	PTI22MFMR**	21.7	550	46
General Electric	PTI22SFMLBS	21.7	550	46
General Electric	PTI22SFMRBS	21.7	550	46
Bottom freezers				
Kenmore	7295*	18.52	475	39
Kenmore	7225*	21.92	490	41
Kenmore	7228*	21.92	490	41
Side-by-side less than 25 cubic feet				
Kitchen Aid	KSRA22KK**0*	21.7	540	45
Kitchen Aid	KSSS36QM*0*	20.96	566	47
Kenmore	5320*20*	21.91	572	47
Kenmore	5329*20*	21.91	572	47
LG Electronics	LRS*C20##**	19.53	578	48
Kenmore	5225*10*	21.91	598	50
Kenmore	5226*10*	21.91	598	50
Kenmore	5325*20*	21.91	598	50
Kenmore	5326*20*	21.91	598	50
GE Monogram	ZIS*360DM*	21.71	615	51
LG Electronics	LRS*C23##**	22.78	615	51
Maytag	MSD2456GE*	23.55	625	52
Side-by-side greater than 25 cubic feet				
Kenmore	5360*20*	25.57	582	48
Kenmore	5369*20*	25.57	582	48
Kenmore	5468*30*	25.57	582	48
Kenmore	5469*30*	25.57	582	48
General Electric	PSF26NGN**	25.5	613	51
General Electric	PSW26SGN**	25.5	613	51
General Electric	ESS25LGN	25.38	613	51
General Electric	ESS25LSN**	25.38	613	51
General Electric	GSS25SXN**	25.38	613	51
General Electric	ESS25GXN	25.38	613	51
General Electric	PSS25MGN**	25.38	613	51
General Electric	PSS25NGN**	25.27	613	51
General Electric	PSS25SGN**	25.27	613	51

[†] Annual energy cost based on U.S. national average electricity cost of 8.28 cents per kWh.

MOST EFFICIENT REFRIGERATORS AND FREEZERS (cont.)

Brand	Model	Volume	Energy Use (kWh/yr)	Annual Energy Cost ($)[†]
Side-by-side greater than 25 cubic feet (cont.)				
Kenmore	5346*	25.6	617	51
Kenmore	5365*30*	25.41	617	51
Kenmore	5366*30*	25.41	617	51
Kenmore	5355*20*	25.46	617	51
Kenmore	5356*20*	25.46	617	51
Kenmore	5255*10*	25.47	618	51
Kenmore	5256*10*	25.47	618	51
Kenmore	5260*10*	25.55	618	51
Kenmore	5269*10*	25.55	618	51
Whirlpool	GS6SHA*K*0*	25.55	619	51
Whirlpool	GS6SHA*L*0*	25.55	619	51
Kenmore	5370*20*	26.92	632	52
Kenmore	5379*20*	26.92	632	52
Samsung	RS2555SL	25.18	633	52
Samsung	RS2555SW	25.18	633	52
Kenmore	5375*20*	26.88	647	54
Kenmore	5376*20*	26.88	647	54
Kenmore	5270*10*	26.98	647	54
Kenmore	5279*10*	26.98	647	54
GE Monogram	ZIS*420DM*	26.11	655	54
Kitchen Aid	KSSS48QM*0*	29.78	659	55
Single-door, refrigerator only, automatic defrost, all sizes				
Sun Frost	R-19	16.14	204	17
Crosley	FFCR17/G	16.8	372	31
Wood's	RFA17NAD**	16.8	372	31
Sub-Zero	601R*	19.94	417	35
General Electric	ZIR36ND-LH	21.85	438	36
General Electric	ZIR36ND-RH	21.85	438	36
General Electric	ZIRS36ND-LH	21.85	438	36
General Electric	ZIRS36ND-RH	21.85	438	36
Compact & small refrigerator-freezers, less than 10.5 cubic feet				
Absocold	GARD562MG10R/L	5.6	268	22
Avanti	1201W-1	11.0	277	23
Absocold	ARD492AS10R/L	4.9	316	26
Kenmore	91499100	4.9	316	26
Kenmore	93491100	4.9	316	26
Sanyo	SR-4910	4.9	316	26

MOST EFFICIENT REFRIGERATORS AND FREEZERS (cont.)

Brand	Model	Volume	Energy Use (kWh/yr)	Annual Energy Cost ($)†
Compact & small refrigerators, less than 10.5 cubic feet				
Avanti	RM901W	8.7	230	19
Avanti	BCA902W	8.87	247	20
BSH Home Appliances	RC29	9.98	274	23
U-Line	75R	5.7	305	25
U-Line	2015R	3.1	307	25
Sub-Zero	249RP*	4.9	334	28
U-Line	2075R	5.5	339	28
Upright freezer, automatic & manual defrost, all sizes				
Avanti	VM799W	7.5	292	24
Wood's	V10NAE*	10.4	353	29
Wood's	V15NAE*	15.0	409	34
Crosley	WCV17/E	16.9	430	36
Wood's	V17NAE	16.9	430	36
Crosley	WCF15/E	15.0	582	48
Wood's	F15NAE**	15.0	582	48
Kenmore	23724	16.7	615	51
Kenmore	23725	16.7	615	51
Wood's	F17NAE**	16.7	616	51
Crosley	WCF20/E	19.6	671	56
Wood's	F20NAE**	19.6	671	56
Chest freezer, manual defrost, all sizes				
Wood's	C09NAD	9.0	251	21
Crosley	WCC10/E	10.0	282	23
Wood's	C10NAE	10.0	282	23
Crosley	WCC12/E	12.2	298	25
Crosley	WCC12/G	12.2	298	25
Wood's	C12NAD	12.2	298	25
Crosley	WCC15O/G	14.8	354	29
Wood's	C15NAE	14.8	354	29
Crosley	WCC17/E	16.5	360	30
Wood's	C17NAD	16.5	360	30
Wood's	C17NAE	16.5	360	30
Wood's	C20NAD	20.3	415	34
Wood's	C22NAE	21.7	460	38

† Annual energy cost based on U.S. national average electricity cost of 8.28 cents per kWh.

DISHWASHERS

Most of the energy used by dishwashers and clothes washers is actually the energy required for heating the water they consume. An efficient dishwasher uses less water to do the job. Virtually all dishwashers available today use booster heaters to further heat the water supplied by the water heater to the higher temperatures required for dishwashing, so you can reduce the temperature of your water heater to 120° for additional energy savings. All of the models listed here exceed the ENERGY STAR requirements and are at least 50% more efficient than the federal minimum standard. Many of the newer models also use significantly less water—as much as one-half less—than hand washing.

Many of the dishwashers on the market today incorporate soil-sensors to adjust water use depending on how dirty the dishes are in each load washed. It is important to note that the energy use estimates listed below and presented on EnergyGuide labels are based on a test procedure that uses clean dishes. As a result, the actual energy use of soil-sensing models may deviate significantly from these estimates, particularly when dishes are not pre-rinsed. A new test procedure currently under development would better estimate the energy consumption of soil-sensing dishwasher models. Until this new procedure is adopted, the data presented here and on the EnergyGuide may not allow for accurate comparisons among models.

Recent studies demonstrate that most new dishwashers do a great job cleaning even the dirtiest dishes without pre-rinsing. So give yourself a break and skip the unnecessary step of pre-rinsing—you'll save money along with precious water, energy, and time.

MOST EFFICIENT DISHWASHERS				
Brand	Model	Energy Factor	kWh/yr (elec.wtr.htr.)	Annual Energy Cost ($)*
Equator	PLS600	1.29	204	17
Equator	PLS600NF	1.29	204	17
Equator	PLS600NFV	1.29	204	17
Equator	PLS600V	1.29	204	17
Equator	PLS602NF	1.29	204	17
Equator	PLS602NFV	1.29	204	17
Equator	PLS602S	1.29	204	17
Equator	PLS602SV	1.29	204	17
Asko	1805FI	0.94	282	23
Asko	1375	0.85	309	26
Asko	1585	0.85	309	26
Asko	D1976	0.85	312	26

	MOST EFFICIENT DISHWASHERS (cont.)			
Brand	Model	Energy Factor	kWh/yr (elec.wtr.htr.)	Annual Energy Cost ($)*
Viking	VUD141	0.84	316	26
Asko	D1876	0.82	321	27
Asko	D1796	0.82	321	27
Asko	D1776	0.81	325	27
Viking	DFUD140	0.79	333	28
Asko	D1996	0.78	338	28
Asko	1385	0.77	341	28
Asko	1485	0.77	341	28
Asko	1595	0.77	341	28
Asko	1805	0.77	341	28
Asko	1885	0.77	341	28
Asko	1895	0.77	341	28
Asko	D1716	0.77	341	28
Frigidaire	MDR251RH	0.76	348	29
Frigidaire	MDS251RH	0.76	348	29
Viking	VUD040	0.75	354	29
Eurotech	EDW174E	0.74	355	29
Miele	G832	0.73	364	30
Fisher & Paykel	DD603-USA	0.72	366	30
Asko	D1706	0.72	367	30
GE/Monogram	ZBD6400G**	0.72	367	30
GE/Monogram	ZBD6500GSS	0.72	367	30
GE/Monogram	ZBD6600GSS	0.72	367	30
GE/Monogram	ZBD6700G**	0.72	367	30
GE/Monogram	ZBD6900GSS	0.72	367	30
GE/Monogram	ZBD7000GII	0.72	367	30
GE/Monogram	ZBD7100GSS	0.72	367	30
General Electric	PDW8000G**	0.72	367	30
General Electric	PDW8060GSS	0.72	367	30
Eurotech	EDW154E	0.72	368	30
Miele	G818	0.71	372	31
Frigidaire	MDB124BA	0.70	380	31
Smeg	CSU2001B	0.69	383	32
Smeg	CSU2001W	0.69	383	32

*Annual energy cost based on U.S. national average electricity cost of 8.28 cents per kWh.

CLOTHES WASHERS

Many new energy-efficient, water-conserving clothes washers have been introduced over the past few years. These resource-efficient washers are available in a variety of sizes and configurations offering consumers a wide range of front-loading and top-loading styles in many different price ranges.

The clothes washers below are listed in order of their modified energy factor (MEF), which is a measure of efficiency that combines tub capacity and energy use. The higher the MEF, the more efficient the washer. In addition to saving energy by reducing water use, the washers listed below spin clothes faster than conventional machines, leaving less moisture in the clothes and reducing the time and energy needed in the clothes dryer. These dryer savings are incorporated in the MEF rating.

Water use is a growing concern in many communities. Reducing the water used in the clothes washer saves both water and energy. Most of the energy consumed to wash clothes is required to heat the water used in the washer. The list below includes the water factor (WF) for each model. The lower the WF, the less water used by the machine.

Stricter new federal standards for clothes washers will take effect in two stages beginning with an interim standard in 2004, which will be further strengthened in 2007. All of the models listed below exceed the 2007 minimum standard.

MOST EFFICIENT CLOTHES WASHERS

Brand	Model	Capacity (cubic feet)	Modified Energy Factor (MEF)	Water Factor	kWh/year (elec.wtr.htr.)
Fisher & Paykel	GWL10	3.00	2.20	8.80	298
LG Electronics	WD 324 * RHD	1.96	2.10	5.04	115
Bosch	WFR2460UC	1.85	2.08	5.73	184
Equator	EZ 1612 V	1.92	2.04	4.85	135
Splendide	WDC 6200 CEE	1.92	2.04	4.85	155
LG Electronics	WD-327*RHD	2.05	2.02	5.21	155
Equator	EZ 3612 CEE	1.92	1.92	5.00	143
Asko	W660	1.90	1.92	8.22	176
Fisher & Paykel	GWL11	3.00	1.91	8.45	217
Kenmore	4304	2.65	1.9	5.86	196
Kenmore	4305	2.65	1.9	5.86	196
Kenmore	4314	2.65	1.9	5.86	196
Asko	W640	1.90	1.88	7.71	181
LG Electronics	WM2411H*	3.22	1.87	3.99	225
LG Electronics	WM2432H*	3.22	1.87	3.99	225
Kenmore	4204	2.65	1.86	7.15	196

Brand	Model	Capacity (cubic feet)	Modified Energy Factor (MEF)	Water Factor	kWh/year (elec.wtr.htr.)
			MOST EFFICIENT CLOTHES WASHERS (cont.)		
Kenmore	4205	2.65	1.86	7.15	196
Kenmore	4214*	2.65	1.86	7.15	196
Softline	XQG65-11	2.01	1.85	5.70	203
Thor	XQG65-11	2.01	1.85	5.70	203
Asko	W6761	1.96	1.84	7.48	189
LG Electronics	WM0532H*	3.22	1.83	4.00	221
LG Electronics	WM2011H*	3.22	1.83	4.00	221
LG Electronics	WM2032H*	3.22	1.83	4.00	221
Equator	EZ 2512 CEE	1.60	1.83	6.00	125
Splendide	WDC 5200 CEE	1.60	1.83	6.00	125
Splendide	WD 2000S	1.60	1.83	6.00	125
Bosch	WFL2060UC	1.85	1.80	6.47	194
LG Electronics	WM1811C*	3.22	1.76	4.26	215
LG Electronics	WM1832C*	3.22	1.76	4.26	215
Asko	W6641	1.96	1.74	7.48	189
Maytag	MAH4000	2.90	1.72	7.66	282
Kenmore	4292*	3.18	1.70	4.43	286
Kenmore	4293*	3.18	1.70	4.43	286
Kenmore	4390*20+	3.18	1.70	4.43	286
Kenmore	4493*20+	3.18	1.70	4.43	286
Whirlpool	GHW9100L*	3.18	1.69	4.28	282
Maytag	MLE2000 (stack unit)	2.90	1.69	7.98	314
Maytag	MLG2000 (stack unit)	2.90	1.69	7.98	314
Whirlpool	GHW9200L*	3.18	1.68	4.36	294
Frigidaire	FWT645RH	2.65	1.68	9.43	259
Frigidaire	FTF1040A	2.65	1.68	9.43	259
Frigidaire	FTF630A	2.65	1.68	9.43	259
Frigidaire	FTR630A	2.65	1.68	9.43	259
Frigidaire	GLTF1040A	2.65	1.68	9.43	259
Imperial	LFW201E	2.65	1.68	9.43	259
Maytag	MAH7500*	2.90	1.66	8.10	362
Samsung	P1092	1.77	1.66	8.83	177
Asko	W6021	1.96	1.66	7.48	209
Miele	W1926	2.01	1.64	7.57	279
Maytag	MAH5500	2.90	1.64	8.10	282
Miele	W1918	1.69	1.64	8.34	267
Miele	W1930	1.69	1.64	8.34	267
Asko	W620	1.90	1.63	8.43	177
Asko	W600	1.90	1.62	8.05	182
Kenmore	4282*	3.18	1.60	4.36	282
Kenmore	4283*	3.18	1.60	4.36	282
Kenmore	4483*20+	3.18	1.60	4.36	282
Quietline	WD9900	1.57	1.59	7.44	217

MOST EFFICIENT CLOTHES WASHERS (cont.)

Brand	Model	Capacity (cubic feet)	Modified Energy Factor (MEF)	Water Factor	kWh/year (elec.wtr.htr.)
Thor	WD9900	1.57	1.59	7.44	217
General Electric	WSXH208A	2.65	1.59	9.45	259
Asko	W6221	1.96	1.58	7.48	209
Frigidaire	39012	2.65	1.57	9.10	259
Frigidaire	39022	2.65	1.57	9.10	259
Maytag	MAH6500	2.90	1.55	8.23	388
Whirlpool	GVW9959K	2.99	1.53	8.11	337
Eurotech	EWF172	2.50	1.52	8.04	306
Kenmore	2106*	3.01	1.50	8.11	337
Kenmore	2108*	3.01	1.50	8.11	337
Kenmore	2206*	3.01	1.50	8.11	337
Kenmore	2208*	3.01	1.50	8.11	337
Kenmore	2408*20	3.01	1.50	8.11	337
Staber	HXW2304	2.00	1.48	7.11	265
Maytag	MAH5500B	2.90	1.47	8.47	288
Maytag	MAH55FLB	2.90	1.47	8.47	288
General Electric	WPXH214A**	2.65	1.47	9.47	351
General Electric	WPGT9350C***	3.53	1.45	6.97	422

WATER HEATERS

The federal efficiency standards for water heaters took effect in 1990, assuring consumers that all new water heaters meet certain minimum-efficiency levels. New standards, set to take effect in 2004, will increase the minimum-efficiency levels of these products. Water heater efficiency is reported in terms of the energy factor (EF). The higher the EF, the more efficient the water heater. All of the water heaters listed here exceed the 2004 standard.

The yellow EnergyGuide labels for water heaters provide estimates of the energy use of each model based on the overall efficiency of the unit and the assumption that 64 gallons of hot water is used per day. Energy use by electric water heaters (including heat pump water heaters) is given in kilowatt-hours per year; energy use by gas water heaters is given in therms per year; and energy use by oil water heaters is given in gallons per year. Estimated annual water heating costs are provided as well. Your actual energy use and cost will vary depending on how much hot water your family uses and the cost of electricity or fuel in your area. There is little difference between the most efficient electric resistance storage water heaters and the minimum-efficiency standard that will take effect in January 2004. As a result, we no longer list specific electric-resistance models. The lists below provide details on the most efficient gas- and oil-fired storage water heaters on the market today including gas-fired combination water heater/space heaters. Combination units are rated by their combined annual efficiency (C_{AE}), a measure of both water and space heating efficiency. The higher the C_{AE}, the more efficient the unit.

Of course, the capacity of a water heater is an important consideration. The water heater should provide enough hot water at the busiest time of the day. For example, a household of two adults may never use more than 30 gallons of hot water in an hour, but a family of six may use as much as 70 gallons in an hour. The ability of a water heater to meet peak demands for hot water is indicated by its "first hour rating." This rating accounts for the effects of tank size and the speed by which cold water is heated. The models below are grouped by their tank size and listed in order of efficiency and first hour rating.

MOST EFFICIENT GAS WATER HEATERS

Manufacturer (Brand)	Model	1st Hour Rating (gallons)	Energy Factor	Storage Tank (gallons)	Therms/Year
Approximately 30 Gallon Storage Tank					
A. O. Smith	FGR-30T-248	67	0.62	30	242
A. O. Smith	FGR-30T-248D	67	0.62	30	242
A. O. Smith	PGR-30-248	67	0.62	30	242
Approximately 40 Gallon Storage Tank					
A. O. Smith	FPSE-40-230E	75	0.65	40	230
Bradford White	M-4-403T***N-13	79	0.64	40	234
Maytag	HN4**40X	76	0.64	40	234
Maytag	HN5**40X	76	0.64	40	234
Bradford White	M-I-TW40L***N-13	72	0.64	40	234
Bradford White	M-4-40T***N-13	67	0.64	40	234
Bradford White	M-4-403T***N-12	79	0.63	40	238
A. O. Smith	CTG-40-226	76	0.63	40	238
A. O. Smith	PGCG-40-226	76	0.63	40	238
Reliance	** 40 NXRTL*** W	76	0.63	40	238
Sears (Kenmore)	153.330401 HA	76	0.63	40	238
Sears (Kenmore)	153.330402HA	76	0.63	40	238
Sears (Kenmore)	153.330451	76	0.63	40	238
Sears (Kenmore)	153.330452	76	0.63	40	238
Maytag	HJ640NOCT52W	73	0.63	40	238
Reliance	** 40 NOCT*** 52W	73	0.63	40	238
State	PR* 40 NOCT*** 52W	73	0.63	40	238
Bradford White	M-4-40T***N-12	67	0.63	40	238
Approximately 50 Gallon Storage Tank					
Bradford White	M-II-TW50T***N-10	105	0.65	48	230
Maytag	HN4**50X	84	0.64	50	234
Maytag	HN5**50X	84	0.64	50	234
Bradford White	M-I-TW50L***N-12	85	0.63	48	238
Bradford White	M-4-50S***N-13	85	0.63	50	238
Apollo	A**50NXRTL2W	84	0.63	50	238
Reliance	**50NXRTL2W	84	0.63	50	238
State	PR* 50 NXRT*** 2W	84	0.63	50	238
State	PR*50NXRTL2W	84	0.63	50	238
A. O. Smith	PGCG-40-246	81	0.63	50	238
Greater than 60 Gallon Storage Tank					
Bradford White	M-II-TW75T***N-10	145	0.64	75	234
Bradford White	M-II-TW65T***N-10	129	0.62	65	242
Lochinvar	PVN075	130	0.60	73	250
Lochinvar	DVN065	120	0.60	65	250

MOST EFFICIENT GAS COMBINATION WATER HEATER/SPACE HEATERS

Manufacturer (Brand)	Model	Heating Capacity (Btu/hr)	Combined Annual Efficiency	Storage Tank (gallons)
American Water Heater (Polaris)	PBG*2-34S100-2N	90	0.90	34
Lennox (Complete Heat)	HM30-100	90	0.90	34
Lennox (Complete Heat)	HM30-150	135	0.90	34
American Water Heater (Polaris)	PBG*2-50T100-2N	90	0.88	50

MOST EFFICIENT OIL WATER HEATERS

Manufacturer	Model	1st Hour Rating (gallons)	Energy Factor	Storage Tank (gallons)	Oil Use (gal/yr)
Bock	32PP**	132	0.68	32	159
Bock	32E**	130	0.66	32	164
GSW	JW 327	150	0.62	30	174
GSW	JW 317	150	0.62	30	174
Heat Transfer	SJ-30 CWB	101	0.62	30	174
GSW	JWF 307	110	0.60	32	180
GSW	JWF 307V	110	0.60	32	180

ROOM AIR CONDITIONERS

Room air conditioners are rated by their energy efficiency ratio (EER), which is the cooling output divided by the power consumption. The higher the EER, the more efficient the air conditioner. All of the models listed below exceed the new standards for room air conditioners, which took effect in October 2000.

MOST EFFICIENT ROOM AIR CONDITIONERS

Manufacturer	Brand	Model	Capacity (Btu/hr)	EER
Less than 6,000 Btu/hr cooling capacity				
Electrolux	Carrier	ACA051T	5,400	11.2
Electrolux	Frigidaire	FAA056M7A	5,400	11.2
LG Electronics	Kenmore	72059	5,700	11.2
LG Electronics	Kenmore	720592	5,700	11.2
LG Electronics	LG Electronics	LWJ0516UGF	5,700	11.2
Sharp	Sharp	AF-P50CX	5,000	11.0
Sharp	Sharp	AF-S50CX	5,000	11.0
Sharp	Sharp	AF-S50DX	5,000	11.0
Sharp	Sharp	AF-S55CX	5,000	11.0
Electrolux	Carrier	ACA051B	5,200	11.0
Electrolux	Frigidaire	FAA053M7A	5,200	11.0
Electrolux	Frigidaire	FAA055M7A	5,200	11.0
LG Electronics	Goldstar	WG5200E	5,200	11.0
LG Electronics	LG Electronics	KG5200ER	5,200	11.0
LG Electronics	LG Electronics	LWJ0512PCG	5,200	11.0
LG Electronics	LG Electronics	M5203ER	5,200	11.0
LG Electronics	LG Electronics	M5203L	5,200	11.0
Electrolux	White-Westinghouse	WAA053M7A	5,200	11.0
Fedders	Airtemp	B7X05F2A	5,600	11.0
Carrier	Carrier	GCA061T	5,600	11.0
Electrolux	Kenmore	72055	5,600	11.0
Electrolux	Kenmore	73055	5,600	11.0
Panasonic	Panasonic	CW-C60YU	5,800	11.0
Panasonic	Panasonic	CW-XC60YU	5,800	11.0
Panasonic	Quasar	HQ2061QH	5,800	11.0
6,000 to 7,999 Btu/hr cooling capacity				
LG Electronics	LG Electronics	LWK0710WGL	7,000	11.7
Friedrich	Friedrich	SQ06J10B	6,200	11.0
Friedrich	Friedrich	XQ06J10	6,200	11.0
LG Electronics	LG Electronics	LWG0812ACG	7,800	11.0
LG Electronics	LG Electronics	M8003L	7,800	11.0
Panasonic	Panasonic	CW-XC80YU	7,800	11.0

MOST EFFICIENT ROOM AIR CONDITIONERS (cont.)

Manufacturer	Brand	Model	Capacity (Btu/hr)	EER
6,000 to 7,999 Btu/hr cooling capacity (cont.)				
Panasonic	Panasonic	CW-C80YU	7,800	11.0
Panasonic	Quasar	HQ2081QH	7,800	11.0
Sharp	Sharp	AF-S60DX	6,000	11.0
Sharp	Sharp	AF-06CSL	6,000	11.0
Sharp	Sharp	AF-P60CX	6,000	11.0
Sharp	Sharp	AF-S60CX	6,000	11.0
8,000 to 9,999 Btu/hr cooling capacity				
Friedrich	Friedrich	SS08J10R	8,200	11.0
LG Electronics	Goldstar	WG8000E	8,000	11.0
LG Electronics	LG Electronics	M1003L	9,800	11.0
Sharp	Sharp	AF-P80CX	8,000	11.0
Sharp	Sharp	AF-S80CX	8,000	11.0
Sharp	Sharp	AF-S80DX	8,000	11.0
10,000 to 12,999 Btu/hr cooling capacity				
Friedrich	Friedrich	SS10J10AR	10,200	11.4
Friedrich	Friedrich	RS10J10	10,000	11.0
Friedrich	Friedrich	RS12J10A	11,750	11.0
Friedrich	Friedrich	SS12J10AR	11,750	11.0
Friedrich	Friedrich	SS12J30D	12,000	11.0
LG Electronics	LG Electronics	LW1000ERY3	10,000	11.0
LG Electronics	LG Electronics	LW1000PRY3	10,000	11.0
LG Electronics	LG Electronics	LWL1010PCL	10,000	11.0
LG Electronics	LG Electronics	LWL1010PGL	10,000	11.0
LG Electronics	LG Electronics	LWL1010WGL	10,000	11.0
Sharp	Sharp	AF-S100DX	10,000	11.0
13,000 to 16,999 Btu/hr cooling capacity				
LG Electronics	LG Electronics	LW1500ER	15,000	11.5
LG Electronics	LG Electronics	LW1500PRY3	15,000	11.5
LG Electronics	LG Electronics	LWP1510PCL	15,000	11.5
LG Electronics	LG Electronics	LWP1510PGL	15,000	11.5
LG Electronics	LG Electronics	LWP1510WGL	15,000	11.5
Friedrich	Friedrich	RS15J10	14,500	11.1
Friedrich	Friedrich	KS15J10	14,500	10.9
Daewoo	Daewoo	DWA-146R	14,320	10.8
LG Electronics	General Electric	AGF14AA	13,800	10.8
LG Electronics	General Electric	AGM14AA	13,800	10.8
LG Electronics	General Electric	AGM14AB	13,800	10.8
LG Electronics	Hampton Bay	HBLG1400E	13,800	10.8
Daewoo	Hampton Bay	267-633	14,320	10.8
LG Electronics	Hampton Bay	HBLG1453E	14,500	10.8

MOST EFFICIENT ROOM AIR CONDITIONERS (cont.)

Manufacturer	Brand	Model	Capacity (Btu/hr)	EER
Greater than 17,000 Btu/hr cooling capacity				
Heat Controller	Comfort Aire	RADS-181	17,300	11.0
LG Electronics	Kenmore	731893	17,500	10.8
LG Electronics	Kenmore	72189	18,000	10.8
LG Electronics	LG Electronics	LW1800ERY3	17,500	10.8
LG Electronics	LG Electronics	LW1800PRY3	17,500	10.8
LG Electronics	LG Electronics	LW1800ER	18,000	10.8
LG Electronics	LG Electronics	LWL1830PCL	18,000	10.8
LG Electronics	LG Electronics	LWL1830PGL	18,000	10.8
LG Electronics	LG Electronics	LWL1830WGL	18,000	10.8
LG Electronics	LG Electronics	LWP1830WGR	18,000	10.8

CENTRAL AIR CONDITIONERS

Central air conditioners (CACs) are rated according to their seasonal energy efficiency ratio (SEER). This is the cooling output divided by the power input for a hypothetical average U.S. climate. The higher the SEER, the more efficient the air conditioner. The national efficiency standard for CACs took effect in 1992, requiring a minimum SEER of 10. New standards, set to take effect in 2006, will raise the SEER requirement by at least 20%. Many older CACs have SEERs of only 6 or 7.

Unfortunately, SEER doesn't tell the whole story. For best possible performance, follow these steps: (1) Get your contractor to perform a complete load calculation to make sure you get a properly sized unit. An oversized CAC will give less comfort because it will not control humidity well. (2) Buy a matched system of condenser, indoor unit, and even the thermostat. In general, older indoor coils are too small to deliver efficiency. (3) For efficiency when it is needed most (on the hottest days), be sure that the unit has a TXV (thermal expansion valve) plus an EER (high temperature rating) greater than 11.6. (4) A variable speed air handler will improve comfort and efficiency and allow continuous air filtering at minimum energy cost. (5) Have your contractor check that all ducts are sealed and insulated (where outside the building envelope) with supply and return systems balanced.

The list below provides manufacturer, trade name, and condenser model. Depending on the indoor unit (or blower coil) installed, SEER and EER can vary significantly within the ranges provided below. When purchasing a new system, check with your contractor or visit the Air-Conditioning and Refrigeration Institute (www.ari.org) to see the specific SEER and EER values for the combination you are considering. For the most efficient system, ACEEE recommends SEER of at least 14.5.

MOST EFFICIENT CENTRAL AIR-CONDITIONERS

Manufacturer	Trade Name	Condenser Model	SEER range min	max	EER range min	max
Cooling Capacity: Approximately 2.0 Tons						
Amana	Prestige Ultra	RCE24A2*	14.60	16.50	12.85	14.55
York	Stealth	H4TS024S06	15.00	16.20	13.00	14.25
Bryant	Quantum Plus 556A	556AN024-A/C/D/E	13.00	15.60	11.40	13.50
Carrier	WeatherMaker 38TSA	38TSA02432	13.00	15.60	11.40	13.50
Fraser-Johnston, Luxaire	HBE Series, Atlas-Butler	HABE-F024S	13.80	15.50	12.30	14.15

MOST EFFICIENT CENTRAL AIR-CONDITIONERS (cont.)

Manufacturer	Trade Name	Condenser Model	SEER range min	SEER range max	EER range min	EER range max
Cooling Capacity: Approximately 2.0 Tons (cont.)						
York	HRE Series	H1RE024S06	13.80	15.50	12.30	14.15
AirPro, Coleman, Coleman-Evcon, Guardian, Kenmore, United Refrigeration	AirPro 14, Coleman 14, Coleman-Evcon 14, Guardian, Kenmore 14, NCP	FRCS0241BD	13.80	15.50	12.30	13.90
Trane	B. XL 1400	TTY024B	11.85	15.50	10.95	13.55
American Standard	B. Allegiance 14	7A4024B	11.85	15.50	10.95	13.55
Arcoaire, Comfortmaker, United Refrigeration	AJ Series	AJ024*KA*	15.00	15.00	13.0	13.00
Bryant	Bryant Puron Two Speed Plus	598BN024-A*	14.00	15.00	10.80	11.85
Carrier	WeatherMaker Two Speed w/Puron	38TDB02430	14.00	15.00	10.80	11.85
Goodman, GmC, Janitrol	CKQ Series	CKQ24-1	13.50	15.00	12.50	13.80
Arcoaire, Comfortmaker, United Refrigeration	AJ Series	AJ024*GA*	13.05	15.00	11.35	13.00
Airquest, Heil, Kenmore, Tempstar, United Refrigeration	9600 AC Series, NCP	CA9624*KB*	13.05	15.00	11.35	13.00
Kenmore, Tempstar	Kenmore Supreme, SmartComfort 2400	TCA424AKA**	12.80	15.00	11.40	13.20
Airquest, Arcoaire, Heil, Kenmore, Maratherm	HAC Series	HAC424AKA**	12.80	15.00	11.40	13.20
Comfortmaker, Everest	CAC Series	CAC424A(G)KA**	12.80	15.00	11.40	13.20
Lennox	Elite 14	HS27-024-1P	12.80	15.00	11.55	13.20
Cooling Capacity: Approximately 2.5 Tons						
York	Stealth	H4TS030S06	13.50	16.00	12.00	14.44
Amana	Prestige Ultra	RCE30A2*	13.50	16.00	12.70	13.55
Lennox	Elite 14	HS27-030-1P	13.00	16.00	11.40	13.95
Bryant	Quantum Plus 556A	556AN030-A/C/D/E	13.50	15.75	11.70	14.00
Carrier	WeatherMaker 38TSA	38TSA03032	13.50	15.75	11.70	14.00
York	HRE Series	H1RE030S06	13.50	15.50	12.40	14.00
AirPro, Coleman, Coleman-Evcon, Guardian, Kenmore, United Refrigeration	AirPro14, Coleman 14, Coleman-Evcon 14, Guardian, Kenmore 14, NCP	FRCS0301BD	13.50	15.50	12.40	14.00

MOST EFFICIENT CENTRAL AIR-CONDITIONERS (cont.)

Manufacturer	Trade Name	Condenser Model	SEER range min	SEER range max	EER range min	EER range max
Cooling Capacity: Approximately 2.5 Tons (cont.)						
Fraser-Johnston, Luxaire	HBE Series, Atlas-Butler	HABE-F030S	13.50	15.50	12.40	14.00
Trane	B. XL 1400	TTY030B	11.80	15.35	10.95	13.60
American Standard	B. Allegiance 14	7A4030B	11.80	15.35	10.85	13.60
Arcoaire, Comfortmaker, United Refrigeration	AJ Series	AJ030*GB*	13.05	15.05	11.30	12.70
Airquest, Heil, Kenmore, Tempstar	9600 AC Series	CA9630*KC*	12.70	15.05	11.20	12.70
Kenmore, Tempstar	Kenmore Supreme, SmartComfort 2400	TCA430*KA*	13.60	15.00	12.70	13.40
Goodman, GmC, Janitrol	CKQ Series	CKQ30-1A	13.50	15.00	12.50	13.80
Kenmore, Tempstar	Kenmore Supreme, SmartComfort 2400	TCA430AKA**	13.20	15.00	12.50	13.90
Airquest, Arcoaire, Heil, Kenmore, Maratherm	HAC Series	HAC430AKA**	13.20	15.00	12.40	13.90
Comfortmaker, Everest	CAC Series	CAC430A(G)KA**	13.20	15.00	12.40	12.40
American Standard	A1. Allegiance 14	4A7A4030A1	12.00	15.00	10.60	12.65
Trane	A0. XL 14i	4TTX4030A1	12.00	15.00	10.60	12.65
Cooling Capacity: Approximately 3.0 Tons						
Trane	A. XL 1800	TTZ036A	15.85	18.00	11.35	13.20
Carrier	WeatherMaker Two Speed w/Puron	38TDB037300	15.50	18.00	11.45	13.15
American Standard	A. Allegiance 16	7A6036A	15.20	17.20	11.00	11.00
Carrier	Synergy 2000	38TDA03630	15.00	17.10	10.05	12.00
Carrier	WeatherMaker Two Speed w/Puron	38TDB03630	14.50	16.50	10.65	12.85
Bryant	Bryant Puron Two Speed Plus	598BN036-A 598BN036-A*	14.50	16.50	10.65	12.85
Amana	Prestige Ultra	RCE36A2*	13.60	16.50	11.95	11.95
York	Stealth	H4TS036S06	15.00	16.00	13.35	14.40
Carrier	WeatherMaker Two Speed w/Puron	38TDB036030	15.00	16.00	11.55	12.60
Bryant	Two Speed Plus	598AN036-C/D	14.00	16.00	10.10	11.95
Fraser-Johnston, Luxaire	HBE Series, Atlas-Butler	HABE-F036S	13.30	16.00	11.90	14.35

MOST EFFICIENT CENTRAL AIR-CONDITIONERS (cont.)

Manufacturer	Trade Name	Condenser Model	SEER range min	max	EER range min	max
Cooling Capacity: Approximately 3.0 Tons (cont.)						
AirPro, Coleman, Coleman-Evcon, Guardian, Kenmore, United Refrigeration	AirPro14, Coleman 14, Coleman-Evcon 14, Guardian, Kenmore 14, NCP	FRCS0361CD	13.30	16.00	11.90	14.35
York	HRE Series	H1RE036S06	13.30	16.00	11.90	14.35
Trane	B. XL 1400	TTY036B	12.40	15.80	11.35	13.85
Bryant	Quantum Plus 556A	556AN036-A/C/D/E	13.20	15.75	11.60	14.10
Carrier	WeatherMaker 38TSA	38TSA03632	13.20	15.75	11.60	14.05
Lennox	Power Saver	HS21-036-*P HS21-411-1P,2P	11.60	15.75	9.40	11.15
Trane	A1. XR1400 Earth*Wise™	RTY036A	14.05	15.60	12.25	13.25
Lennox	Elite 14	HS27-036-1P	13.00	15.60	11.25	13.50
American Standard	B. Allegiance 14	7A4036B	12.35	15.55	11.25	13.60
Carrier	WeatherMaker Two Speed w/Puron	38TDB036	15.50	15.50	11.25	11.25
Lennox	Elite 13 w/R-410A Refrigerant	HS32-036-1P	13.05	15.15	11.05	12.80
Goodman, GmC, Janitrol	CKQ Series	CKQ36-1A	13.50	15.00	12.50	13.80
Cooling Capacity: Approximately 3.5 Tons						
Amana	Prestige Ultra	RCE42A2*	14.00	16.00	12.10	14.00
AirPro, Coleman, Coleman-Evcon, Guardian, Kenmore, United Refrigeration	AirPro 14, Coleman 14, Coleman-Evcon 14, Guardian, Kenmore 14, NCP	FRCS0421CE	13.25	15.50	11.30	13.20
York	HRE Series	H2RE042S06	13.25	15.50	11.30	13.20
Fraser-Johnston, Luxaire	HBE Series, Atlas-Butler	HBBE-F042S	13.25	15.50	11.30	13.20
Airquest, Arcoaire, Heil, Kenmore, Maratherm	HAC Series	HAC442AKA**	13.50	15.40	11.90	13.10
Comfortmaker, Everest	CAC Series	CAC442A(G)KA**	13.50	15.40	11.90	13.10
Kenmore, Tempstar	Kenmore Supreme, SmartComfort 2400	TCA442AKA**	13.50	15.40	11.90	13.10
Lennox	Elite 14	HS27-042-1P	13.00	15.35	11.35	13.20
Carrier	WeatherMaker 38TSA	38TSA04232	13.20	15.10	11.50	13.60
Bryant	Quantum Plus 556A	556AN042-A/C/D/E	13.20	15.10	11.50	13.60
American Standard	A1. Allegiance 14	4A7A4042A1	12.00	15.00	10.60	12.25
Trane	A0. XL 14i	4TTX4042A1	12.00	15.00	10.65	12.25

MOST EFFICIENT CENTRAL AIR-CONDITIONERS (cont.)

Manufacturer	Trade Name	Condenser Model	SEER range min	SEER range max	EER range min	EER range max
Cooling Capacity: Approximately 4.0 Tons						
Trane	A. XL 1800	TTZ048A	15.15	16.50	10.75	12.30
American Standard	A. Allegiance 16	7A6048A	15.10	16.40	10.15	11.60
York	Stealth	H4TS048S06	14.00	16.00	12.20	14.50
Rheem	Rheem RANB Series	RANB-049JA	11.20	15.60	9.90	13.00
Ruud	Ruud UANB Series	UANB-049JA	11.20	15.60	9.90	13.00
Carrier	WeatherMaker Two Speed w/Puron	38TDB04830	14.00	15.50	10.15	11.85
Bryant	Bryant Puron Two Speed Plus	598BN048-A 598BN048-A*	13.50	15.50	9.70	11.85
Amana	Prestige Ultra	RCE48A2*	13.20	15.50	11.65	13.55
AirPro, Coleman, Coleman-Evcon, Guardian, Kenmore, United Refrigeration	AirPro 14, Coleman 14, Coleman-Evcon 14, Guardian, Kenmore 14, NCP	FRCS0481CE	13.00	15.50	11.25	13.65
York	HRE Series	H2RE048S06	13.00	15.50	11.25	13.25
Fraser-Johnston, Luxaire	HBE Series, Atlas-Butler	HBBE-F048S	13.00	15.50	11.25	13.25
Carrier	Synergy 2000	38TDA04830	13.80	15.30	9.50	10.80
Trane	A1. XR1400 Earth*Wise™	RTY048A	13.85	15.15	11.85	12.90
Cooling Capacity: Approximately 5.0 Tons						
Trane	A. XL 1800	TTZ060A	14.35	16.40	9.95	10.90
American Standard	A. Allegiance 16	7A6060A	14.85	15.80	9.80	10.35
York	Stealth	H4TS060S06	13.50	15.50	12.00	14.00
AirPro, Coleman, Coleman-Evcon, Kenmore	AirPro 14, Coleman 14, Coleman-Evcon 14, Kenmore 14	FRCS0601CE	13.00	15.25	11.60	13.70
York	HRE Series	H1RE060S06	13.00	15.25	11.60	13.70
Fraser-Johnston, Luxaire	HBE Series, Atlas-Butler	HABE-F060S	13.00	15.25	11.60	13.70
Carrier	WeatherMaker Two Speed w/Puron	38TDB06030	14.00	15.00	9.45	10.80
Bryant	Bryant Puron Two Speed Plus	598BN060-A 598BN060-A*	13.50	15.00	9.15	10.80
Amana	Prestige Ultra	RCE60A2*	13.00	14.50	11.05	13.10

CENTRAL HEAT PUMPS

Central heat pumps provide both cooling in the summer and heating in the winter. However, heat pumps generally do not perform well over extended periods of sub-freezing temperatures. The cooling performance of heat pumps, like that of central air conditioners, is rated as a SEER. Heating performance is measured by the heating season performance factor (HSPF), a ratio of the estimated seasonal heating output divided by the seasonal power consumption for an average U.S. climate. The current national efficiency standard for new heat pumps requires a minimum HSPF of 6.8 and a minimum SEER of 10. In 2006, a new standard for central air conditioners and heat pumps will take effect, but the final performance level has not been set because of ongoing litigation.

The heat pumps listed below are grouped by their heating and cooling capacities. In warmer climates, SEER and EER are more important than HSPF; in colder climates, focus on getting the highest HSPF feasible. In addition to this list, you can find guidance on high-performance products at www.energystar.gov and www.cee1.org. For the most efficient equipment, ACEEE recommends SEER at least 14.5 and HSPF in the range of 9.0.

The list below provides manufacturer, trade name, and condenser model. Depending on the indoor unit installed, SEER and HSPF can vary significantly within the ranges provided below. When purchasing a new system, check with your contractor or visit the Air-Conditioning and Refrigeration Institute (www.ari.org) to see the specific SEER and HSPF values for the combination you are considering.

MOST EFFICIENT CONVENTIONAL (AIR SOURCE) HEAT PUMPS								
			SEER range		EER range		HSPF range	
Manufacturer	Trade Name	Condenser Model	min	max	min	max	min	max
Cooling Capacity: Approximately 2.0 Tons								
York	ERE Series	E1RE024S06	14.00	16.00	12.15	13.70	8.50	9.00
Fraser-Johnston, Luxaire	EBE Series, Atlas-Butler	EABE-F024S	14.00	16.00	12.15	13.70	8.50	9.00
Airpro, Coleman, Coleman-Evcon, Guardian, Kenmore, United Refrigeration	AirPro 14, Coleman 14, Coleman-Evcon 14, Guardian, Kenmore 14, NCP	FRHS0241CD	14.00	16.00	12.15	13.70	8.50	9.00
Lennox	Elite 14	HP27-024-*P	13.25	15.05	11.40	12.95	8.25	9.00
Comfortmaker, Everest	CHP Series	CHP424A(G)KA*	14.00	15.00	12.25	13.40	7.95	8.10
Airquest, Arcoaire, Heil, Kenmore, Maratherm	HHP Series	HHP424AKA*	14.00	15.00	12.25	13.40	7.95	8.10

MOST EFFICIENT CONVENTIONAL (AIR SOURCE) HEAT PUMPS (cont.)

Manufacturer	Trade Name	Condenser Model	SEER range min	max	EER range min	max	HSPF range min	max
Cooling Capacity: Approximately 2.0 Tons (cont.)								
Kenmore, Tempstar	Kenmore Supreme, SmartComfort 2400	TCH424AKA*	14.00	15.00	12.25	13.40	7.95	8.10
Amana	TempAssure Ultra	RHF24A2A	12.75	15.00	12.25	14.30	8.00	8.50
American Standard	Heritage 14	4A6H4024A1	11.75	15.00	10.85	13.20	7.35	8.40
Trane	XL14i Weathertron	4TWX4024A1	11.75	15.00	10.85	13.20	7.35	8.40
Carrier	Tech 2000 38YSA	38YSA02431 38YSA02432	12.50	14.70	11.20	12.80	8.00	8.60
Carrier	WeatherMaker 38YXA	38YXA02432	12.50	14.50	10.95	12.60	7.40	8.00
Bryant	Quantum Plus 650A	650AN024-D	12.50	14.50	10.95	12.60	7.40	8.00
Rheem	Rheem RPPA Series	RPPA-025JA	12.00	14.40	10.70	12.35	8.40	8.75
Ruud	Ruud UPPA Series	UPPA-025JA	12.00	14.40	10.70	12.35	8.40	8.75
Weatherking	WeatherKing WPPA Series	WPPA-025JA	12.00	14.40	10.70	12.35	8.40	8.75
Cooling Capacity: Approximately 2.5 Tons								
Carrier	Tech 2000 38YSA	38YSA03031 38YSA03032	13.00	15.50	11.05	12.85	7.80	9.00
Lennox	Elite 14	HP27-030*P	13.30	15.25	11.70	13.05	8.50	9.15
Amana	TempAssure Ultra	RHF30A2A	13.40	15.00	11.60	12.85	8.30	8.85
Comfortmaker, Everest	CHP Series	CHP430A(G)KA*	13.40	15.00	12.25	13.85	7.95	8.30
Airquest, Arcoaire, Heil, Kenmore, Maratherm	HHP Series	HHP430AKA*	13.40	15.00	12.25	13.85	7.95	8.30
Kenmore, Tempstar	Kenmore Supreme, SmartComfort 2400	TCH430AKA*	13.40	15.00	12.25	13.85	7.95	8.30
Fraser-Johnston, Luxaire	EBE Series, Atlas-Butler	EABE-F030S	13.00	15.00	11.65	13.10	8.00	9.25
Airpro, Coleman, Coleman-Evcon, Guardian, Kenmore, United Refrigeration	AirPro 14, Coleman 14, Coleman-Evcon 14, Guardian, Kenmore 14, NCP	FRHS0301CD	13.00	15.00	11.65	13.10	8.00	9.25
York	ERE Series	E1RE030S06	13.00	15.00	11.65	13.10	8.00	9.20
Lennox	Elite 13 with R-410A Refrigerant	HP32-30-230* HPXA15-030-230*	12.50	14.75	10.55	12.35	7.50	8.30
American Standard	Heritage 14	4A6H4030A1	11.75	14.75	10.70	12.55	7.65	9.00
Trane	XL14i Weathertron	4TWX4030A1	11.75	14.75	10.70	12.55	7.65	9.00
Lennox	Elite 13	HP26-030-*P	12.80	14.70	11.20	12.65	8.30	8.85
Carrier	WeatherMaker 38YXA	38YXA03032	12.20	14.50	10.75	12.55	7.40	8.10
Bryant	Quantum Plus 650A	650AN030-D	12.20	14.50	10.75	12.55	7.40	8.10

MOST EFFICIENT CONVENTIONAL (AIR SOURCE) HEAT PUMPS (cont.)

Manufacturer	Trade Name	Condenser Model	SEER range min	max	EER range min	max	HSPF range min	max
		Cooling Capacity: Approximately 3.0 Tons						
Trane	XL 1800 Weathertron	TWZ036A	16.05	17.65	11.60	12.90	8.10	8.55
American Standard	Heritage 16	6H6036A	16.00	17.35	11.20	12.45	8.00	8.50
Carrier	WeatherMaker Two Speed w/Puron	38YDB03730	16.00	17.00	12.35	13.00	8.60	9.50
Amana	TempAssure Ultra	RHF36A2A	13.20	16.00	12.00	13.90	7.80	8.80
Carrier	WeatherMaker Two Speed w/Puron	38YDB03630	12.50	16.00	10.30	11.75	7.70	8.80
Bryant	Bryant Puron Two Speed Plus	698BN036-A	12.50	16.00	10.30	11.75	7.70	8.80
York	ERE Series	E1RE036S06	13.00	15.60	11.55	13.40	8.00	9.00
Fraser-Johnston, Luxaire	EBE Series, Atlas-Butler	EABE-F036S	13.00	15.60	11.55	13.40	8.00	9.00
Airpro, Coleman, Coleman-Evcon, Guardian, Kenmore, United Refrigeration	AirPro 14, Coleman 14, Coleman-Evcon 14, Guardian, Kenmore 14, NCP	FRHS0361CD	13.00	15.60	11.55	13.40	8.00	9.00
Comfortmaker, Everest	CHP Series	CHP436A(G)KA*	13.70	15.00	11.90	13.00	8.95	9.10
Airquest, Arcoaire, Heil, Kenmore, Maratherm	HHP Series	HHP436AKA*	13.70	15.00	11.90	13.00	8.95	9.10
Kenmore, Tempstar	Kenmore Supreme, SmartComfort 2400	TCH436AKA*	13.70	15.00	11.90	13.00	8.95	9.10
Lennox	Elite 14	HP27-036-*P	13.50	15.00	11.40	12.70	8.00	8.80
American Standard	Heritage 14	4A6H4036A1	12.00	15.00	10.80	12.65	7.85	9.85
Trane	XL14i Weathertron	4TWX4036A1	12.00	15.00	10.80	12.65	7.85	9.85
Carrier	Tech 2000 38YSA	38YSA03631 38YSA03632	12.50	14.70	10.75	12.40	7.30	9.40
Lennox	Power Saver	HP21-36-230*	12.00	14.65	9.20	10.35	7.55	8.50
Carrier	WeatherMaker 38YXA	38YXA03632	12.25	14.50	10.40	12.25	7.30	9.00
Bryant	Quantum Plus 650A	650AN036-D	12.25	14.50	10.40	12.25	7.30	9.00
		Cooling Capacity: Approximately 3.5 Tons						
Lennox	Power Saver	HP21-48-230-*	12.05	16.15	9.75	11.80	7.20	8.50
York	ERE Series	E1RE042S06	13.00	15.20	11.10	13.15	8.00	9.25
Fraser-Johnston, Luxaire	EBE Series, Atlas-Butler	EABE-F042S	13.00	15.20	11.10	13.15	8.50	9.25
Airpro, Coleman, Coleman-Evcon, Guardian, Kenmore, United Refrigeration	AirPro 14, Coleman 14, Coleman-Evcon 14, Guardian, Kenmore 14, NCP	FRHS0421CD	13.00	15.20	11.10	13.15	8.50	9.25

MOST EFFICIENT CONVENTIONAL (AIR SOURCE) HEAT PUMPS (cont.)

Manufacturer	Trade Name	Condenser Model	SEER range		EER range		HSPF range	
			min	max	min	max	min	max
Cooling Capacity: Approximately 3.5 Tons (cont.)								
Amana	TempAssure Ultra	RHF42A2A	13.00	15.20	11.80	14.25	7.80	8.80
American Standard	Heritage 14	4A6H4042A1	12.00	14.25	10.40	12.20	7.55	9.70
Trane	XL14i Weathertron	4TWX4042A1	12.00	14.25	10.40	12.20	7.55	9.70
Lennox	Elite 14	HP27-042-*P	12.40	14.20	10.30	11.80	7.80	8.50
Carrier	Tech 2000 38YSA	38YSA04231 38YSA04232	12.20	14.20	10.65	12.05	7.50	8.80
Cooling Capacity: Approximately 4.0 Tons								
American Standard	Heritage 16	6H6048A	14.50	16.30	10.20	11.60	7.75	8.65
Trane	XL 1800 Weathertron	TWZ048A	14.70	16.15	9.95	11.30	7.75	8.25
York	ERE Series	E1RE048S06	12.65	15.30	11.10	13.35	7.85	9.20
Fraser-Johnston, Luxaire	EBE Series, Atlas-Butler	EABE-F048S	12.65	15.30	11.10	13.35	7.85	9.20
Airpro, Coleman, Coleman-Evcon, Guardian, Kenmore, United Refrigeration	AirPro 14, Coleman 14, Coleman-Evcon 14, Guardian, Kenmore 14, NCP	FRHS0481BD	12.65	15.30	11.10	13.35	7.85	9.20
Amana	TempAssure Ultra	RHF48A2A	13.00	15.00	11.65	13.15	7.30	9.00
Carrier	WeatherMaker Two Speed w/Puron	38YDB04830	12.00	14.50	9.55	11.10	8.00	9.10
Bryant	Bryant Puron Two Speed Plus	698BN048-A	12.00	14.50	9.55	11.10	8.00	9.10
Armstrong	Armstrong, American Aire, Air-Ease, Magic-Pak	SHP14M48A	13.10	14.40	11.30	12.10	7.10	8.00
Cooling Capacity: Approximately 5.0 Tons								
American Standard	Heritage 16	6H6060A	14.25	15.70	9.15	10.20	8.00	8.65
Trane	XL 1800 Weathertron	TWZ060A	14.25	15.30	9.35	9.85	8.00	8.40
American Standard, Trane	American-Standard, Trane Weathertron	WCZ060F100B*	15.05	15.05	10.50	10.50	8.10	8.10
Carrier	WeatherMaker Two Speed w/Puron	38YDB06030	12.00	14.50	8.85	10.25	7.50	8.50
Bryant	Bryant Puron Two Speed Plus	698BN060-A	12.00	14.50	8.85	10.25	7.50	8.50

FURNACES AND BOILERS

The efficiency of new furnaces and boilers is given as the annual fuel utilization efficiency (AFUE), a measure of overall performance. The federal minimum-efficiency standards for furnaces and boilers took effect in 1992, requiring that new furnace units have an AFUE of at least 78% and new boiler units have an AFUE of at least 80%. In comparison, many old furnaces and boilers have AFUE ratings of only 55–65%.

Most new gas furnaces tend to be grouped in one of two general classes of efficiency: power combustion at 80–82% AFUE and "condensing" furnaces that are at least 90% efficient. Condensing furnaces are more economical in cold regions. Furthermore, condensing furnaces are much less likely to suffer from corrosion caused by condensation in the unit or its flue and chimney. Only a few oil-fired condensing furnaces and boilers are available.

When buying a new furnace, make sure its heating capacity is appropriate for your home. If the insulation and/or windows in your home have been upgraded since the old heating equipment was installed, you can probably use a much less powerful furnace or boiler. Oversized furnaces operate less efficiently because they cycle on and off more frequently; in addition, larger furnaces are more expensive to buy. Two-speed or modulating furnaces tend to work better and are less sensitive to oversizing. Insist that your contractor do a heat loss analysis of your home to size your new heating equipment properly, whether fixed-capacity or modulating.

A furnace can also use a significant amount of electricity to power its motors and fans to move air through your house. We list below the estimated amount of electricity that will be used in an average heating season by each model. The actual amount of electricity used in your home will vary with your local weather and home characteristics.

The models listed are appropriate for cold climates. "Southern" models are equipped with larger fans (for use with central air conditioning during the cooling season) and will use more electricity. At this time, the best advice for Southern installations is to select a cooling system with a high SEER (at least 14.5) and EER (at least 11.6), and to specify a variable speed blower motor. Additional information on specific models can be found on the Gas Appliance Manufacturers Association's website (www.gamanet.org).

MOST EFFICIENT GAS FURNACES

Manufacturer	Trade Name	Model Number	Capacity (Btu/hr)	Electric Energy (kWh/yr)	AFUE
25,000 to 42,000 Btu/hr heating capacity					
Bryant	Bryant, Plus 90I	355MAV042040-L	25,000	84	96.6
Carrier	Carrier, Weathermaker (Infinity)	58MVP040-14-L	25,000	84	96.6
Bryant	Bryant, Plus 90I	355MAV042040	38,000	105	96.6
Carrier	Carrier, Weathermaker (Infinity)	58MVP040-14	38,000	105	96.6
Bryant	Bryant, Plus 90I	355MAV042040-L**	25,000	85	96.1
Carrier	Carrier, Weathermaker (Infinity)	58MVP040-14-L**	25,000	85	96.1
Bryant	Bryant, Plus 90I	355MAV042040**	37,000	106	96.1
Carrier	Carrier, Weathermaker (Infinity)	58MVP040-14**	37,000	106	96.1
Bryant	Bryant, Plus 90I	355MAV042040-L*	25,000	86	95.0
Carrier	Carrier, Weathermaker (Infinity)	58MVP040-14-L*	25,000	86	95.0
Bryant	Bryant, Plus 90I	355MAV042040*	37,000	107	95.0
Carrier	Carrier, Weathermaker (Infinity)	58MVP040-14*	37,000	107	95.0
Armstrong	Armstrong, Air-Ease, American Aire	G2D95AC040V12B*-***	38,000	180	94.5
Armstrong	Armstrong, Air-Ease, American Aire	G2D95AU040V12B*-***	38,000	180	94.5
43,000 to 59,000 Btu/hr heating capacity					
Amana	Amana	GUVA045*30	45,000	165	96.0
Buy Max	Xenon Heating and Air Conditioning	XF9V0453A	45,000	165	96.0
Armstrong	Armstrong, Air-Ease, American Aire	G2D95AC060V14B*-***	57,000	202	94.5
Armstrong	Armstrong, Air-Ease, American Aire	G2D95AU060V14C*-***	57,000	202	94.5
Thermo-Products	Thermo Pride	CHBI-50	47,000	309	94.5
Bryant	Bryant, Plus 90I	355MAV060080-L	49,000	84	94.1
Carrier	Carrier, Weathermaker (Infinity)	58MVP080-20-L	49,000	84	94.1
Bryant	Bryant, Plus 90I	355MAV042060	57,000	95	94.1
Carrier	Carrier, Weathermaker (Infinity)	58MVP060-14	57,000	95	94.1
Bryant	Bryant, Plus 90I	355MAV042080-L	49,000	96	94.1
Carrier	Carrier, Weathermaker (Infinity)	58MVP080-14-L	49,000	96	94.1
Rheem	Rheem	RGFD-06(E,N)MCKS	56,000	351	94.1
Ruud	Ruud	UGFD-06(E,N)MCKS	56,000	351	94.1
Coleman	Coleman-Evcon, AirPro, Guardian, NCP, Red T, Coleman	G9V06012UPB11	57,000	243	94.0
Fraser-Johnston	Fraser-Johnston	G9V06012UPB11	57,000	243	94.0
Luxaire	Luxaire	G9V06012UPB11	57,000	243	94.0
York	York, Stellar, Diamond, Sunline	P1XUB12V05501	57,000	243	94.0
60,000 to 76,000 Btu/hr heating capacity					
Amana	Amana	GUVA070*X40	67,000	275	95.5
Buy Max	Xenon Heating and Air Conditioning	XF9V0704A	67,000	275	95.5
Thermo Products	Thermo Pride	CHX1-75N	71,000	173	94.5

MOST EFFICIENT GAS FURNACES (cont.)

Manufacturer	Trade Name	Model Number	Capacity (Btu/hr)	Electric Energy (kWh/yr)	AFUE
60,000 to 76,000 Btu/hr heating capacity (cont.)					
Armstrong	Armstrong, Air-Ease, American Aire	G2D95AC080V16C*-***	76,000	250	94.5
Armstrong	Armstrong, Air-Ease, American Aire	G2D95AU080V16C*-***	76,000	250	94.5
Armstrong	Armstrong, Air-Ease, American Aire	G2D95AC080V20C*-***	76,000	280	94.5
Armstrong	Armstrong, Air-Ease, American Aire	G2D95AU080V20C*-***	76,000	280	94.5
Bryant	Bryant, Plus 90I	355MAV060080	75,000	103	94.1
Carrier	Carrier, Weathermaker (Infinity)	58MVP080-20	75,000	103	94.1
Bryant	Bryant, Plus 90I	355MAV060100-L	61,000	161	94.1
Carrier	Carrier, Weathermaker (Infinity)	58MVP100-20-L	61,000	161	94.1
Bryant	Bryant, Plus 90I	355MAV060120-L	73,000	161	94.1
Carrier	Carrier, Weathermaker (Infinity)	58MVP120-20-L	73,000	161	94.1
Lennox	3Dimension	G32V3-75-**	71,000	315	94.0
77,000 to 93,000 Btu/hr heating capacity					
Amana	Amana	GUVA090*X50	90,000	333	95.7
Buy Max	Xenon Heating and Air Conditioning	XF9V0905A	90,000	333	95.7
Bryant	Bryant, Plus 90I	355MAV042080	75,000	118	94.1
Carrier	Carrier, Weathermaker (Infinity)	58MVP080-14	80,000	118	94.1
Rheem	Rheem	RGFD-09(E,N)ZCMS**	85,000	386	94.1
Ruud	Ruud	UGFD-09(E,N)ZCMS**	85,000	386	94.1
94,000 to 110,000 Btu/hr heating capacity					
Amana	Amana	GUVA115*X50	109,000	397	95.8
Buy Max	Xenon Heating and Air Conditioning	XF9V1155A	109,000	397	95.8
Armstrong	Armstrong, Air-Ease, American Aire	G2D95AC100V20D*-***	95,000	280	94.5
Armstrong	Armstrong, Air-Ease, American Aire	G2D95AU100V20D*-***	95,000	280	94.5
Thermo-Products	Thermo Pride	CHX1-100N	100,000	340	94.5
Carrier	Carrier, Weathermaker (Infinity)	58MVP100-20	94,000	225	94.1
Bryant	Bryant, Plus 90I	355MAV060100	94,000	225	94.1
Lennox	3Dimension	G32V5-100-**	95,000	599	94.0
111,000 to 127,000 Btu/hr heating capacity					
Lennox	3Dimension	G32V5-125-**	118,000	547	94.2
Bryant	Bryant, Plus 90I	355MAV060120	113,000	258	94.1
Carrier	Carrier, Weathermaker (Infinity)	58MVP120-20	113,000	258	94.1
Thermo-Products	Thermo Pride	CHX1-125N	117,000	359	94.0
Armstrong	Armstrong, Air-Ease, American Aire	G2D95AC125V20D*-***	118,000	370	94.0
Armstrong	Armstrong, Air-Ease, American Aire	G2D95AU125V20D*-***	118,000	370	94.0
York	York, Stellar, Diamond, Sunline	P1XUD20V11201	112,000	740	94.0

MOST EFFICIENT GAS HOT WATER BOILERS

Manufacturer	Trade Name	Model Number	Capacity (Btu/hr)	Electric Energy (kWh/yr)	AFUE
Less than 43,000 Btu/hr Heating Capacity					
GlowCore	GlowCore	GB040A	35,520		94.1
Slant/Fin	Slant/Fin Prodigy 21 Series	KC45	38,000	134	86.3
Slant/Fin	Slant/Fin Concept 21 Series	CB-45	39,000	188	85.6
Weil-McLain	Weil-McLain	AHE-45	38,000	136	85.3
Slant/Fin	Slant/Fin Victory II Series	VHS-30EP	26,000	276	84.5
Waterpik Technologies	Laars, Mini-Therm	JVS050ND(I,L)	42,000	98	84.4
Carrier	Carrier, Bryant, Day and Night, Payne	BW3AAN000042ABAA	36,000	269	84.4
Dunkirk	Dunkirk	XEB-2	36,000	269	84.4
Lennox	Lennox	GWB8-0421E	36,000	269	84.4
Pennco	Pennco	FSB-2	36,000	269	84.4
Sears	Kenmore	229.965520	36,000	269	84.4
43,000 to 59,000 Btu/hr Heating Capacity					
Burnham	Opus	G1-50	47,000	341	99.0
GlowCore	GlowCore	GB060A	53,400		94.1
Carrier	Carrier, Bryant, Day and Night, Payne	BW9AAN0000050AAAA	45,000	194	90.0
Dunkirk	Dunkirk Quantum 90	Q90-50	45,000	195	90.0
Lennox	Conservator 90	GWB9-050IH	45,000	195	90.0
Sears	Kenmore	K90-50	45,000	195	90.0
Burnham	Burnham Revolution	RV3(N,P)S(L,P)-	55,000	225	88.0
Slant/Fin	Slant/Fin Prodigy 21	KC50	43,000	233	87.3
Utica	Utica	USC-3	44,000	228	87.0
Slant/Fin	Slant/Fin Prodigy 21	KCS-50	43,000	252	86.0
Weil-McLain	Weil-McLain	AHE-60	51,000	153	85.5
Weil-McLain	Weil-McLain	CGs-3-PIN	57,000	274	85.3
International Comfort Products	Comfort Maker, Heil, Tempstar	GWS-063N-I	54,000	291	85.3
Williamson-Thermoflo	Thermoflo, Williamson	GWS-063N-I	54,000	291	85.3
60,000 to 76,000 Btu/hr Heating Capacity					
Burnham	Opus	G1-125 (75)	70,000	309	98.0
Heat Transfer Products	Munchkin	80M	74,000	76	92.0
Peerless	Pinnacle	PI 80	74,000	76	92.0
Carrier	Carrier, Bryant, Day and Night, Payne	BW9AAN000075AAAA	68,000	174	90.0
Dunkirk	Dunkirk Quantum 90	Q90-75	68,000	174	90.0
Lennox	Conservator 90	GWB9-075IH	68,000	174	90.0
Sears	Kenmore	K90-75	68,000	174	90.0
Energy Kinetics	System 2000	EK-1	69,000	236	88.0

MOST EFFICIENT GAS HOT WATER BOILERS (cont.)

Manufacturer	Trade Name	Model Number	Capacity (Btu/hr)	Electric Energy (kWh/yr)	AFUE
60,000 to 76,000 Btu/hr Heating Capacity (cont.)					
Weil-McLain	Weil-Mclain	GV-3	61,000	243	87.5
Slant/Fin	Slant/Fin Prodigy 21	KC90	75,000	181	85.8
Viessmann	Viessmann Vitogas 100	GSI-22	76,000	130	85.6
Dunkirk	Dunkirk EV	DPFG-3T-70	60,000	276	85.0
Ultimate	Ultimate	PFG-3T-70	60,000	276	85.0
Buderus	Buderus	G124X-18DI	63,000	311	85.0
77,000 to 93,000 Btu/hr Heating Capacity					
Viessmann	Viessmann Vitodens 200	WB2 6-24	81,000	483	94.2
GlowCore	GlowCore	GB090A	79,920	n/a	92.6
Hydrotherm	Hydrotherm Hydro-Pulse	AM-100	90,000	77	90.4
Dunkirk	Dunkirk Quantum 90	Q90-100	90,000	164	90.0
Lennox	Conservator 90	GWB9-100IH	90,000	164	90.0
Sears	Kenmore	K90-100	90,000	164	90.0
Carrier	Carrier, Bryant, Day and Night, Payne	BW9AAN0000100AAAA	100,000	164	90.0
Energy Kinetics	System 2000	EK-1	85,000	217	88.0
Burnham	Burnham Revolution	RV4(N,P)S(L,P)-	84,000	232	87.6
Slant/Fin	Slant/Fin Prodigy 21	KC100	86,000	195	87.5
Weil-McLain	Weil-Mclain	GV-4	92,000	204	87.3
Utica	Utica	USC-4	87,000	192	87.0
Slant/Fin	Slant/Fin Prodigy 21	KCS-100	87,000	221	86.0
Slant/Fin	Slant/Fin Concept 21	CB-90	77,000	241	85.4
Buderus	Buderus	GA124-23	79,000	n/a	85.1
Dunkirk	Dunkirk	DPFG-4T-91	78,000	266	85.0
Ultimate	Ultimate	PFG-4T-91	78,000	266	85.0
Peerless	Peerless	PDE-04-HS	84,000	272	85.0
Buderus	Buderus	G124X-25DI	87,000	280	85.0
94,000 to 110,000 Btu/hr Heating Capacity					
Burnham	Opus	G1-125 (100)	94,000	349	98.0
Dunkirk	Dunkirk Quantum Leap	QL-100	95,000	205	95.0
Energy Kinetics	System 2000	EK-1	101,000	189	87.0
Viessmann	Viessman Vitogas 100	GSI-29	98,000	134	85.5
Waterpik Technologies	Laars, Endurance	EBP 110	94,000	360	85.5
Waterpik Technologies	Laars, Endurance	EDP 110	94,000	360	85.5
Buderus	Buderus	GA124-30	104,000	n/a	85.0
Dunkirk	Dunkirk EV	DPFG-5T-112	96,000	260	85.0
Ultimate	Ultimate	PFG-5T-112	96,000	260	85.0
Buderus	Buderus	G124X-32II	110,000	111	84.6
Slant/Fin	Slant/Fin Sentry	S-120ED	101,000	123	84.1

MOST EFFICIENT GAS HOT WATER BOILERS (cont.)

Manufacturer	Trade Name	Model Number	Capacity (Btu/hr)	Electric Energy (kWh/yr)	AFUE
		111,000 to 140,000 Btu/hr Heating Capacity			
Burnham	Opus	G1-125	117,000	326	98.0
Burnham	Opus	G1-250 (150)	140,000	314	97.0
Viessmann	Viessman Vitodens 200	WB2 8-32	112,000	483	94.1
GlowCore	GlowCore	GB130A	115,400	n/a	92.6
Heat Transfer Products	Munchkin	140M	129,000	89	92.0
Peerless	Pinnacle	PI 140	129,000	89	92.0
Hydrotherm	Hydrotherm Hydro-Pulse	AM-150	135,000	82	90.6
Dunkirk	Dunkirk Quantum 90	Q90-125	112,000	n/a	89.6
Sears	Kenmore	K90-125	112,000	n/a	89.6
Dunkirk	Dunkirk Quantum 90	Q90-150	134,000	n/a	89.6
Sears	Kenmore	K90-150	134,000	n/a	89.6
Waterpik Technologies	Laars, Heatmaker	CB-M2-150	135,000	286	88.6
Burnham	Burnham Revolution	RV5(N,P)S(L,P)-	114,000	238	87.4
Weil-McLain	Weil-Mclain	GV-5	122,000	214	87.2
Utica	Utica	USC-5	122,000	192	87.0

MOST EFFICIENT GAS STEAM BOILERS

Manufacturer	Trade Name	Model Number	Capacity (Btu/hr)	Electric Energy (kWh/yr)[†]	AFUE
		Less than 93,000 Btu/hr Heating Capacity			
Weil-McLain	Weil-McLain	PEG-35-PIDN-S	83,000		82.9
Weil-McLain	Weil-McLain	EG-35-PIDN-S	83,000		82.9
Burnham	Burnham Independence	IN4PVNI-	87,000	83	82.2
Burnham	Burnham Independence	IN4(S,L)(N,P)(I,S)-	87,000		82.0
New Yorker	New Yorker	CGS40A(N,P)I-	86,000		81.4
Crown Boiler	Crown	JSI103E	84,000	161	81.4
		94,000 to 110,000 Btu/hr Heating Capacity			
Weil-McLain	Weil-McLain	EG-40-PIDN-S	104,000		82.9
Weil-McLain	Weil-McLain	PEG-40-PIDN-S	104,000		82.6
Weil-McLain	Weil-McLain	PEG-40-SPDN-S	104,000		81.5
Weil-McLain	Weil-McLain	EG-40-SPDN-S	104,000		81.5
Williamson-Thermoflo	Thermoflo, Williamson	GSA-125N-S	104,000		81.5
Hydrotherm	Hydrotherm	VS-135BS-PV	110,000	113	81.5
Smith Cast Iron Boilers	Smith Cast Iron Boilers	GB200-S-4H-INTD	110,000	113	81.5

[†] **Electric energy consumption data is available for a limited number of gas-fired steam boilers.**

MOST EFFICIENT GAS STEAM BOILERS (cont.)

Manufacturer	Trade Name	Model Number	Capacity (Btu/hr)	Electric Energy (kWh/yr)[†]	AFUE
111,000 to 127,000 Btu/hr Heating Capacity					
Weil-McLain	Weil-McLain	EG-45-PIDN-S	125,000		82.9
Weil-McLain	Weil-McLain	PEG-45-PIDN-S	125,000		82.6
Burnham	Burnham Independence	IN5PVNI-	116,000	78	82.2
Burnham	Burnham Independence	IN5(S,L)(N,P)(I,S)-	115,000		82.0
Weil-McLain	Weil-McLain	PEG-45-SPDN-S	125,000		81.6
Weil-McLain	Weil-McLain	EG-45-SPDN-S	125,000		81.6
Williamson-Thermoflo	Thermoflo, Williamson	GSA-150N-S	125,000		81.6
New Yorker	New Yorker	CGS50A(N,P)I-	115,000		81.4
Crown Boiler	Crown	JSI138E	112,000	169	81.4
128,000 to 144,000 Btu/hr Heating Capacity					
Burnham	Burnham Independence	IN6(S,L)(N,P)(I,S)-	144,000		82.1
New Yorker	New Yorker	CGS60A(N,P)I-	143,000		81.4
Crown Boiler	Crown	JSI172E	140,000	155	81.4
Hydrotherm	Hydrotherm	VGA-175BS-PV	142,000	117	81.3
Smith Cast Iron Boilers	Smith Cast Iron Boilers	GB250-S-5L-INTD	142,000	117	81.3
Hydrotherm	Hydrotherm	VS-165BS-PV	134,000	124	81.2
Smith Cast Iron Boilers	Smith Cast Iron Boilers	GB200-S-5-INTD	134,000	124	81.2
Slant/Fin	Slant/Fin Galaxy	GXH-170EDPZ	137,000		81.1
145,000 to 178,000 Btu/hr Heating Capacity					
Weil-McLain	Weil-McLain	PEG-50-PIDN-S	145,000		82.8
Weil-McLain	Weil-McLain	EG-50-PIDN-S	145,000		82.8
Weil-McLain	Weil-McLain	PEG-55-PIDN-S	167,000		82.8
Weil-McLain	Weil-McLain	EG-55-PIDN-S	167,000		82.8
Burnham	Burnham Independence	IN6PVNI-	145,000	80	82.2
Burnham	Burnham Independence	IN7(S,L)(N,P)(I,S)-	173,000		82.1
Weil-McLain	Weil-Mclain	PEG-50-SPDN-S	145,000		81.9
Weil-McLain	Weil-Mclain	EG-50-SPDN-S	145,000		81.9
Williamson-Thermoflo	Thermoflo, Williamson	GSA-175N-S	145,000		81.9
Weil-McLain	Weil-Mclain	PEG-55-SPDN-S	167,000		81.9
Weil-McLain	Weil-Mclain	EG-55-SPDN-S	167,000		81.9
Williamson-Thermoflo	Thermoflo, Williamson	GSA-200N-S	167,000		81.9
Hydrotherm	Hydrotherm	VGA-200BS-PV	163,000	128	81.6

MOST EFFICIENT GAS STEAM BOILERS (cont.)

Manufacturer	Trade Name	Model Number	Capacity (Btu/hr)	Electric Energy (kWh/yr)[†]	AFUE
145,000 to 178,000 Btu/hr Heating Capacity (cont.)					
Smith Cast Iron Boilers	Smith Cast Iron Boilers	GB250-S-5H-INTD	163,000	128	81.6
New Yorker	New Yorker	CGS70A(N,P)I-	172,000		81.5
Crown Boiler	Crown	JSE207E	169,000	161	81.5
Slant/Fin	Slant/Fin Galaxy	GXH-210EDPZ	172,000		81.2

MOST EFFICIENT OIL FURNACES

Manufacturer	Trade Name	Model Number	Capacity (Btu/hr)	Electric Energy (kWh/yr)	AFUE
60,000 to 76,000 Btu/hr heating capacity					
Adams Manufacturing	Adams Manufacturing	AHEO 70-2.5 ASHEO 70-2.5	66,500	n/a	95.0
Dornback	Dornback	HEO 70-2.5 SHEO 70-2.5	66,500	n/a	95.0
Crown Boiler	Crown	CHC68-96*-85	71,000	605	84.6
Thermo-Products	ValPro, Xenon	VC-A-84	71,000	605	84.6
77,000 to 93,000 Btu/hr heating capacity					
Adams Manufacturing	Adams Manufacturing	AHEO 90-3.5 ASHEO 90-3.5	85,500	n/a	95.0
Dornback	Dornback	HEO 90-3.5 SHEO 90-3.5	85,500	n/a	95.0
Thermo-Products	Thermo Pride	OC5-85-V	83,000	561	86.0
Thermo-Products	Thermo Pride	OH5-85M	91,000	674	86.0
Thermo-Products	Thermo Pride	OH5-85-V	83,000	608	85.0
Crown Boiler	Crown	CHC68-96*-105	89,000	659	84.8
Thermo-Products	ValPro, Xenon	VC-A-105	89,000	659	84.8
94,000 to 110,000 Btu/hr heating capacity					
Adams Manufacturing	Adams Manufacturing	AHEO 105-4 ASHEO 105-4	99,750	n/a	95.0
Dornback	Dornback	HEO 105-4 SHEO 105-4	99,750	n/a	95.0
Thermo-Products	Thermo Pride	OH11-105M	107,000	610	85.0
Crown Boiler	Crown	CHC68-96*-120	100,000	782	84.5
Thermo-Products	ValPro, Xenon	VC-A-119	100,000	782	84.5

[†] **Electric energy consumption data is available for a limited number of gas-fired steam boilers.**

MOST EFFICIENT OIL FURNACES (cont.)

Manufacturer	Trade Name	Model Number	Capacity (Btu/hr)	Electric Energy (kWh/yr)	AFUE
111,000 to 130,000 Btu/hr heating capacity					
Williamson-Thermoflo	Thermoflo, Williamson	CHB-140*-1	116,000	1113	85.0
Williamson-Thermoflo	Thermoflo, Williamson	CCF-140*-1	116,000	1113	84.2
Thermo-Products	ValPro, Xenon	VC-A-140	116,000	830	84.0
Boyertown Furnace	Hallmark	HBD115*	114,000	936	83.2
Columbia Boiler	Columbia Warm Air Furnaces	CHB115*	114,000	936	83.2
Greater than 130,000 Btu/hr heating capacity					
Boyertown Furnace	Hallmark	HB145*/HB145C*	145,000	1328	85.9
Columbia Boiler	Columbia Warm Air Furnaces	CHB145*/CHB145C*	145,000	1328	85.9
Boyertown Furnace	Hallmark	HB160*/HB160C*	155,000	1244	85.1
Columbia Boiler	Columbia Warm Air Furnaces	CHB160*/CHB160C*	155,000	1244	85.1
Williamson-Thermoflo	Thermoflo, Williamson	CHB-140*-2	144,000	1136	84.2
Williamson-Thermoflo	Thermoflo, Williamson	CCF-140-2	144,000	1136	84.2

MOST EFFICIENT OIL HOT WATER BOILERS

Manufacturer	Trade Name	Model Number	Capacity (Btu/hr)	Electric Energy (kWh/yr)	AFUE
60,000 to 76,000 Btu/hr Heating Capacity					
Burnham	Opus	O1-1-60	76,000	230	90.1
Dunkirk Boilers	Dunkirk	DPFO-3T-.50	62,000	359	87.6
Melvin	Memco	CSTO-3T-.50	62,000	359	87.6
Ultimate	Ultimate	PFO-3T-.50	62,000	359	87.6
Dunkirk Boilers	Dunkirk	DPFO-4-.60	74,000	300	87.5
Melvin	Memco	CSTO-4-.60	74,000	300	87.5
Ultimate	Ultimate	PFO-4-.60	74,000	300	87.5
Viessmann	Viessmann	VB2-18*	72,000	248	87.1
Viessmann	Viessmann	VR2-18	67,000	251	86.7
Burnham	Burnham	LEDV1- /LE1-	74,000	538	86.7
New Yorker	New Yorker	MICROTEK3-1 MICROTEKDV-1	74,000	538	86.7
Buderus	Buderus	115-21	74,000	321	86.5
Viessmann	Viessmann	VB2-18	72,000	251	86.2
Pennco	Pennco	3K0.60	74,000	194	86.1
Peerless	Peerless	WBV-03-085R-W	74,000	314	86.1
77,000 to 93,000 Btu/hr Heating Capacity					
Newmac	Newmac	NBR 90V	91,000	271	89.1
Newmac	Newmac	NBR 91	92,000	291	88.3
Axeman-Anderson	Axeman-Anderson Olympia	OL-91D	80,000	374	88.0

MOST EFFICIENT OIL HOT WATER BOILERS (cont.)

Manufacturer	Trade Name	Model Number	Capacity (Btu/hr)	Electric Energy (kWh/yr)	AFUE
77,000 to 93,000 Btu/hr Heating Capacity (cont.)					
Energy Kinetics	System 2000	EK-1	83,000	270	87.9
Energy Kinetics	System 2000	EK-1	90,000	248	87.7
Crown Boiler	Crown Freeport	CTPR-3	92,000	274	87.6
Dunkirk Boilers	Dunkirk	DPFO-5-.75	93,000	301	87.5
Melvin	Memco	CSTO-5-.75	93,000	301	87.5
Ultimate	Ultimate	PFO-5-.75	93,000	301	87.5
Dunkirk Boilers	Dunkirk	DPFO-4T-.65	80,000	347	87.5
Melvin	Memco	CSTO-4T-.65	80,000	347	87.5
Ultimate	Ultimate	PFO-4T-.65	80,000	347	87.5
Viessmann	Viessmann Vitola 200	VB2-22*	92,000	241	87.2
Axeman-Anderson	Axeman-Anderson Olympia	OL-105D	92,000	332	87.2
Waterpik Technologies	Laars, Max	MAX 75	91,000	275	87.0
Waterpik Technologies	Laars, Max	DMAX 75	91,000	275	87.0
Viessmann	Viessmann Vitorond 220	VR2-22	80,000	244	86.8
Viessmann	Viessmann Vitorond 220	VR2-27	92,000	271	86.8
Crown Boiler	Crown Freeport	CTPB-3	92,000	278	86.6
Peerless	Peerless	EC/ECT-03-075W	92,000	313	86.6
94,000 to 110,000 Btu/hr Heating Capacity					
Burnham	Opus	O1-1-75	94,000	279	89.3
Newmac	Newmac	NBR 98V	98,000	300	88.9
Axeman-Anderson	Axeman-Anderson Co.	74NPO-UD	105,000	342	88.7
Newmac	Newmac	NBR 96V	97,000	322	88.6
Newmac	Newmac	NBR 100	100,000	316	88.0
New Yorker	New Yorker	FRHGS	100,000	357	87.8
Energy Kinetics	System 2000	EK-1	104,000	216	87.5
Dunkirk Boilers	Dunkirk	DPFO-5T-.80	99,000	339	87.5
Melvin	Memco	CSTO-5T-.80	99,000	339	87.5
Ultimate	Ultimate	PFO-5T-.80	99,000	339	87.5
Buderus	Buderus	115-28	98,000	361	86.8
Axeman-Anderson	Axeman-Anderson Vesta	PVT-119HD	102,000	350	86.7
Axeman-Anderson	Axeman-Anderson Co.	74NPO-U	105,000	350	86.5
New Yorker	New Yorker	FR98	104,000	342	86.4
Axeman-Anderson	Axeman-Anderson Olympia	OL-119D	103,000	351	86.4
Thermo-Dynamics	Thermo-Dynamics	CWL-85D	102,000	345	86.3
Thermo-Dynamics	Thermo-Dynamics	S-85D	101,000	346	86.3
Weil-McLain	Weil-McLain	WGO-3R	98,000	294	86.2
Weil-McLain	Weil-McLain	WTGO-3R	98,000	294	86.2
111,000 - 127,000 Btu/hr Heating Capacity					
Burnham	Opus	O1-1-90	112,000	274	88.7
Dunkirk Boilers	Dunkirk	DPFO-6T-.95	117,000	343	87.5
Melvin	Memco	CSTO-6T-.95	117,000	343	87.5

MOST EFFICIENT OIL HOT WATER BOILERS (cont.)

Manufacturer	Trade Name	Model Number	Capacity (Btu/hr)	Electric Energy (kWh/yr)	AFUE
111,000 to 127,000 Btu/hr Heating Capacity					
Newmac	Newmac	NBR 126V	127,000	279	87.8
Newmac	Newmac	NBR 122V	125,000	296	87.6
Newmac	Newmac	NBR 113	115,000	321	87.6
Newmac	Newmac	NBR 111V	112,000	308	88.4
Newmac	Newmac	NBR 109V	111,000	329	88.1
Waterpik Technologies	Laars, Max	DMAX 100	121,000	335	86.5
Waterpik Technologies	Laars, Max	MAX 100	121,000	335	86.5
Thermo-Dynamics	Thermo-Dynamics	NYS-100	122,000	340	86.7
Ultimate	Ultimate	PFO-6T-.95	117,000	343	87.5
Viessmann	Viessmann Vitola 200	VB2-33*	116,000	268	87.2
Viessmann	Viessmann Vitorond 200	VR2-33	122,000	277	86.8
128,000 to 144,000 Btu/hr Heating Capacity					
Burnham	Opus	O1-2-105	132,000	264	90.0
Dunkirk Boilers	Dunkirk	DPFO-7-1.05	130,000	345	87.6
Melvin	Memco	CSTO-7-1.05	130,000	345	87.6
Ultimate	Ultimate	PFO-7-1.05	130,000	345	87.6
Axeman-Anderson	Axeman-Anderson Co.	87NPO-UD	134,000	359	87.2
Newmac	Newmac	NBR 127	129,000	324	87.1
Viessmann	Viessmann Vitorond 200	VR2-40	140,000	262	86.9
Axeman-Anderson	Axeman-Anderson Co.	74NPOD	133,000	362	86.6
Thermo-Dynamics	Thermo-Dynamics	NYS-110	133,000	378	86.6
145,000 to 178,000 Btu/hr heating capacity					
Burnham	Opus	O1-2-125	156,000	252	89.2
Energy Kinetics	System 2000	EK-2	147,000	304	87.6
Dunkirk Boilers	Dunkirk	DPFO-9-1.35	167,000	355	87.6
Melvin	Memco	CSTO-9-1.35	167,000	355	87.6
Ultimate	Ultimate	PFO-9-1.35	167,000	355	87.6
Melvin	Memco	CSTO-8T-1.25	154,000	246	87.4
Dunkirk Boilers	Dunkirk	DPFO-8T-1.25	154,000	346	87.4
Ultimate	Ultimate	PFO-8T-1.25	154,000	346	87.4
Axeman-Anderson	Axeman-Anderson Co.	108NPO-UD	153,000	355	87.4
Viessmann	Viessmann Vitola 200	VB2-40*	146,000	274	87.3

MOST EFFICIENT OIL STEAM BOILERS

Manufacturer	Trade Name	Model Number	Input (Btu/hr)	Electric Energy (kWh/yr)	AFUE
77,000 to 93,0000 Btu/hr heating capacity					
Hydrotherm	Hydrotherm	PB-105S	90,000	208	85.6
Smith Cast Iron Boilers	Smith Cast Iron Boilers	8-S-3L	90,000	208	85.6
Peerless	Peerless	EC/ECT-03-075S	91,000	204	85.4
Burnham	Burnham	V83	91,000	128	85.1
Crown Boiler	Crown	KSZ065	78,000	826	84.9
Crown Boiler	Crown	KSZ075	90,000	723	84.5
Columbia Boiler	Columbia	CSFH-365*	78,000	n/a	84.0
Utica Boilers	Utica Starfire 3	SFH365S	78,000	381	84.0
94,0000 to 127,000 Btu/hr heating capacity					
Burnham	Burnham	V84	127,000	128	85.3
Crown Boiler	Crown	KSZ090	108,000	723	84.9
Peerless	Peerless	EC/ECT-03-100S	120,000	217	84.4
New Yorker	New Yorker	CL5SR	108,000	561	84.0
New Yorker	New Yorker	CL4SR	96,000	629	84.0
Weil-McLain	Weil-McLain	*-SGO-3	114,000	297	83.8
Crown Boiler	Crown	KSZ100	119,000	774	83.5
Hydrotherm	Hydrotherm	PB-120S	112,000	241	83.4
Smith Cast Iron Boilers	Smith Cast Iron Boilers	8-S-3H	112,000	241	83.4
Peerless	Peerless	WBV-03-085-S	101,000	222	83.1
128,0000 to 161,000 Btu/hr heating capacity					
Hydrotherm	Hydrotherm	PB-150S	132,000	240	85.5
Smith Cast Iron Boilers	Smith Cast Iron Boilers	8-S-4L	132,000	240	85.5
Peerless	Peerless	EC/ECT-04-125S	151,000	222	85.1
Hydrotherm	Hydrotherm	PB-180S	149,000	246	84.7
Smith Cast Iron Boilers	Smith Cast Iron Boilers	8-S-4H	149,000	246	84.7
Crown Boiler	Crown	KSZ120	144,000	731	84.5
Crown Boiler	Crown	KSZ125	149,000	793	84.2
Slant/Fin	Slant/Fin Liberty	LD30PZ	134,000	255	84.1
Weil-McLain	Weil-McLain	*-SGO-4	144,000	269	84.0
New Yorker	New Yorker	CL6SR	138,000	588	84.0
Peerless	Peerless	WBV-04-125-S	149,000	227	83.0
Peerless	Peerless	EC/ECT-03-120S	142,000	210	82.9
Greater than 161,000 Btu/hr heating capacity					
Burnham	Burnham	V85	164,000	142	85.4
Hydrotherm	Hydrotherm	PB-200S	168,000	248	85.3
Smith Cast Iron Boilers	Smith Cast Iron Boilers	8-S-5L	168,000	248	85.3
Weil-McLain	Weil-McLain	*-SGO-5	174,000	279	83.9

SOURCES

The listings in this guide were derived from product directories published by the Air-conditioning and Refrigeration Institute, the Association of Home Appliance Manufacturers, and the Gas Appliance Manufacturers Association. Additional information was obtained from the U.S. Department of Energy and the Environmental Protection Agency's ENERGY STAR appliance listings as well as product manufacturers.

Please bear in mind that manufacturers continuously introduce new models while withdrawing other models from the market. Use these listings as a guide to identify efficient models, not a bible.

APPENDIX 1
CO_2 Emissions and Energy Savings

The CO_2 emissions that result from using different types of fuel are listed in Table A.1. With this information, it's easy to calculate just how much CO_2 you are introducing into the atmosphere through your energy use. Simply look at your energy bills to find out how much fuel you are using: gallons of oil, therms of natural gas, kilowatt-hours of electricity, etc. Multiply that value by the quantity of CO_2 produced per unit of fuel in Table A.1.

TABLE A.1

CO_2 EMISSIONS FROM DIFFERENT ENERGY SOURCES

	CO_2 produced per unit of fuel	Lbs. of CO_2 produced per million Btus
Fuel Oil	26.4 lbs. CO_2/gallon	190
Natural Gas	12.1 lbs. CO_2/therm	118
Gasoline	23.8 lbs. CO_2/gallon	190
Coal (direct combustion)	2.48 tons CO_2/ton	210
Wood[1]	2.59 tons CO_2/cord	216
Electricity (from coal)	2.37 lbs. CO_2/kWh	694
Electricity (from oil)	2.14 lbs. CO_2/kWh	628
Electricity (from natural gas)	1.32 lbs. CO_2/kWh	388
Electricity (weighted national average including all generation)	1.54 lbs. CO_2/kWh	450

1. If the wood is harvested on a sustainable basis, there is no net CO_2 emission because the growing trees absorb more CO_2 than is released when burning the wood.

For example, if you use 1,300 gallons of fuel oil during a heating season, you are responsible for the release of 34,320 lbs. of CO_2 emissions. If you carry out energy conservation measures that reduce your oil use from 1,300 down to 1,000 gallons per year, you will have reduced your CO_2 emissions by almost 8,000 lbs. (300 gal. × 26.4 lbs. CO_2/gal.). Similarly, if you cut your annual electricity use from 9,000 kWh to 6,000 kWh, you would be responsible for about 7,000 lbs. less CO_2 emissions, if your utility company burned coal to produce electricity. The CO_2 savings would not be as great if your utility company used a fuel other than coal.

If you use wood as a heating fuel and if the wood is grown on a sustained yield basis (i.e., the woodlot is left intact and younger trees replace those that are cut), there is no net contribution of CO_2 because the growing trees absorb CO_2 out of the atmosphere.

APPENDIX 2
Understanding EnergyGuide Labels

Federal law requires that EnergyGuide labels be placed on all new refrigerators, freezers, water heaters, dishwashers, clothes washers, room air conditioners, central air conditioners, heat pumps, and furnaces and boilers. These labels are bright yellow with black lettering. This section describes the labels, and provides guidance for using the information they contain.

WHAT INFORMATION IS ON THE LABEL?

Sample EnergyGuide labels are reproduced here for a refrigerator, a room air conditioner, a clothes washer, a water heater, a heat pump, and a furnace. For the first two sample labels, see the numbered lists for a brief description of key label elements.

HOW DO YOU USE THE LABEL?

The line scale in the middle of the label shows how that particular model compares in energy efficiency with other models on the market of comparable size and type. You will see a range of lowest to highest.

For refrigerators, freezers, water heaters, dishwashers, and clothes washers, the range shows annual energy consumption (in kWh/year for electricity or therms/year for gas). The most efficient models will have labels showing energy consumption (represented by the downward-pointing triangle labeled "This Model Uses"), at or near the left-hand end of the range. It will be close to the words "Uses Least Energy."

For room air conditioners, central air conditioners, heat pumps, and furnaces and boilers, the range is not energy consumption, but rather the energy efficiency ratings for these products (EER, SEER, HSPF & SEER, and AFUE, respectively). Therefore, labels on the most efficient models will show "This Model's Efficiency" at or near the right-hand end of the range, close to the words "Most Efficient."

The label will not tell you who makes the more efficient models, or if they are available locally. To find out about the most efficient models, look at the listings in this book. Some manufacturers now include the ENERGY STAR on the EnergyGuide label for qualifying products.

A word of caution—the ranges shown on the labels are not updated frequently, and manufacturers are constantly introducing new appliances. For example, it is possible to find a model that is more efficient than the most efficient end of the range. Similarly, it is possible to find a model that is less efficient than the least efficient end of the range. On such a product, the label will include a statement explaining that the consumption or efficiency of that particular model was not available at the time the range was published.

The labels showing estimated annual energy consumption also show estimated annual operating costs, near the bottom of the label. This estimated cost is based on recent national average prices of electricity and/or natural gas, and assumes typical operating characteristics. For example, the energy use and cost estimates for dishwashers are based on six dishwasher loads per week; the estimates for clothes washers assume eight loads of laundry per week.

New furnaces and boilers must carry EnergyGuide labels showing their annual fuel utilization efficiency (AFUE), the energy efficiency rating for these products. EnergyGuide labels on heating and cooling equipment refer customers to manufacturer's fact sheets available from the seller or installer. These fact sheets give further information about the efficiency and operating cost of the equipment under consideration.

EnergyGuide labels are not required on kitchen ranges, microwave ovens, clothes dryers, portable space heaters, and lights. For these products, look for the energy-conserving features discussed throughout this book.

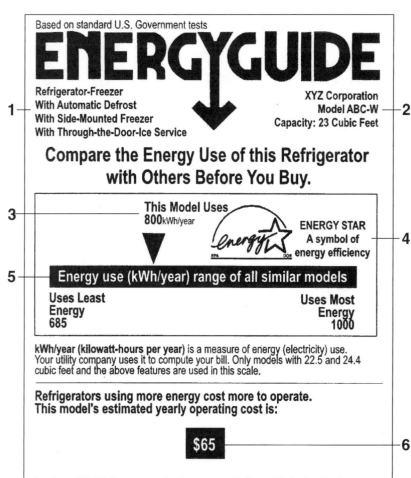

1. Type of appliance.
2. Size, make and model number.
3. This model's annual energy consumption.
4. ENERGY STAR label. The label can be used only on models that qualify for ENERGY STAR.
5. Scale indicating range of annual energy consumption for models similar in size and type.
6. This model's estimated yearly operating cost.

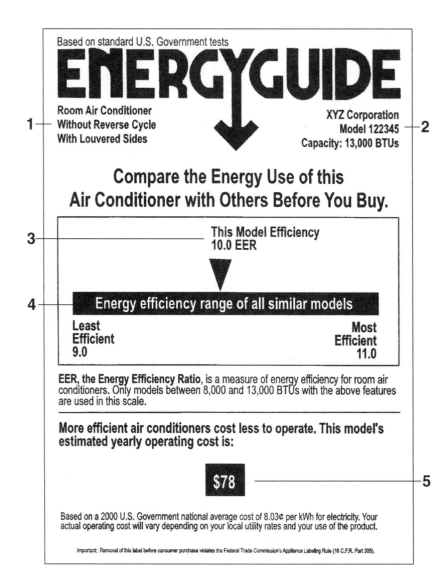

1. Type of appliance.
2. Size, make and model number.
3. This model's energy efficiency rating.
4. Scale indicating range of efficiency ratings for models similar in size and type.
5. This model's estimated yearly operating cost.

Based on standard U.S. Government tests

ENERGYGUIDE

Clothes Washer
Capacity: Standard

XYZ Corporation
Model(s) MR328, XL12, NAA83

Compare the Energy Use of this Clothes Washer with Others Before You Buy.

This Model Uses
873kWh/year

Energy use (kWh/year) range of all similar models

Uses Least
Energy
156

Uses Most
Energy
1154

kWh/year (kilowatt-hours per year) is a measure of energy (electricity) use. Your utility company uses it to compute your bill. Only standard size clothes washers are used in this scale.

Clothes washers using more energy cost more to operate.
This model's estimated yearly operating cost is:

$70

$33

when used with an electric water heater

when used with a natural gas water heater

Based on eight loads of clothes a week and a 2000 U.S. Government national average cost of 8.03¢ per kWh for electricity and 68.8¢ per therm for natural gas. Your actual operating cost will vary depending on your local utility rates and your use of the product.

Important: Removal of this label before consumer purchase violates the Federal Trade Commission's Appliance Labeling Rule (16 C.F.R. Part 305).

Label on a clothes washer. Note the cost comparison between electric and gas water heating at the bottom of the label. As of 2000, the top-loading and front-loading clothes washer categories were combined, allowing a direct comparison of these models. This is a relatively inefficient model.

Based on standard U.S. Government tests

ENERGYGUIDE

Water Heater – Natural Gas
Capacity (first hour rating):
60 gallons

XYZ Corporation
Model(s) RP23
RP38

Compare the Energy Use of this Water Heater with Others Before You Buy.

This Model Uses
240 Therms/year

Energy use (Therms/year) range of all similar models

Uses Least
Energy
245

Uses Most
Energy
295

The Estimated Annual Energy Consumption of this model was not
available at the time the range was published.

Therms/year is a measure of energy use. Your utility company uses it to compute
your bill. Only models with first hour ratings of 56 to 64 gallons are used in this scale.

Natural gas water heaters that use fewer therms/year cost less to
operate. This model's estimated yearly operating cost is:

$165

Based on a 2000 U.S. Government national average cost of 68.8¢ per therm for natural gas. Your
actual operating cost will vary depending on your local utility rates and your use of the product.

Important: Removal of this label before consumer purchase violates the Federal Trade Commission's Appliance Labeling Rule (16 C.F.R. Part 305).

This energy-efficient gas water heater's energy use is off the
low end of the range, indicating that it is more efficient than all
models in prior years.

Based on standard U.S. Government tests

ENERGYGUIDE

Heat Pump
Cooling and Heating
Split System

XYZ Corporation
Model 12345

Compare the Energy Efficiency of this Heat Pump with Others Before You Buy.

This Model (Cooling)
12.0SEER

Energy efficiency range of all similar models

Least
Efficient
10.0

Most
Efficient
16.4

SEER, the Seasonal Energy Efficiency Ratio, is a measure of energy efficiency for central air conditioners.

This Model (Cooling)
7.5HSPF

Energy efficiency range of all similar models

Least
Efficient
6.8

Most
Efficient
10.2

HSPF, the Heating Seasonal Performance Factor, is a measure of energy efficiency for heat pumps when heating.

- These energy ratings are based on U.S. Government standard tests of this condenser model combined with the most common coil. The ratings will vary slightly with different coils

- Federal law requires the seller or installer of this appliance to make available a fact sheet or directory giving further information about the efficiency and operating cost of this equipment. Ask for this information.

Important: Removal of this label before consumer purchase violates the Federal Trade Commission's Appliance Labeling Rule (16 C.F.R. Part 305).

**Labels on heat pumps
show both cooling efficiency (SEER)
and heating efficiency (HSPF).**

Based on standard U.S. Government tests

ENERGYGUIDE

Furnace – Natural Gas

XYZ Corporation
Model 2345X

Compare the Energy Efficiency of this Furnace with Others Before You Buy.

This Model's Efficiency
80.7 AFUE

Energy efficiency range of all similar models

Least Efficient 78.0	Most Efficient 97.0

The **AFUE, Annual Fuel Utilization Efficiency,** is a measure of energy efficiency for furnaces and boilers. Only furnaces fueled by natural gas are used in this scale.

Natural gas furnaces that have higher AFUEs are more energy efficient.

Federal law requires the seller or installer of this appliance to make available a fact sheet or directory giving further information about the efficiency and operating cost of this equipment.

Ask for this information.

Important: Removal of this label before consumer purchase violates the Federal Trade Commission's Appliance Labeling Rule (16 C.F.R. Part 305).

**Furnace label shows annual fuel utilization efficiency (AFUE).
This particular model is not very efficient.**

APPENDIX 3
List of Manufacturers

This appendix lists phone numbers (and web sites, when available) for manufacturers and brand names of the high-efficiency equipment listed in this book. Toll-free numbers are listed when available.

We suggest you call the manufacturer if you cannot find a listed model in your local area. In most cases the manufacturer will refer you to its distributor in your area.

These numbers were compiled from the latest available information and verified for accuracy. However, we caution the reader that there has been quite a bit of consolidation among makers of space heating and water heating equipment in recent years, and the numbers here may change if mergers and acquisitions continue in these industries.

This list does not repeat the company phone numbers provided in the text for lighting products, ground source heat pumps, instantaneous water heaters, heat pump water heaters, and solar water heating systems; please refer back to those sections for complete information on those products.

Manufacturer	Phone Number	Web Site
A.O. Smith	800-527-1953	www.hotwater.com
Absocold	800-843-3714	www.absocold.com
Adams Manufacturing	216-587-6801	
Air-Ease	419-483-4840	www.airease.com
Airpro	877-874-7378	www.york.com
AirQuest	800-458-6650	www.icpusa.com
Air Temp	217-342-3901	www.fedders.com
Amana	800-843-0304	www.amana.com
American Aire	800-598-1175	www.americanaire.com
American Standard	419-483-3557	www.americanstandard.com
American Water Heater	800-456-9805	www.americanwaterheater.com
Applied Energy Recovery/E-Tech	770-734-9696	www.aeretech.com
Arcoaire	800-458-6650	www.arcoaire.com
Armstrong	419-483-4840	www.armstrongair.com

Manufacturer	Phone Number	Web Site
Asko	800-898-1879	www.askousa.com
Avanti	305-592-7834	www.avantiproducts.com
Axeman-Anderson	570-326-9114	
Bock	800-794-2491	www.bockwaterheaters.com
Bosch/BSH Home Appliances	800-944-2904	www.boschappliances.com
Boyertown Furnace	610-369-1450	
Bradford-White	215-641-9400	www.bradfordwhite.com
Bryant	800-468-7253	www.bryant.com
Buderus	800-283-3787	www.buderus.net
Burnham	717-397-4701	www.burnham.com
Buy Max	877-428-9629	www.4buymax.com
Carrier	800-227-7437	www.carrier.com
Coleman	877-874-7378	www.colemanac.com
Coleman-Evcon	877-874-7378	www.york.com
Columbia Boiler	610-473-8457	www.columbiaboiler.com
Comfort Aire	517-787-2100	www.heatcontroller.com
Comfortmaker	800-458-6650	www.comfortmaker.com
Crosley	336-761-1212	www.crosley.com
Crown Boiler	215-535-8900	www.crownboiler.com
Daewoo	800-323-9668	www.e-daewoo.com
Day & Night	800-428-4326	www.bryant.com
Dornback Furnace	216-662-1600	
Dunkirk	716-366-5500	www.dunkirk.com
Electrolux	216-898-1800	www.electrolux.com
Endurance	805-529-2000	www.laars.com
Energy Kinetics	800-323-2066	www.energykinetics.com
Equator	713-464-3422	www.equatorappl.com
Estate	800-253-1301	www.estateappliances.com
Eurotech	800-898-1879	www.eurotechappliances.com
Everest	800-458-6650	www.comfortmaker.com
Fedders	217-342-3901	www.fedders.com
Fisher & Paykel	888-936-7872	www.usafisherpaykel.com
Fraser-Johnston	877-874-7378	www.york.com
Friedrich	210-357-4400	www.friedrich.com
Frigidaire	800-451-7007	www.frigidaire.com
General Electric	800-626-2000	www.geappliances.com
Gibson	800-458-1445	www.frigidaire.com/gibson.asp
Glowcore	800-676-4546	www.glowcoreac.com

Manufacturer	Phone Number	Web Site
GmC	888-593-9988	www.goodmanmfg.com
Goldstar	877-714-7486	www.lgappliances.com
Goodman	888-593-9988	www.goodmanmfg.com
GSW Water Heating	888-479-8324	www.gsw-wh.com
Guardian	877-874-7378	www.york.com
Hallmark	610-369-1450	
Hampton Bay	877-714-7486	www.lgappliances.com
Heat Controller	517-787-2100	www.heatcontroller.com
Heat Transfer Products	800-323-9651	www.htproducts.com
Heil	800-458-6650	www.heil-hvac.com
Hydrotherm	413-568-9571	www.hydrotherm.com
Imperial	216-898-1800	www.electrolux.com
Int'l Comfort Products	800-458-6650	www.icpusa.com
Janitrol	888-593-9988	www.goodmanmfg.com
Jenn-Air	800-688-1100	www.jennair.com
Kenmore (Sears)	800-349-4358	www.kenmore.com
KitchenAid	800-422-1230	www.kitchenaid.com
Laars	805-529-2000	www.laars.com
Lennox	800-953-6669	www.lennox.com
LG Electronics	877-714-7486	www.lgappliances.com
Lochinvar	615-889-8900	www.lochinvar.com
Luxaire	877-874-7378	www.luxaire.com
Magic Chef	800-688-9900	www.maytag.com
Maratherm	800-458-6650	www.icpusa.com
Marathon	800-321-6718	www.marathonheaters.com
Maytag	800-688-9900	www.maytag.com
Melvin/Memco	207-645-4212	
Miele	800-843-7231	www.mieleusa.com
Mini-Therm	805-529-2000	www.laars.com
Munchkin	800-323-9651	www.htproducts.com
Newmac	902-662-3840	www.newmacfurnaces.com
New Yorker Boiler	215-855-8055	www.newyorkerboiler.com
Oneida Royal	315-797-1310	www.uticaboilers.com
Opus	717-397-4701	www.burnham.com
Panasonic	800-211-7262	www.panasonic.com
Payne	888-417-2963	www.payne.com
Pennco	315-797-1310	www.ecrinternational.com
Peerless Heater Co.	800-858-5844	www.peerless-heater.com
Polaris	800-456-9805	www.americanwaterheater.com

Manufacturer	Phone Number	Web Site
Quantum/Quantum Leap	716-366-5500	www.dunkirk.com
Quasar	800-211-7262	www.panasonic.com
Quietline	800-884-8635	www.quietline.com
Reliance Water Heater	800-365-8170	www.stateind.com
Rheem	501-648-4900	www.rheem.com
Roper	800-447-6737	www.roperappliances.com
Ruud	501-648-4900	www.rheem.com
Samsung	973-601-6000	www.samsungusa.com
Sanyo	800-421-5013	www.sanyo.com
Sears	800-349-4358	www.sears.com
Sharp	800-237-4277	www.sharp-usa.com
Slant/Fin	516-484-2600	www.slantfin.com
Smeg	416 646 2500	www.smeg.it
Smith Cast Iron	413-562-9631	www.smithboiler.com
Softline	877-877-0540	www.specializedappliances.com
Speed Queen	800-345-5649	www.speedqueen.com
Splendide	800-356-0766	www.splendide.com
Staber Industries	800-848-6200	www.staber.com
State Industries	800-365-8170	www.stateind.com
Sub-Zero	800-222-7820	www.subzero.com
Sun Frost	707-822-9095	www.sunfrost.com
System 2000	800-323-2066	www.energykinetics.com
Tempstar	800-458-6650	www.tempstar.com
Thermo-Dynamics	570-385-0731	www.thermodynamicsboiler.com
Thermoflo	800-736-2378	www.williamson-thermoflo.com
Thermo Pride/ Thermo-Products	574-896-2133	www.thermopride.com
Thor	877-877-0540	www.specializedappliances.com
Trane	903-581-3200	www.trane.com
U-Line	414-354-0300	www.u-line.com
Ultimate	716-366-5500	www.dunkirk.com
United Refrigeration	888-578-9100	www.uri.com
U.S. Craftmaster	800-999-9515	www.uscraftmaster.com
Utica Boilers	315-797-1310	www.uticaboilers.com
ValPro	877-324-3444	www.eainet.net
Viessmann	401-732-0667	www.viessmann.us
Viking	888-845-4641	www.vikingrange.com
Waterpik Tech	949-719-3700	www.waterpik.com
Weatherking	817-442-0655	www.weatherking.com

Manufacturer	Phone Number	Web Site
Weathermaker	800-227-7437	www.carrier.com
Weil-McLain	219-879-6561	www.weil-mclain.com
Whirlpool	800-253-1301	www.whirlpool.com
White-Westinghouse	216-898-1800	www.electrolux.com
Williamson-Thermoflo	800-736-2378	www.williamson-thermoflo.com
Wood's	419-523-9663	www.wcwood.com
Xenon Heating & AC	877-428-9629	www.4buymax.com
York	877-874-7378	www.york.com

APPENDIX 4
For More Information

If you have additional questions or concerns that have not been answered in this book, we encourage you to check out the resources listed below. Government agencies, consumer and environmental organizations, trade associations, and private businesses can provide a wealth of information to help answer questions about home energy conservation, renewable energy resources, energy suppliers, and related matters. In addition, a range of energy-efficient products and services can be purchased through on-line and print catalogs. Many more web resources can be located through the "Energy Efficiency-Related Web Sites" page on the ACEEE web site (http://aceee.org).

GOVERNMENT RESOURCES

The **U.S. Department of Energy (DOE)** offers information to the public through the **Energy Efficiency and Renewable Energy Clearinghouse (EREC)**. EREC has a toll-free number and professional staff to assist consumers with questions about home energy use, renewable energy, recycling, and related issues. Call 800-363-3732.

DOE also provides useful consumer information through the **Energy Efficiency and Renewable Energy Network** web site. The site includes information on getting a home energy audit, tips for saving energy throughout the home, guidance on using solar energy, suggestions for remodelers and apartment dwellers, and a buying guide for purchasing energy-efficient appliances. Visit the site at http://www.eere.energy.gov/ buildings/homes.

The **Environmental Protection Agency (EPA)** and DOE maintain a web site with information about ENERGY STAR programs and products. The site describes each ENERGY STAR program, provides news and updates on products, and allows users to search for ENERGY STAR-qualifying products by brand, type, size, or model number. Check out the site at http://www.energystar.gov. Information and questions about ENERGY STAR products can also be obtained by calling the toll-free ENERGY STAR hotline at 888-STAR-YES.

Lawrence Berkeley National Laboratory offers information on energy-efficient appliances, residential energy software, utility programs, home energy ratings, and financing options as well as numerous reports, case studies, and newsletters (http://eetd.lbl.gov). The lab also offers an on-line interactive tool, the Home Energy Advisor, to analyze your home for energy savings (http://hes.lbl.gov).

We also suggest you contact your state energy office and/or county extension service. These local agencies may have information of particular interest to your location.

CONSUMER AND ENVIRONMENTAL ORGANIZATIONS

The **Alliance to Save Energy** is a coalition of prominent business, government, environment, and consumer leaders. Energy-saving tips and information for consumers can be found at http://www.ase.org/consumer. The site also provides information for educators and the media. Call 202-857-0666 for additional information.

The **Consumer Federation of America/Consumer Research Council** provides information on ways to save energy and money throughout the home and answers to common questions about purchasing energy-efficient products and services. Call the Council at 202-387-6121 or visit their web site at http://www.buyenergyefficient.org.

Consumers Union publishes the well-respected Consumer Reports, a valuable resource for information on a range of products, including home appliances and consumer electronics. Product reviews provide ratings of key features, performance, repair history, and pricing in addition to information on energy use and efficiency. A web-based version of the magazine, along with an archive of product evaluations and reports, can be accessed for a modest fee at http://www.consumerreports.org.

Environmental Defense maintains the Green Advisor web site as a resource for consumers interested in making environmentally sound purchasing decisions. The site (http://www.greenadvisor.org) links to information and educational resources from a wide variety of environmental groups and offers tips on buying environmentally friendly products; cooking and eating a green diet; recycling and waste reduction; and green travel and recreation.

The **Natural Resources Defense Council (NRDC)** is a nonprofit organization dedicated to protecting the world's resources and ensuring a safe and healthy environment for all. Visit NRDC on-line at http://www.nrdc.org to learn more about the connection between energy use and the environment, clean power sources, air pollution, and much more.

TRADE ASSOCIATIONS

The **Association of Home Appliance Manufacturers (AHAM)** provides information on a wide range of appliances through its "Just for Consumers" web site. The site also offers advice from the experts on appliance purchasing, use, maintenance, and repair. Visit the site at http://www.aham.org/consumerhome/home.cfm.

Utilities and manufacturers are also useful sources of information. See Appendix 3 for phone numbers and web sites of manufacturers referenced in this book. Contact your local utility for information relevant to your location.

ENERGY SERVICES AND
ENERGY-EFFICIENT PRODUCTS

ENERGYguide sells a growing list of high-quality products to help reduce your energy costs along with the information you need to guide your decisions. Enter your zipcode and the site will determine what, if any, utility rebates apply to your locale and apply the rebate directly to your purchase. The site can also help consumers find a contractor or select an energy supplier. See http://www.energyguide.com.

Energy Federation Incorporated (EFI) offers a wide variety of water and energy saving products in their on-line catalog. The site will apply any applicable utility rebates directly to your purchase. Visit its site at http://www.efi.org.

Iris Communications maintains the Oikos web site offering information on energy-efficient products and a database of 1,900 companies that make or distribute them. The site also has an on-line catalog of books, videos, and software for sustainable, environmentally sound construction. Visit its site at http://www.oikos.com or call for a free print catalog (800-346-0104).

LightSite.net is a web site dedicated to making lighting cleaner, safer, and more affordable. This site has information about energy-efficient lighting alternatives plus a savings calculator to demonstrate the potential energy and dollar savings from efficient lighting products. The site offers a retail locator to help consumers find retailers selling energy-efficient lighting products. Visit its site at http://www.lightsite.net.

Real Goods has been a leader in the sustainable products market offering goods, services, and advice on saving energy and using renewable energy in the home for more than 20 years. Over 10,000 products ranging from air and water purification devices to clothing, lighting, batteries, and toys are available on its web site (http://www.realgoods.com). Call 800-762-7325 for more information or to order a copy of the print catalog.

APPENDIX 5
Choosing Heating and Air Conditioning Contractors

Choosing a good contractor to install a new furnace or central air conditioner can be as important as the equipment you choose, because proper installation and maintenance is needed for the equipment to operate safely, reliably, and at maximum efficiency. Here are some suggestions for selecting a contractor, adapted in part from *Contracting Business* magazine.

■ If you already know a reputable heating and air conditioning contractor, that is a good place to start. If you don't, friends and relatives in the area can often give you recommendations.

■ Do not give your business to a company offering to give you an estimate over the phone without ever looking at the job to be done.

■ A well-trained, up-to-date contractor will not try to discourage you from purchasing high-efficiency equipment. Less-qualified companies may not keep their employees current with the latest technology, and therefore they may discourage you from new and better designs.

■ A good estimator will do a survey of your home and base his or her proposal on a heat-load calculation (or cooling-load calculation for air conditioning).

■ Many furnaces and central air conditioners are not properly sized for the homes they serve, because of improper sizing years ago and/or energy efficiency improvements to the building since the old equipment was installed. Better contractors will not use your existing equipment to size your new heating or cooling system.

■ A good estimator should also ask about any heating or cooling problems you have had with your old equipment, and offer understandable explanations or solutions.

■ Using their heat-load and/or cooling-load calculations, good contractors should be able to estimate the annual operating costs (energy bills) for the equipment they are proposing for your home.

■ A good company will give you a written bid (or proposal) outlining the equipment to be installed, the work to be done, and the price, including labor costs.

■ We suggest you get estimates from multiple contractors, but try not to let the lowest price be the main reason for selecting a contractor. Better contractors may charge more, but they probably offer greater value. Be skeptical of extremely low bids; those contractors may not be including all routine services and customary warranties, or they may be trying to unload outdated or unreliable equipment.

■ Reliable contractors are professional. Their people are prompt and courteous. How a company treats you now reflects how they will treat you if there is a problem. They should have an office or shop facility, and they should not be ashamed to have you visit them. An office or shop is an indication that the company has been in business and intends to remain in business.

INDEX

AFUE (see Annual fuel utilization efficiency)

Air conditioners, 77–96
central, 77–89
installation, 85–87
maintenance, 87–89
most efficient
central, 85, 195–199
room, 84, 192–194
room, 78–85
sizing, 81–82
standards, 82–83
types, 78–80
variable-speed, 84

Air leakage, 11–21
caulk, 13–18
common sites, 13–21
importance of reducing, 11–12
weatherstripping, 19–21
windows, 17–21, 29–32, 35–36, 40–41

American Society of Heating, Refrigeration, and Air Conditioning Engineers (ASHRAE), 89

Andersen Windows, 32, 38

Annual fuel utilization efficiency (AFUE), 48, 52–53, 57–58, 65, 75, 106, 204–215, 219–220, 226
savings from improvements in, 52

Aquariums, 165–167

Aquastat, 46, 70, 73–75

Argon gas–filled windows, 3, 32, 37

Asbestos, 57

Asterisks (*), meaning of, 8, 178

Attic ventilation, 91, 94–95

Attics,
air leakage into, 13–16
insulation, 21–25, 91
ventilation of, 91, 94–95

Back-drafting (combustion appliances), 56, 105, 125

Ballasts, fluorescent lighting, 147–154

Block heaters, 171

Boilers, 43–48
most efficient, 58
gas, 207–211
oil, 212–215
savings from more efficient, 51–52
sizing, 54–55

Booster heater (dishwasher), 114, 131–132

British thermal unit (Btu), (defined), 55

Carbon dioxide (CO_2), 1–4, 26
emissions from different fuels, 217–218
emissions from heating systems, 43, 65
emissions resulting from air conditioning, 77

Caulk, 13–18

Ceiling fans, 87, 89, 95, 166–167

Clock thermostats,
space heating, 72–74
Clothes dryers, 139, 141–144,
220
Clothes washers, 137–144
controls, 140–141
cost of a load of laundry, 140
energy factor, 139
most efficient, 186–188
water temperature, 139–140,
143
Coefficient of performance (COP),
49, 59–60
Color rendition index (CRI), 152
Combination water heaters/space
heaters, 100–101, 106, 108,
191
Combined annual efficiency, 106
Combustion
by–products (pollutants), 45,
51, 55–56, 105
efficiency, 47–48, 52, 57
sealed, 55
Comfort, 11–12, 73–74, 89
Compact fluorescent lighting, 2–3,
90, 145–151, 154–155, 157–
160, 161–162
bulb manufacturers, 148
lifecycle costs, 150–151
savings from use of, 2–3, 145–
146, 150–151
torchiere, 154–155
Compressors, air conditioner, 78,
85–86
location, 85–86
replacement and proper
matching, 86–87
Computers, energy use by, 166–
167, 170
Conduction (defined), 31
Contractors,
air conditioning, 80–81, 85–88,
96, 237–238

heating system, 53–58, 60, 62,
64–66, 68–72, 76, 237–
238
home performance, 11–12
insulation, 21–25
water heaters, 110–111
window installation, 36
Convection (defined), 31
Convection ovens, 126–127
Cooking, 123–129
comparative costs by method,
127
Cooktops (ranges), 123–24, 127–
129
Cooling, 77–96 (see also Air
conditioners)
recommendations, 95–96
without air conditioning, 89–95
COP (see Coefficient of performance)
CRI (color rendition index), 152

Daylighting, 158–159
DC power supplies (transformers),
165–169
Demand (instantaneous) water
heaters, 97–99, 103, 106–
107, 110, 220
Dehumidification, 84
Dishwashers
booster heaters in, 131–132,
134, 184
most efficient, 133, 184–185
water temperature, 131–132,
184
Dishwashing, 131–135
DOE, 2, 77, 233
Doors, 17, 21, 36
Dryers (see Clothes dryers)
Duct insulation, 67
Duct sealing, 68, 76

Economics (see also Lifecycle costs)
of compact fluorescent bulbs, 150–151
of improvements to building shell, 25–26
of improving heating systems, 51–53
of water heater options, 108–110

Electric blankets, 166–167, 171

Electric heat
heat pumps, 48–50, 59–61, 75, 200–203
resistance, 26, 48, 51, 53, 75

Energy audits, 11–12

Energy efficiency rating (EER), 59–60, 82–84, 96, 192–203, 219

Energy factor (EF)
clothes washers, 139, 186–188
water heaters, 105–106, 189–191

EnergyGuide labels, 6–8, 83, 133, 139, 177–178, 184, 188, 219–226

ENERGY STAR, 4–6, 58–59, 75, 82–83, 85, 96, 117–119, 121, 133, 139, 146–147, 150– 151, 155, 165, 168, 170, 177–179, 184, 221, 233

Environment, energy use & the, 1–6, 26, 43, 50, 77, 217–218

EPA, 2, 50, 177, 233

Evaporative cooler (swamp cooler), 79–80

Fans,
ceiling, 87, 89, 95, 166–167
furnace, 56, 58, 74, 166–167, 169, 204

fusible link, 94–95
whole-house, 94–95, 166–167
window, 94, 166–167

Fenestration, 36

Filters,
heating system, 62, 76
cooling system, 83, 87–88

First-hour rating, 103

Flame retention oil burner, 69

Flue economizer, 71

Fluorescent lighting (see also Compact fluorescent lighting; Lighting)
compact, 90–91, 145–151, 159–162
tube, 151–153

Freezers, 117–121, 179–183

Front–loading clothes washers (see Horizontal-axis clothes washers)

Fuel switching, 51–53

Furnaces (see also Heating systems)
condensing, 56
fan, 56, 58, 74, 166–167, 169, 204
filters, 62, 76
most efficient
gas, 58, 204–206
oil, 58, 211–212
savings from more efficient, 3, 43, 51–53

Fusible link, 94–95

Geothermal Heat Pump Consortium, 61

Geothermal heat pumps (see Ground–source heat pumps)

Global warming, 1–5

Ground–source heat pumps, 49, 59–61

Halogen cooking elements, 124
Halogen lighting, 154
Halogen torchieres, 154–155
Heat gain (unwanted), 33, 39–40, 90–96
Heat pumps (space heating), 48–50, 59–61
  air-source, 48–50, 59
  ground-source, 50, 59–61
  most efficient
    air-source, 59, 200–203
    ground-source, 59–61
    water-source, 60–61
Heat pump water heaters, 99, 106, 108, 110
Heating season performance factor (HSPF), 49, 59, 200–203, 219, 225
Heating systems, 43–76 (see also Furnaces; Boilers; Heat pumps)
  AFUE, 47–48, 52, 57–58, 65, 75, 204–215, 219, 226
  aquastats, 46, 70, 73, 76
  distribution systems, 53, 65–68
  fuel choices, 44, 53
  installation, 56–58
  integrated water heating, 100–101, 106, 108, 189, 191
  maintenance, 62–66
  modifications, 66–72
  operation, 73–75
  radiators, 44–45, 53, 63, 66–68, 71–72, 75–76
  recommendations, 75–76
  replacement, 51–58
  return on investment of new, 51–53
  sizing, 54–55, 68–69, 237
  thermostats, 46, 72–76
  tune-ups, 64–66
  type, 44–50
  vent dampers, 70
Home-performance contractors, 11–12, 237–238

Horizontal-axis clothes washers, 137–140
Hot tubs, 165–167, 169–170
House doctors, 12
Humidity, 84, 87–89, 95
Hydronic heating systems, 44–48

Indirect water heaters, 100, 110
Infiltration (see also Air leakage) 90–91, 125
  windows and, 31–32, 34–35, 38–40
Infrared radiation (heat), 29
Instantaneous water heaters, 97–99, 103, 106–107, 110, 220
Insulation, 11, 14, 21–27, 90–91
  attic, 21–24, 90–91
  basement, 24–25
  crawl space, 24–25
  duct, 67
  foundation, 24
  pipe, 66–67, 113–115
  savings from additional, 3
  wall, 21–22
Integrated (combination) water heaters, 100–101, 106, 108, 191
International Ground Source Heat Pump Assoc., 61

Laundry, 137–144 (see also Clothes dryers; Clothes washers)
  comparative costs, 140
  recommendations, 143–144
Lawrence Berkeley National Laboratory, 3, 166–167
Lifecycle costs, 4–6
  compact fluorescent lighting, 150–151
  water heater comparison, 108–110

Lighting, 145–163
   color rendition index (CRI), 152
   compact fluorescent, 2–3, 90–
      91, 145–151, 155, 159–
      162
   controls, 156–158
   daylighting, 158–159
   efficacy, 152
   ENERGY STAR fixtures,
      150, 155
   halogen, 154–155
   high intensity discharge (HID),
      152–154
   lifecycle cost of, 150–151
   lumens, 151–153
   mail order sales, 156, 162
   occupancy sensors, 157, 161
   solar, 155–156, 161
   task, 159–160
   tube fluorescent, 151–153, 157
Low-emissivity (low–e) windows,
   31–33, 39–41, 93
Low-flow showerheads, 111–112,
   115
Lumens, 151, 153

Mastic, 67–68, 96
Microwave ovens, 123, 125–127,
   129
Modulating temperature control, 98

National Fenestration Rating
   Council (NFRC), 29, 35
   window labeling program, 36–
      41
Natural lighting, 158–159

Occupancy sensors, 157, 161
Office equipment, 170
Oil imports, 4–5
Ovens, 125–129

Passive solar heating, 29, 31, 33,
   39–41, 159

Photovoltaic lighting, 155–156
Pipe insulation, 66–67, 113–115
Pool pumps, 165–167

Radiant barriers (attic), 91
Radiant floor heating, 45
Radiant heat (explained), 31
Radiators, 44–45, 63, 67–68, 70–
   72
   bleeding, 63
Ranges (cooking), 123–129
Rebates, 5–6, 117, 138, 162, 176
Refrigerators, 117–121, 219–221
   maintenance, 119–121
   most efficient, 118–119, 179–
      183
Remaining moisture content
   (RMC), 138–139
Room air conditioners (see also
   Air conditioners; Cooling),
   78, 82–84
   most efficient, 192–194

Seasonal energy efficiency ratio
   (SEER), 59, 82–83, 85–86,
   96, 195–203, 219, 225
Shading, 92–93, 96
   air conditioners, 85–86
   coefficient (windows), 40
Small appliances, energy use by,
   165–171
Solar heat gain coefficient (SHGC),
   31, 33, 38–41, 93
Solar lighting, 155–156
Solar water heaters, 101–102, 104,
   109–110
Standards, appliance efficiency, 2,
   175–176
   air conditioners
      central, 82, 195

Standards, appliance efficiency
air conditioners (cont.)
room, 82–83, 192
boilers, 204
clothes washers, 139, 186
dishwashers, 133, 184
freezers, 118, 179
furnaces, 204
heat pumps, 200
refrigerators, 117, 179
showerheads, 112
water heaters, 105–106, 189
Storm windows, 19–21
Swamp cooler, 79–80

Tankless coil water heaters, 72,
99–100
Task lighting, 159–160
Technicians (see Contractors)
Televisions, 165–169
Thermostats, 73–74, 76, 87, 96
Tyvek, 25

Unvented fireplaces, 50–51
Unvented gas heaters, 50–51
U.S. Department of Energy (DOE),
2, 177, 233
U.S. Environmental Protection
Agency (EPA), 2, 50, 177,
233
Utility programs, 60
energy audits, 11–12
rebates, 5–6, 117, 138, 162,
176
U–factor (see U–value)
U–value, 31, 33, 37–39, 41

Variable–speed fans, 56, 84, 96
Vent–free appliances, 50–51
Vent damper, automatic, 70

Ventilation, 91–95, 124–125
attic, 91, 94–95
ceiling fans, 87, 89, 95, 166–
167
range hoods, 124–125
whole-house fans, 94–95, 166–
167
window fans, 94, 166–167
Video cassette recorders (VCRs),
165–169
Visible light transmittance, 39–40

Wall insulation, 21–22
Water heaters, 97–115
energy factor, 105–106, 189–
191
first-hour rating, 103
fuel choices, 104–105
heat pump, 99, 106, 108, 110
installation, 110–111
instantaneous, 97–99, 103,
106–107, 110, 220
integrated space heating, 100–
101, 106, 108, 191
insulation, 97, 112–113
lifecycle costs, 108–110
most efficient, 106–107, 189–
191
combination, 189, 191
electric resistance, 106, 189
electric heat pump, 106, 189
gas, 106, 189–190
oil, 106, 189, 191
power venting, 105
recommendations, 114–115
replacement, 102–105
sizing, 103–104
solar, 101–102, 104, 109–110
thermostat, 114
types, 97–102
Waterbeds, 166–167, 170–171
Water use and conservation, 111–
112, 115
peak hourly demand, 103–104

Weatherization, 11–25

Well pumps, 166–167, 169–170

Windows, 17–21, 29–42
    argon gas in, 3, 32, 37
    edge spacers, 33–34, 36
    ENERGY STAR windows,
        40–41
    gas-fill, 32, 37, 41
    improving efficiency of, 17–21
    low-e, 31–33, 39–41, 93
    NFRC labels (ratings), 36–41
    selection of, 32, 41–42
    storm, 19–21
    tinted coatings, 32
    U–values, 31, 33, 37–39, 41

Wood heat, 50, 217–218

About the Authors

ALEX WILSON is the editor and publisher of *Environmental Building News*, a highly regarded newsletter on environmentally sustainable design and construction, based in Brattleboro, Vermont. He has also written extensively on energy and building technology; his articles have appeared in such magazines as *Architecture, Journal of Light Construction, Progressive Architecture, Home Mechanix, Home,* and *Popular Science.*

JENNIFER THORNE is on the staff of the American Council for an Energy-Efficient Economy. She has authored numerous articles and reports on energy use in buildings, appliances, and consumer products. She also has experience educating citizens on a range of environmental and consumer issues. She received a bachelor's degree from Trinity University and a master's degree from the Yale School of Forestry and Environmental Studies.

JOHN MORRILL is the energy manager for Arlington County, Virginia. Prior to joining the county government in 2000, he enjoyed 15 years in a variety of roles with the American Council for an Energy-Efficient Economy. He is also coauthor of *Residential Indoor Air Quality and Energy Efficiency.* He received his bachelor's degree from Clark University and a master's degree from the University of Virginia.

ACEEE's Green Book®:
The Environmental Guide to
Cars and Trucks,
Model Year 2003 (updated annually)
by John DeCicco and James Kliesch

"...the country's preeminent guide to environmentally friendly passenger cars and trucks." — John O'Dell, *Los Angeles Times*

"Start any new car purchase by investing in ACEEE's Green Book®...it's the equivalent of the Kelley Blue Book guide to auto prices—it's also a readable, no-nonsense primer on how car choice affects the environment. It's far more than just a fuel economy guide." — Tom Horton, *Baltimore Sun*

"...for anyone who wants to ponder our automotive footprint on the earth or argue the merits of cleaner cars, this is a must read." —Royal Ford, *Boston Globe*

This unique buyers' guide ranks all cars and trucks according to environmental friendliness. Shoppers can compare cars, vans, pickups, and SUVs by their environmental impacts on air pollution, global warming, and fuel efficiency. Inside the guide:

- "Green Scores" for all makes and models, listed by class—compact, mid-size, and large cars; vans; pickups; and sport utilities
- "Best of 2003" section featuring the "greenest" models in each class
- "Green by Design" chapter highlighting technologies providing superior "green" performance
- Overview and analysis of hybrid-electric vehicles
- How to buy the cleanest and most efficient vehicle that meets your needs
- Tips on keeping your vehicle running cleanly and efficiently
- Handy index for cross-referencing all 2003 model year cars and trucks by make and class
- The environmental impacts of vehicles, including global warming and the health effects of vehicle pollution

Published by the American Council for an Energy-Efficient Economy

ISBN: 0-918249-51-1
Soft cover, 6"x 9," 150 pages, illustrated, 2003, $8.95

Bulk purchase discounts available.

The Most Energy-Efficient Appliances 2002-2003

ACEEE's annual listing of the top-rated residential equipment on the U.S. market contains the latest compilation of the most efficient appliances. The booklet details the best in energy-efficient refrigerators, dishwashers, clothes washers, water heaters, central and room air conditioners, central heat pumps, and furnaces and boilers. Utilities and energy offices across the country have used this compact booklet to educate consumers about making wise appliance purchase choices.

Soft cover, 5-1/2" x 8-1/2," 32 pages, 2002, $4.00
Bulk purchase discounts available.